Praise for *When to Worry*

"No other book provides such breadth and depth of information on teenage difficulties in language that is easy to understand."

—Carol Klenow, Ed.D., President,
School Board of Education, Utica Community Schools

"Dr. Lisa says things that EVERY parent of a teen should hear about. This important book brings it all together."

—Kerby T. Alvy, Ph.D., Founder and Director of the Center for the
Improvement of Child Caring; Founding Board Member
of the National Effective Parenting Initiative

"Dr. Lisa, well-versed in adolescence, brings understanding of troubled teens to new heights. The resource section alone is invaluable to parents and professionals."

—Barbara Leiner, Director, FosterParents.com

"Parents will get the answers they desperately desire, and educational professionals will gain tools to help their struggling students. Highly recommended!"

—Nancy Lander, Middle School Principal for 15 Years (retired)

"You may pick up this book to read about a specific teen issue, but will end up reading it cover to cover! The case examples bring the information to life, and the solutions are solid."

—Ronna Harris, M.S.W., Social Worker,
Adoption and Family Care Services

"Engaging and practical, *When to Worry* should be mandatory reading for all parents and adults who spend time with adolescents. Lives can be saved with the information in this book."

—Donna G. Noonan, M.P.H., Youth Suicide
Prevention Coordinator, Oregon Public Health Division

more . . .

"This book is a wonderful resource, and we will recommend it to all of the parents and families that we work with."

—Dr. Candice Seti, Psy.D.,
Clinical Psychologist, San Diego Family Services

"This state-of-the art book addresses cultural issues, gender issues, and the tough questions parents and professionals want answers to regarding teens who struggle. Parents, teachers, counselors, physicians, and nurses NEED this book. Fantastic!"

—Jacquelyn Evans, R.N., Alta Bates Medical Center

"Dr. Boesky's book will serve as an invaluable resource for school personnel that work closely with troubled students. All of our staff will be referring parents to this highly enlightening book."

—Gregory Minter, M.A., Associate Principal, Prospect High School

"*When to Worry* is long overdue. Worried, frustrated, or confused parents will feel relief within the first few pages. And the book just keeps getting better from there. Excellent resource, and SO needed!"

—Laurie J. Hall, Licensed Clinical Social Worker and Bilingual Therapist

"In my 20 years as a family therapist, the most frequently asked question is, 'Is my teen normal and should I be worried?' Dr. Lisa's long-awaited book addresses this question in a poignant and matter-of-fact manner. This is an easy must-read for all parents struggling with teen issues."

—Heather Parker, M.S.W., Executive Director,
AMCAL Family Services, Montreal, Canada

When to Worry

Worry

How to Tell if Your Teen Needs Help—and What to Do About It

Lisa Boesky, Ph.D.

Special discounts on bulk quantities of *When to Worry* are available
to schools, agencies, professional associations, and other organizations.
For details, contact Special Sales at specialsales@whentoworry.com

Symptoms listed throughout this book are based on the *Diagnostic and Statistical Manual of
Mental Disorders, Fourth Edition,* Text Revision (Washington, D.C.: American Psychiatric
Association, 2000).

Boesky, Lisa.
    When to worry: how to tell if your teen needs help—and what to do about it / Lisa
Boesky.
        p.   cm.
    Includes bibliographical references and index.
    ISBN-13: 978-0-8144-7363-4
    ISBN-10: 0-8144-7363-6
    1. Adolescent psychopathology.   2. Teenagers—Mental health.   3. Teenagers—
Mental health services.   4. Parent and teenager.   5. Problem youth.   I. Title.

RJ503.B64   2007
616.8900835—dc22

                                                                    2007000580

10   9   8   7   6   5   4   3   2

To my mother and father, may they rest in peace

CONTENTS

The Answers Are
Finally Here

Congratulations. By picking up this book, you have just taken the first step toward understanding your teenager better and bringing more peace into your family.

Perhaps your sweet, compliant child has become a moody, unfocused, unpredictable, angry, defiant, lazy, or overly sensitive teenager. Maybe minor idiosyncrasies you noticed during childhood are becoming troublesome now that your teen is older. Or your teen may struggle in areas where classmates and siblings are doing fine. In any of these situations, it is natural to wonder if your child's behavior reflects normal adolescence or if "something's just not right." It is just as likely that you are a desperate parent of an out-of-control teenager who knows something is wrong but does not know where to turn.

Children do not stop needing their parents once they hit puberty; in fact, as children move through the teen years, you are as pivotal as ever. Parents know their teens better than anyone, so trust your gut or intuition when concerns arise regarding your child. Those around you may accuse you of being overprotective or overreactive. Or just the opposite: others may be concerned about your teen, but you don't see a problem. Either way, this book will give you essential information to help determine whether you currently need to worry about your teen—and if so, what next steps are important for you to take.

Who Will Benefit from This Book

The material in this book is relevant to a wide range of parents, including but not limited to those who:

- Think their teen is fine, but just want to make sure.
- Worry their teen *may* be struggling and want to get an idea as to what may be going on.
- Know their teen is experiencing some difficulties but aren't sure what to do about it.
- Feel alarmed and frightened by their teen's behavior and want guidance.
- Have tried to get help for their teen in the past, but the situation did not improve.
- Have found help for their teen and want to be certain they are on the right track.

Every type of parent can benefit from this book—married parents, single parents, divorced parents, stepparents, adoptive parents, foster parents, and even grandparents.

Although I use language directed at primary caregivers, the information is just as helpful for professionals who interact with teenagers: teachers, school counselors, pediatricians, family practice physicians, nurses, mental health practitioners, substance abuse specialists, juvenile probation officers, judges, attorneys, law enforcement officials, juvenile correction officers, child protective service workers, case managers, residential treatment providers, wilderness program personnel, big brothers and big sisters, mentors, coaches, and youth directors.

The Purpose of This Book

Although we do not have exact numbers, it appears that close to one in five teenagers has an emotional or behavioral problem that affects his or her ability to develop and maintain relationships with peers, achieve in school, or get along with family members—and the majority of these teens are not receiving the specialized services they need.[1, 2]

When faced with a teenage child who does things that don't make sense—particularly if these behaviors are bothersome—parents naturally feel confused, frustrated, and even upset. The entire family is affected when teens experience difficulties. Parents want to do the right thing for their children but often cannot tell what's "normal" during the teenage years and when something is amiss. And even when parents know something is wrong, it is not easy to figure out who to see, where to go, and what to do. This book is designed to help parents become as educated and informed as possible regarding their teen's behavior so that they can make effective and strategic

---

1. *Mental Health: A Report of the Surgeon General—Executive Summary* (Rockville, Md.: U.S. Department of Health and Human Services, Substance Abuse and Mental Health Services Administration, Center for Mental Health Services, National Institutes of Health, National Institute of Mental Health, 1999.)

2. G. Canino, et al, "The DSM-IV rates of child and adolescent disorders in Puerto Rico: Prevalence, correlates, service use, and the effects of impairment," *Archives of General Psychiatry*, 61, 83–93, 2004.

decisions should their teen require assistance. Although it sounds clichéd, *knowledge truly is power when dealing with a struggling teenager.*

The goal of this book is to bring together my eighteen years of education, clinical training, and professional experience with decades of research on problematic teen behavior and to present the result in a practical and easy-to-access format.

By the end of Section I, I hope you will experience one of the following reactions:

- *Relief.* Your teen seems to be doing fine and is not exhibiting problematic behavior

- *Validation.* Not only were you right to be concerned, but there may actually be a name for what your teen is going through and specific strategies known to be effective for your teen's issues. You may also be a bit scared since what you feared may actually be true. However, do not be frightened. This book walks you through the steps you need to take to help your child. Parents should be scared of *not knowing* because when you don't know what is wrong, there is no way to improve things. By the end of this book, you will be one of the most prepared parents around and one step closer to reducing your child's (and family's) suffering.

- *Mixed Emotions, but Mostly Relief.* Your teen exhibits some of the warning signs in the book, but not enough to indicate that it is "time to worry." Throughout the book, you will learn exactly what behaviors to keep a close eye on as your teen develops, matures, and moves through the obstacles of adolescence. If your teen's behavior worsens, you can refer back to the book for specific recommendations regarding what to do.

Even when your teen's behavior has not reached a level where outside assistance is needed, this book can help you discuss important topics with your teen to let them him or her know that you are aware and you care.

Although warning signs of serious conditions are provided, this book was not written to help you diagnose your child. You definitely should *not* do that. As you will discover, diagnoses are much more than a checklist of symptoms. You will find out exactly who can make a diagnosis, how a diagnosis is made, and when these types of diagnoses should be given. The warning signs give you a jump start as to what your teen's specific issue(s) may be. *My intention is to provide you with the tools to identify when you can relax about your child's behavior (and just let your teen be a teen) versus when additional assistance may be warranted. And if your teen needs help, this book will make the process easier and more effective for you and your teen.*

You may have already been down the path of trying to get assistance for your son or daughter. If you did this alone and did not have someone warning you of the complexities involved, you may have ended up frustrated and resigned. This book will reveal another road to travel.

Although the material is designed to be straightforward, I hope you also find it compassionate and reassuring. I know how stressful and exhausting raising a teen who struggles can be. There is hope and there are solutions, once you have the tools.

Why I Wrote This Book

Day after day, year after year, I see what happens when teens don't get the help they need. As a clinical psychologist, I spent the first part of my career working in mental health hospitals and juvenile justice facilities, where I had the privilege to work with some of the most challenging and troubled teens in the country. Not one of those young people developed severe, and sometimes dangerous, emotional or behavioral problems overnight. Each had shown indications of suffering months, and often years, before an arrest or hospital admission. But, it can be difficult to hear the cries of teenagers, because they usually don't say, "I need help." If anything, their words often communicate just the opposite.

Some of the parents of the adolescents I worked with knew that something was not right with their child but were told "She's just going through a phase" or "Don't worry, he's acting like a typical teen." So they took a "wait and see" approach. And things got worse. The parents who tried to get assistance from the start found it was fairly easy to have their teen diagnosed and given a prescription for medication or a referral for talk therapy. The difficulty was in finding someone or something that truly helped their son or daughter—no one or nothing seemed to get to the root of what was wrong. So the teens continued to suffer, as did their families.

My heart broke a little each day. Had these teen's difficulties been correctly identified and appropriately addressed early on, the course of their lives could have been dramatically different.

Consequently, I devoted the second half of my career to traveling the country speaking to large audiences of parents and educational, juvenile justice, mental health, substance abuse, child welfare, and health care professionals, teaching them to recognize the subtle and obvious signs of teens who are struggling—and the specific things they can do to help them. An overriding theme is that too many "sick teens in need of treatment" are viewed as "bad teens in need of punishment." Extreme defiance, rebellion, and acting out are typically much more than they appear—and much can be done to decrease this negative behavior.

I have spoken to tens of thousands of parents and professionals who serve youth across the United States and internationally, yet, at the end of each talk, I always heard the same comments: "This workshop forever changed the way I look at teenagers," "I wish I had this information *years* ago," "Why is so little written about this critical topic?" and "How can I take you home with me?" Parents and professionals continually asked me to recommend a resource that contained all of the information I had spoken about so that they could refer to it whenever issues with teenagers came up. I never found an in-depth book that covered the full spectrum of emotional and behavioral difficulties that affect adolescents, the wide variety of solutions available, and the specific steps to take should a particular teen need help. Eventually, I realized I needed to write that book.

Warning

If you are tempted to blame yourself, don't do it. You did the best you could with the information you had at the time (and some of that information may have even come from well-meaning professionals). Do what you can now.

If you feel yourself getting overwhelmed, take a breath. This book contains a large amount of information. Some of it may apply to your child, or none of it may apply. Even if you recognize your teen in some of the pages of this book, you do not have to take action this second. Unless adolescents are at imminent risk of hurting themselves or others, you have some time to strategically plan the best action to take.

Lisa Boesky, Ph.D.
www.drlisab.com

SECTION I

What's Normal and What's Not

CHAPTER ONE

Is My Teen Normal?

Teens Displaying Typical Behavior vs. When to Worry

Isn't adolescence itself one big emotional disorder?

- Matthew, sixteen, smelled of beer when he came home from a party. He has been staying out past curfew and refusing to do his chores.

- Mara, fifteen, has become sad and withdrawn since her boyfriend broke up with her. She has lost weight and is preoccupied with the notion that she "will never fall in love again."

- Sarah, fourteen, started wearing black clothes, wants her tongue pierced, and writes poems about feeling invisible.

- Evan, sixteen, may not graduate high school due to failing grades and disruptive behavior in the classroom. His teachers say he is a daydreamer and a troublemaker. Evan says he just hates school.

Should the parents of these adolescents worry about their behavior, or are they behaving like typical teens? *It can be difficult to distinguish what is normal during the teenage years and what is cause for worry.* Every adolescent is unique, and all teens have their own personal quirks, habits, strengths, and vulnerabilities. Although there is no true definition of "normal" behavior," we do know the usual or expected way most teenagers behave—and it is different from the stereotypes you see on TV. Adolescence is not necessarily a period of emotional turmoil. In fact, most young people pass through their teenage years without major problems.

It is easy to forget how many physical, emotional, intellectual, and social changes occur during adolescence. For some teens, the changes are dramatic; for others, the changes are slow and gradual. As adolescents transition into adulthood, they are discovering who they are, what they like, with whom they want to spend their time, and how they envision their future. The more you understand typical and healthy behavior during adolescence, the better you will be able to detect problematic teen behavior.

Emotional Changes

Teenagers experience their feelings more intensely, and their emotions change more quickly than those of young children or adults (so, no, you aren't imagining it). These changes are likely a result of the ways that adolescents' brains develop. And, because the parts of the brain associated with emotions are not yet fully wired to the parts associated with controlling one's behavior, adolescents may feel as if flooded with feelings. When teens appear to overreact to innocent requests or questions, it may be because of their difficulty interpreting *your* emotions—believing you are angry, upset, or accusatory when you really aren't.

Adolescents typically report more anxiety, loneliness, embarrassment, and self-consciousness than their parents perceive. This is especially true when teens are doing poorly in school, unpopular with peers, or experiencing problems within the family. Although clearly more emotional during adolescence than during other times in their lives, most teens do not have emotional "problems."

Social Changes

Adolescents spend more time with their friends and less time with their families than they did when they were younger. Girls begin sharing their innermost secrets with each other. Peers are essential to helping teens develop their identity.

The term "peer pressure" is somewhat misleading. Teens do feel tremendous pressure to fit in. However, they place just as much pressure on themselves (and sometimes more) than that exerted by their friends. It is often teens' own fears that others will view them as different, uncool, or weak that drives their behavior. In fact, rather than innocent teens being corrupted by bad crowds, adolescents typically *choose* to hang out with peers who hold similar beliefs, values, and interests. This is actually beneficial if your teen's interests include sports, academics, moral behavior, or other pro-social activities. It is concerning if your teen is rebellious or delinquent, hates school, uses alcohol or drugs, or frequently "hooks up" with the opposite sex.

Teenage boys and girls develop crushes on one another, and many begin dating before the end of adolescence. Some will become involved in serious romantic relationships.

Family Changes

Teenagers remain very connected to their parents, despite shying away from physical affection and not wanting to be seen with them in public. Although they want to be independent, adolescents still care about what parents think of them, want to make them proud, and listen to what they have to say (even if they don't follow the advice). Teenagers typically won't ask for your opinion on music, clothing, hairstyles, or the latest technological gadget. However, they still rely on you for morals, values, and emotional support. Parent-teen conflict typically increases in early adolescence and eventually decreases during late adolescence. Most disagreements are related to everyday issues such as chores, curfew, and homework. Despite the rise in arguments, most parents and teenagers describe their relationship as positive and close.

Physical Changes

Adolescence is a time of significant physical changes, which can add to feelings of awkwardness and insecurity. Boys get taller on different schedules; some teens look like men, and others take years to catch up. Girls often panic when their body fat increases with puberty, and those who mature early may be particularly self-conscious because of their increased breast size. Normal physical changes such as acne, pubic hair, and menstruation can be embarrassing and confusing for some teens. Bodies going through this much growth and development need a lot of sleep.

Intellectual Changes

In early adolescence, teens do not think past right now, so problems feel as if they will go on *forever*. As their brains continue to develop, adolescents are increasingly able to think abstractly, imagine the future, and think about things on a much deeper level. Because they can start to understand the many dimensions of theoretical concepts, they experiment with new beliefs regarding religion, politics, injustice, health, and relationships. They explore, change, and map out educational and career goals. Sarcasm, puns, and more sophisticated humor appear.

Although this advanced thinking opens up new realms of possibilities regarding places to go and things to try, it also leads teens to develop a more intense focus on themselves. Once they realize people may be thinking about them, they assume *everyone* is thinking about and judging them *all of the time*. Adolescents view themselves as unique and feel that no one has *ever* gone through or felt what they have (which is why they are convinced you could *never* understand). Teens believe the world is their oyster: they are unstoppable and indestructible. This view often results in the belief that *they* will be the one who won't get pregnant, hooked on drugs, suspended from school, caught by the police, or taken advantage of when experimenting with risky behavior. In addition, as their reflective thinking intensifies, teens may become overly romantic or cynical and anti-mainstream; don't be surprised if they briefly reject your religious and spiritual values or political beliefs.

Rule Changes

The development of abstract thinking means that teens no longer think of right and wrong as black and white. Concern about fairness comes to the forefront, particularly when it comes to teens themselves. This often shows up in adolescents questioning the limits and rules parents have had in place for years. Suddenly, your teen can identify flaws in your reasoning, and "Because I said so" no longer seems to work. Teens want you to state your case to make sure it makes sense. They are also quick to point out your glass of wine at dinner after your lecture on the dangers of alcohol. Although teenagers may appear defiant and oppositional, often they are trying out their newfound logic—and what better place to do that than in the comfort of their own home? Although quick to hold their parents accountable for any misstep, they may find that sticking to their own rules proves to be more difficult. For example, your new vegetarian son may be seen eating ribs. Although the endless questions, debates, and arguments over rules can be exasperating, these are essential in helping teens develop the skills to avoid becoming blind followers as they mature.

Privacy Changes

An important aspect of adolescents becoming independent and separating from their parents is the desire to keep their lives private. Telephone conversations are conducted in a whisper, the computer screen goes blank, and discussions with friends come to a halt when you walk by. Children who couldn't wait to tell you about their day now won't give you more than one-word answers when directly asked. If you press teens to elaborate, they'll accuse you of working for the FBI. Adolescents literally separate themselves from the family by disappearing into the garage, basement, or their bedroom for hours—with the door shut. And don't even think about coming into the room while they are changing clothes—most teens don't want anyone, including you, to look at their developing bodies.

Each child's experience during the adolescent years is individualized and influenced by family, culture, and community. The combination of extreme emotions, increasing intellect, distancing from family, and increased conflict can make the developmental stage of adolescence more difficult for youth (as well as for those closest to them) than either childhood or adulthood. However, despite these challenges, the majority of teenagers:

- Feel positive about their lives.
- Get along with their parents.
- Have friends to whom they feel connected.
- Have a positive view of their future.

The Modern Teen

Even when they don't experience major difficulties, most of today's teens are forced to deal with issues that can make the transition from childhood to adulthood particularly confusing and scary:

- *Exposure to* sexually explicit music and music videos, violent movies and video games, alcohol and drugs at school, the threat of terrorism, sexual predators on the Internet, bullying and harassment, weapons at school, the suicide of friends
- *Pressure to* dress provocatively, engage in sexual behavior, have the "right" clothes, achieve good grades, get into a "good" college, look "perfect"
- *Risks of* sexually transmitted diseases, unplanned pregnancy, car accidents, obesity
- *Exposure to* divorce, remarriage, stepfamilies, addiction of a family member, date violence, date rape, the departure of a loved one for war

Teenagers strive to grow up and to make their own decisions, but they may not have the skills to deal with all that is thrown at them. Consequently, teenagers can feel alone, isolated, and disconnected. Though you are competing with countless outside influences, as a parent you still have the greatest effect on your teen's life.

Teens Outside the Lines

Although most teens (and their families) move through the obstacle course of adolescence fairly unscathed, some youth display emotions or behaviors that require extra support or outside assistance. The following issues *may* be a signal that something has gone awry with a teenager. *Each will be covered throughout this book, with specific suggestions on the most effective ways to respond.*

Emotional Behavior

Extreme moodiness, frequent sadness or misery

Frequent irritability or agitation

Excessive worries or stress

Hostility, belligerence, or verbally assaultive behavior

Sudden personality change

Any talk (including joking) about suicide or wanting to die

Relationship with Parents

Overly dependent

Excessive defiance or continual rebellion

Loathing or hating one's parents

Social Behavior

Social isolation or withdrawal

Lack of friends (despite wanting them)

Sudden change in peer group

Reluctance to have you meet their friends

Physical Issues

Significant weight loss or gain

Preoccupation with weight or body image

Sleep difficulties

Frequent cuts or burns on arms or legs

Intellectual Issues

Poor school grades or sudden decline in grades

Inattention or distractibility

Rigid and inflexible thinking

Odd use of language or speech

Strange or unusual thoughts

Hobbies and Interests

Loss of interest in activities they used to enjoy

Excessive time spent engaged in one activity

Risky Behavior

Overly impulsive or persistent bad judgment

Repeatedly cutting school

Signs of tobacco, alcohol, or other drug use

Sexual behavior with several partners or risky sexual activity

Cruelty to animals or people (including bullying)

Running away from home

Physical aggression or fighting

Arrest or other involvement with law enforcement

When parents attribute potentially problematic behaviors to "typical adolescence," their teens may not get the help they need.

Is Bad Parenting to Blame?

Many parents believe that they must have somehow caused their teen's emotional or behavioral difficulties. If only they didn't get divorced, if only they hadn't waited so long to get divorced, if only they hadn't remarried, if only they had remarried. . . . The "if only" can go on forever. Maybe it would have made a difference. Maybe not. Regardless, it probably was not the sole cause of your teen's difficulties.

In the simplest terms, the conditions in this book typically result from the complex combination of several factors:

- Inherited genes or another type of biological vulnerability
- Exposure to social and environmental stressors
- A teen's particular abilities and coping skills

Many emotional and behavioral conditions run in families. However, this makes it more *likely* that teens will develop a similar condition; it certainly does not *guarantee* it. Other types of biological factors that render teens more vulnerable typically involve a child's developing brain (minimal prenatal care, exposure to toxins in utero, pregnancy or birth complications, and trauma to the head).

Stresses can include, but are not limited to, enduring bullying or harassment at school, living in a chaotic and conflict-filled home, suffering physical or sexual abuse or significant neglect, being a witness to domestic violence, living with a parent with untreated addiction or mental illness or a physical illness or serious injury, enduring frequent moves, witnessing a vicious parental divorce, being removed from the family home as a child, living in poverty, being involved with the juvenile justice system, living in a violent neighborhood, having a physical disability, and losing a family member. Adolescents differ in their responses to stressful life experiences. Some teenagers have survived prolonged or repeated hardship without exhibiting significant problems, while others experience considerable difficulty in response to minor stressors. Most adolescents fall somewhere in the middle.

Having good social skills, high intelligence, and productive coping abilities helps teens better handle negative life events and can protect them from developing emotional and behavioral difficulties. Receiving support from family, pro-social friends, school, and the community serves a similar role.

Stigma: Alive and Well in the Twenty-First Century

Emotional and behavioral conditions are still viewed as less legitimate than physical conditions. Families are not embarrassed to say that their teen has a broken leg, appendicitis, or strep throat. Nobody whispers in the corner when adolescents are diagnosed with chronic conditions such as asthma or diabetes. And parents do not keep teens from using inhalers or insulin for fear of "what others would think." In fact, when parents ask for support, school personnel, coaches, and dance teachers are often willing to accommodate and assist teens in the management of their illness. Emotional and behavioral problems should be no different—especially now that we know that many of these conditions are associated with genetics and other biological factors and not the result of bad parenting.

Unfortunately, because of the stigma imposed by society, parents are frequently reluctant to seek help for their teen's emotional or behavioral symptoms. Some parents do not obtain outside assistance until their child reaches young adulthood, when difficulties interfere with performance at college or on the job or in raising a family. *Treatment is much more effective when symptoms are addressed in the early stages.* One reason for this is that many conditions worsen over time. In addition, adolescents' difficulties usually start to negatively impact their school performance, relationships with family and friends, and self-esteem. Untreated emotional and behavioral problems place teenagers at significant risk for alcohol or drug use, further compromising their health and happiness.

This book is not about labels, although several are mentioned. The intention of the following chapters is to help you determine whether or not you need to worry about your teen—and, if you should, what to do about it. That being said, labels (officially referred to as *diagnoses*) are not something to be fearful of. The label "pneumonia" results in teens receiving life-saving antibiotics; the label "diabetes" results in treatment with life-saving insulin and an individualized eating and exercise plan. Identifying your teen's issue is the first step toward finding the solution. Down the road, a label may or may not come into play. Regardless, the main objective is to understand the complexities of your teen's emotional and behavioral health. Research over the past few decades has provided tremendous tools to help adolescents (and their families) get back on track. Stigma does exist. And it's not right. Please do not let fear of stigma keep your teen from getting help if it is needed.

Sad, Mad, or Bad

Teens Who Are Too Moody

My teen's moods are so extreme. Why does everything have to be such a big deal?

Teenagers experience more frequent mood changes and greater extremes in mood (both positive and negative) than young children or adults. So what is typical teenage moodiness, and when should you worry about a teen's excessive emotional swings?

Every adolescent experiences happiness, sadness, anger, fear, disappointment, frustration, irritability, and excitement—sometimes all in the same day! However, some adolescents experience these feelings so intensely that they become overwhelmed. Their exaggerated and extreme emotional reactions hurt their relationships with family and friends, impair their school performance, and make it difficult for them to keep a job.

It is normal and expected that adolescents go through periods of being down in the dumps, or feeling blue. We worry when these feelings are too intense or last for weeks or months.

Krystal: Typical Teen or Too Insecure and Cranky?

Over the past several weeks, Krystal, fourteen, has begun repeatedly checking herself in the mirror and commenting on how "hideous" she looks. She hates her "big nose," "small eyes," and "fat thighs." Krystal is convinced that everyone at school hates her because she is "disgusting." Out of the blue, she believes her best friend of three years secretly dislikes her and is turning other kids at school against her. She tried to drop one of her new classes because of the teacher's "unfair and outrageous expectations," and it has been almost a month since she attended gymnastics practice regularly. These days, Krystal mostly lies around the house watching television. Instead of inviting her younger brothers to join her, she now finds them annoying. When encouraged to participate in scheduled family activities, she repeatedly states she is "too tired" or says that "it's lame." Krystal's irritation increases when her younger brothers continually ask why she is so "cranky."

It is not unusual for teens to experience *some* of Krystal's behaviors. However, she is experiencing *all* of these behaviors simultaneously—and they are a marked change from how she typically acts. In addition, her new behavior has continued for several weeks and negatively impacts her relationships with peers, family members, school, and hobbies.

Teens with Low Moods

We worry about teens when they appear sad or "bummed out" for more than a couple of weeks. Regardless of what their parents say or do, these youth continue to appear unhappy and miserable. They may tear up easily and cry over small or trivial incidents.

However, not all adolescents with a low mood appear sad or gloomy. It is common for teenagers—especially boys—to express a low mood in irritability or agitation. They report having a "short fuse" or feeling ready to "blow" at any moment. These teens are easily annoyed, and even small comments by others can result in angry outbursts. These irritable teens may go out of their way to provoke parents, other adults, or siblings; yet, they become upset if negative consequences result.

Adolescents who express their low mood with irritability frequently receive write-ups, restrictions, or punishments at school, work, and home because of their negative attitude. Even though they are "sad" kids, they are usually viewed as "bad kids."

One of the most obvious changes parents notice in teens with a low mood is that they appear bored and uninterested in activities they used to enjoy. When questioned about their sudden lack of enthusiasm, typical responses include "That's stupid" or "Only losers play that," even though they recently enjoying these pursuits. These teens are also less interested than before in spending time with friends and family, even those with whom they are particularly close. To avoid social interaction or certain activities, they may pretend they are sick or too tired; some teens are purposely disobedient so that they will be prohibited from participating.

It is normal for adolescents to continuously try new pursuits and then switch to other interests. Their hobbies may heavily depend on the latest trend or what their friends enjoy. It becomes worrisome when teens seem unable to enjoy anything; nothing excites them anymore.

Overeating becomes a way to comfort themselves or fill up feelings of emptiness. They may snack incessantly or eat several portions during mealtime. Other teens with a low mood may lose their appetite, eat little, and drop weight. They say they are not hungry, avoid family meals, or just pick at their food. A significant change in eating habits or weight—up or down—could be a sign of low mood.

Adolescents with a low mood commonly experience one or more disturbances of the sleep-wake cycle. Teens who oversleep may repeatedly nap during the day, even after a full night of rest. They are often difficult—if not impossible—to awaken in the morning. Other teens will toss and turn for hours, unable to fall asleep at night. Some may fall asleep without a problem, but will wake up repeatedly throughout the night or awaken in the very early morning hours, unable to fall back asleep.

Children's moods can greatly affect their physical movements. Teens with a low mood may suddenly move at a slower or quicker pace than before. Their conversational skills may be sluggish; they may talk more slowly than they used to or wait lengthy periods before responding to questions. They often run behind and are unable to "hurry up" when told to do so.

On the other hand, some of these teens become jumpy and nervous. They begin fidgeting with their clothes and other objects. You may find them pacing in place or suddenly appearing revved up.

When adolescents suffer from low moods, they typically feel

tired and appear worn out. They complain of having no energy and view small requests as enormous undertakings. They report feeling bored or "blah" much of the time, and everyday activities become unappealing because of the effort involved. Even when fun or special events occur, these teens often cannot motivate themselves to attend. If their attendance is mandatory, they barely participate once there.

Some adolescents, particularly boys, show signs of low mood physically. They may frequently complain of headaches, stomachaches, or joint pain, despite no evidence of illness. For some of these teens, vague aches and pains continue to reappear, though doctors cannot pinpoint a cause.

Minor mishaps and small errors often cause tremendous distress for teenagers with low moods. They focus too much on what they have done wrong and minimize their accomplishments. When parents unknowingly make a disapproving remark, these youth can obsess about the negative comment for hours or days. Teens with low moods are overly sensitive to criticism and usually perceive any negative feedback as confirmation that they are losers and not as good as others. However, in some cases, these teens compensate with a false and exaggerated sense of bravado, pretending to be completely unconcerned about anyone's view of them.

Adolescents with low moods often feel guilty about their past behavior (regardless of how minor or trivial their infraction) and often refer to themselves in disparaging terms.

Attention and concentration problems are also common among these teenagers. They may have trouble remembering things. Because of these difficulties, schoolwork becomes increasingly difficult. Their grades may slip, and teachers typically report a change in classroom behavior. Adolescents with low moods often fall behind with household chores, in their job, or with other commitments. Parents typically find themselves providing repeated reminders as their teen acts progressively more "spacey"; these youth may require parental or peer assistance to make even small or inconsequential decisions.

Although it is frightening to imagine, teens with low moods may think about death and dying. These thoughts vary in their intensity and specificity, from brief moments of wondering what it would be like to be dead to preoccupation with death and a detailed plan for how to kill themselves. The artwork and writing of these youth frequently contains morbid themes, and they become increasingly interested in what happens when people die, the after-life, or reincarnation.

Statements such as "I wish I could go to sleep and never wake up," "Maybe I should just kill myself," or "I wish I were dead" should be taken very seriously, even if stated in the heat of anger. Marks on a teen's wrist (no matter how superficial) or unexplained pill bottles in a backpack or bedroom demand immediate attention.

A low mood is a significant risk factor for suicide, regardless of whether teens are expressing it with irritability or sadness. *Take very seriously any communication from your teen regarding thoughts about death or wanting to die or any action to kill themselves. Further evaluation is imperative.*

Worry Signs 2.1   Is Your Teen's Mood Too Low?

The following behaviors are important worry signs of teens with *low mood*:

- Seems unhappy and sad or easily irritated and quick to anger.

- Shows decreased interest in hobbies or activities they used to enjoy.

- Gains or loses a considerable amount weight without trying.

- Sleeps too much or has problems falling asleep.

- Moves more slowly or appears more restless than usual.

- Repeatedly complains of being tired, having no energy, or experiencing physical symptoms.

- Is overly self-critical, including a preoccupation with past failures and mistakes.

- Shows increased distractibility or has problems remembering things.

- Has mentioned suicide, wanting to be dead, or "not being able to take it anymore.

- Is attracted to music, books, or poetry containing themes of death or destruction.

Is It Time to Worry That Your Teen's Mood Is Too Low?

All teens get distressed. Adolescence can be full of stressful events: peer pressure, the breakup of a romantic relationship, poor test grades, parental separation or divorce, awkward bodily changes, or death of grandparents. So when is a teen experiencing normal sadness or irritability and when is his or her mood *too* low?

The behaviors listed in Worry Signs 2.1 are symptoms of Major Depression (sometimes called Clinical Depression or MD). If you recognize your teen in one or two of the symptoms just described, do not panic. Even if your child is experiencing three or more of the *symptoms*, that does not necessarily indicate your teen suffers from the *syndrome* of Major Depression. Many adolescents experience such mood and behavior changes at various times and to various degrees. Major Depression is a serious mental health condition and drastically different from the few hours or days of sadness or irritability observed among teenagers in response to disappointment or loss. Temporary feelings of sorrow or anger are normal and expected reactions to upsetting situations. In addition, the symptoms can frequently be explained by causes other than Major Depression.

Your "worry barometer" should rise if your teen shows several of the behaviors for at least a couple of weeks, especially if the problems negatively affect your teen's functioning and are not caused solely by other factors.

There is no magic number of low-mood symptoms that indicates that your teen needs help. Exhibiting the one symptom of wanting to die is more serious than exhibiting all four symptoms of lack of appetite, difficulty sleeping, irritability, and restlessness. The greater the number of symptoms and/or the more severe the symptoms, the more you should worry.

Keep in mind that most teenagers deny they are depressed—even when they truly are. These youth are not necessarily lying; most teens do not know what depression is and often have no idea when they are suffering from it. Therefore, in addition to talking with your son or daughter about changes in mood and behavior, rely on what you *observe*.

Some parents may see their teen in the symptoms listed under Major Depression, yet they may be confused because their adolescent has behaved this way for *years*. The troubling behaviors they observe do not represent a clear-cut "change"; the worry signs reflect how their teen used to behave—and how he or she is currently behaving. In fact, these parents might not remember a time when their child was *not* sad, irritable, or had difficulty sleeping.

Justin: Typical Teenager or Persistent Problem?

Justin's mother does not know what happened to her son. He developed an "attitude" problem when puberty hit at thirteen; his crankiness still has not subsided at age fifteen. Justin is irritated by everything his mother says or does and has no problem verbalizing his annoyance. He challenges his mother on trivial matters, and when she defends her position, Justin loses his temper and an argument ensues. Justin's mother walks on eggshells, choosing her words and actions carefully so as not to aggravate her son. Although Justin complains of always being tired, he cannot fall asleep at night, often lying awake until 3:00 A.M. He views himself as stupid, is not interested in school, and says a high school diploma is a "waste of time." He is commonly overheard saying, "Life sucks."

Because Justin has exhibited these problems for over a year and his behavior is negatively affecting his family life, his mother has every reason to worry.

Teens with Low Moods for Too Long

Dysthymic Disorder (commonly referred to as Dysthymia) is a condition of low mood similar to Major Depression, but there are definite and distinct differences. Dysthymia is a chronic, milder form of depression. Teens with Dysthymia experience symptoms of their illness almost every day, *for at least one year.* Major Depression is usually a short-lived, intense mood disturbance that reappears over time, whereas Dysthymia is a *less intense, but more persistent form of depression; both can involve sadness and/or irritability.* Teens with Dysthymia typically experience less social withdrawal and fewer sleep or appetite problems than teens suffering from Major Depression. Teens with Major Depression are also more likely to experience strong feelings of guilt and are more preoccupied with dark, gloomy subjects. But do not be fooled. Dysthymia still has substantial negative effects on a teen's ability to function in key activities such as school and work and to maintain close relationships with friends and family members.

Worry Signs 2.2   Has Your Teen's Mood Been Too Low for Too Long?

The following behaviors are worry signs of teens who suffer a low mood for *a year or longer.*

- Shows chronic irritability, including being constantly annoyed by everyone and everything.
- Repeatedly uses statements such as "Everyone pisses me off" or "Everyone gets on my nerves."
- Is perpetually cynical, pessimistic, or hopeless.
- Always seems miserable, including low-level sadness that does not go away.
- Has long-standing sleep problems.

- Repeatedly eats too much or has no appetite.

- Constantly complains about low energy or fatigue.

- Suffers unremitting low self-esteem.

- Faces continual problems with concentration or making decisions.

- Shows no significant mood changes in the past year.

A significant percentage of teens with Dysthymic Disorder eventually develop an intense and severe episode of Major Depression; this is referred to as *double depression*. Suffering from Dysthymic Disorder places teens at risk for suicidal thinking and behavior, and this danger increases if Major Depression takes hold. Clearly, early identification and treatment of both of these illnesses is critical.

The teenage years can be filled will periods of excitement, enthusiasm, and giddiness. Adolescents can be extremely passionate about personal beliefs, music, celebrities, and the opposite sex. Emotions sometimes seem unrestrained and volatile. This is normal. But, when is a teen too excited or too emotionally uninhibited? When are their feelings too intense? When do we worry?

Brian: Everyday Moodiness or Out-of-Control Mood Swings?

At sixteen, Brian keeps his friends guessing. One minute he is enthusiastic, excited, and feeling great; the next, he is irritable, easily annoyed, and angry. Friends enjoy Brian and his good mood—his boasting, joke telling, and schemes for new, exciting activities for the group. There is never a dull moment when Brian feels confident, adventurous, and on the hunt for fun. Some of the boys' wildest (and most dangerous) memories resulted from Brian and his "great ideas." However, Brian's friends know that the fun eventually ends. Sooner or later, he loses his zest for life and stays home for several weeks. His self-confidence disappears, and Brian becomes quiet and dull. Sarcasm replaces ideas, and if he does tell a joke, it is typically mean-spirited. During these periods, Brian argues with his parents and becomes verbally abusive toward his mother. Some friends continue to hang around him in this down phase, but most disappear and come back when the "fun" Brian returns.

Many teenagers have changeable emotions—happy one minute and sad the next. However, there appear to be distinct time frames in which Brian feels overly excited or very down and angry. It also seems that there are no situational factors that trigger his mood shifts, and his mood and behavior change is so extreme that his friends not only notice but alter their behavior in response to it.

Teens with Too High Moods

Because most adolescents experience intense feelings and frequent mood changes, we worry only when these emotions are extremely exaggerated and over the top. Teens whose moods are too high may appear excessively happy, giddy, or euphoric, as if they were high on drugs. Other teens with high moods display excessive irritability and anger that are uncharacteristic of their usual behavior. Their agitation can be severe, sometimes to the point of aggressive outbursts and even violence. These teens frequently exhibit major changes in mood for no apparent reason, with days of overexcitement and enthusiasm spontaneously leading to days of rage and misery. Parents of these adolescents find themselves asking their son or daughter, "What is wrong with you?" because their child's emotional reactions seem so disproportionate to the situation.

Feelings of self-importance and superiority are often seen among adolescents whose moods are too high. These teens commonly believe they can overpower anyone regardless of size or status and don't mind provoking others. Teens with high moods often voice their dissatisfaction with expectations and rules, frequently going to great lengths to change them. They may directly challenge authority figures. They typically believe that the rules do not apply to them, that they should receive special favors, and that they are "above" the negative consequences siblings or peers receive. When these teens get into trouble, they commonly shout, "You can't do this to *me*."

These youth may feel so important that they believe they possess extraordinary abilities, talents, and knowledge that no one else does. They frequently tell elaborate stories about personal achievements in areas where they have no skills or training or give detailed advice and specific instructions even without knowledge of a situation or subject. If their thought processes become completely irrational, teens whose moods are too high can develop *delusional* beliefs, in which they truly cannot differentiate between fantasy and reality.

Bounds of endless energy often accompany a mood that is too high. These teens seem driven by a motor; they move and talk rapidly. They frequently go several nights with only two to three hours of sleep, or without any sleep at all. Most sleep-deprived individuals feel drowsy and lethargic and have difficulty concentrating; when teens have too high a mood, they continue to be animated and energized. Because drugs such as methamphetamine and cocaine can cause teens to be "hyped up" and awake for days, make sure drug use is not responsible for signs of a mood that is too high.

Communicating with adolescents when their mood is too high is challenging and sometimes impossible. They often speak so loudly that it seems they are shouting for an entire conversation. Their speech can be so frantic and hurried that others are unable to get a word in edgewise. Some teens with very high moods speak dramatically, overly enunciating each word or suddenly breaking into song; others become argumentative over minor or trivial issues. These youth sometimes become so excited they talk nonstop for hours, regardless of whether anyone is interested. In contrast, other teens with very high moods become hostile and angry in the middle of a pleasant conversation, for no apparent reason.

When their mood is too high, teens' ideas can sound convoluted and confusing; topics may seem only remotely related or have no logical connection. This is referred to as *flight of ideas*. The following vignette illustrates a teenager experiencing flight of ideas:

Denise, seventeen, came home from school yelling for her parents. When asked what the fuss was about, she exclaimed, "Josh was seen kissing my best friend Pam while they ate lasagna outside the cafeteria, but today they were supposed to be serving pizza with tiny cubes of meat on it. I like extra cheese on my pizza, but the overweight woman with the hairnet always gives me the smallest piece, which usually has burnt cheese or no cheese on it at all. Why does that woman wear a hairnet? It looks like a pair of fishnet stockings on her head. I once wore fishnet stockings when I dressed as a 1920s flapper for Halloween. Fishnets feel the same as panty-hose, and I hate wearing pantyhose. And don't worry, I will wear pantyhose when I go out to dinner with Grandpa, but only if he brushes his teeth. Last time his breath smelled like a skunk.

Though their parents are confused, teens who display flight of ideas believe that they make sense and appear to understand what they are communicating. Their abrupt topic changes reflect their disorganized thinking. These youth frequently describe thinking so many thoughts at one time that it is difficult to decide which to speak out loud, as if their ideas occur faster than they can physically release them out of their mouths.

When their mood is too high, they often only half-listen when given instructions or explicit directions. They are easily distracted by anything and everything around them. Background noise, posters on a wall, or a sibling's activity on the other side of the room can completely throw these youth off track.

Teens with extremely high moods constantly formulate innovative and exciting ideas; this often leads to throwing themselves into numerous activities simultaneously. Because of a lack of organization and preparation, however, their actions and plans are usually disorganized and chaotic. Despite their gift for beginning new projects, most of their endeavors remain incomplete as they move on to something novel and more interesting. When their mood is too high, these youth tend to significantly increase activities they enjoy: playing sports, shopping for clothes, playing video games, buying collectibles, bullying others, or using alcohol and other drugs.

Social activity and the desire for socialization can also be heightened and intensified during periods of extremely high mood. These teens want to interact and immediately connect with everyone they come into contact with, which often results in inappropriate relationships. It is common for them to get involved with much older individuals, including those leading dangerous and delinquent lifestyles. Because of an intense need for association and bonding, most teens with very high moods do not realize when they are socially inappropriate; they also do not consider the potential consequences of their actions. For example, they may arrive unannounced at someone's house in the middle of the night or invite strangers to stay at their families' home.

Some teens become overly sexual during periods of extremely high mood. Despite having no history of such behavior, they may make repeated calls to sex telephone hotlines, view large amounts of pornography, engage in elaborate sexual fantasies, experience an insatiable appetite for sex with a romantic partner, or strongly desire sexual relations with an assortment of partners. Their intense need for contact and connection with others when their mood is too high places them at risk for sexual behavior with individuals who could harm them in a variety of ways.

Because they feel invincible, indestructible, and unconcerned about consequences of their actions, teens experiencing a mood that is too high often participate in a variety of high-risk, dangerous, or even deadly activities. Delinquent behavior such as theft, destruction of property, and trespassing are common. When their mood is too high, teens with a history of good judgment and upstanding behavior may go on extensive shopping sprees without money or shoplift, drive recklessly at high speeds, take their parent's car for a cross-country joyride, or break into school to steal a test. They may spend excessive amounts of time partying, overconsume alcohol or other drugs, start gambling, engage in unusual sexual practices, or have unprotected sex, potentially exposing themselves to sexually transmitted diseases, including the Human Immunodeficiency Virus (HIV).

Most teens who experience moods that are too high *also* experience moods that are too low and experience periods of time with symptoms of Major Depression.

Worry Signs 2.3   Is Your Teen's Mood Too High?

The following behaviors are worry signs of teens whose moods are *too high*:

- Acts unusually happy, silly, and enthusiastic for no particular reason; becomes extremely irritable or agitated; experiences severe mood swings.

- Acts overly conceited; holds irrational and completely unrealistic ideas about what he or she wants to do in life, currently or in the future.

- Has astonishing levels of energy and sleeps only a few hours a night or not at all without becoming tired.

- Talks so rapidly that the speech is difficult to interrupt; describes thoughts as "racing" or "going too fast."

- Has difficulty paying attention.

- Becomes involved in too many hobbies or activities at once and wants to interact with as many people as possible, including strangers.

- Engages in extremely reckless activities.

- Suffers from symptoms of Major Depression (MD).

Is It Time to Worry About Your Teen's High Mood?

The behaviors in Worry Signs 2.3 are symptoms of the manic (high) phase of Bipolar Disorder. The term "bipolar" refers to the *two* extreme *poles* of mood (very high and very low) experienced by individuals with this illness. In fact, Bipolar Disorder used to be known as "Manic-Depression," because it is characterized by repeated (and typically alternating) episodes of *mania* and *depression*. Bipolar Disorder can be serious and disabling, and *close to one-third of teens with Major Depression eventually develop Bipolar Disorder.*

However, even if you recognize your teen from the description given, it does not necessarily indicate that he or she suffers from this condition. Your "worry barometer" should rise if your teen shows several of the behaviors for more than a few days, especially if they negatively impact your teen's functioning and are clearly not due to other causes.

The Bipolar Disorder Diagnosis

Adolescents are currently being diagnosed with Bipolar Disorder at the highest rate ever. Although mental health and medical professionals are becoming better at recognizing the disorder among teenagers, I believe there is also a great deal of misdiagnosis occurring. In addition, a considerable number of teens receive a different mental health diagnosis or are labeled as a "behavior problem" when they truly suffer from Bipolar Disorder. Professionals who diagnose young people with Bipolar Disorder should have training and experience with teens and mood disorders, as well as adequate time to conduct a comprehensive and detailed mental health evaluation.

When teens are ill with Bipolar Disorder, they are usually unaware of the substantial changes in their activity and speech; *therefore*, a determination of whether something serious is occurring must be based on the observations of those around them.

For some teens, a manic episode begins suddenly, with a quick increase in symptoms within a few days. For others, mania is preceded by weeks or months of irritability and disruptive (or even delinquent) behavior. A manic episode can last anywhere from a week to a few months.

There is a subset of adolescents with Bipolar Disorder whose mood changes are less intense and striking than those noted earlier. Their manic symptoms are not as hyperactive and disorganized; their overconfidence, poor judgment, and talkativeness are not as extreme. Instead of experiencing full-blown *mania*, these young people suffer from *hypomania*. This less severe, but still serious, form of Bipolar Disorder consists of "hypomanic" episodes interspersed with Major Depressive episodes.

Pattern of Symptoms

The pattern of bipolar symptoms is highly variable. Some teens experience lengthy periods (weeks, months, or years) of normal mood in between episodes of mania and depression. Others become depressed immediately after a manic episode or become manic immediately after their depression lifts. There is also a subset of adolescents with Bipolar Disorder who exhibit symptoms of mania and depression simultaneously. These teens do not have specific and distinct periods of highs and lows but experience rapidly alternating highs and lows several times within the same day.

In severe cases of Bipolar Disorder, teens can become *psychotic*, finding it difficult to differentiate what is real from what is not real. For example, they may hear voices when no one is there, see things that other people cannot see, have very strange and unusual thoughts, or engage in extremely bizarre behavior.

This Sounds Like My Teen, But What Else Could It Be?

Even if your child exhibits many of the worry signs listed in this chapter, there are several possible explanations for the changes in your teen's mood and behavior that are *unrelated* to Major Depression, Dysthymic Disorder, or Bipolar Disorder. However, even if your child does not have a mood disorder, many of the circumstances listed here are serious enough to warrant an evaluation by a qualified medical or mental health professional:

- Loss or stressful event
- Use of alcohol or other drugs
- Presence of a medical condition or medication

- Presence of other factors related to weight gain or loss
- Continuing overexertion or underexertion
- Difficult family environment
- Presence of learning difficulties or problems with attention and impulsivity
- Physical trauma
- Injury to the brain

Frequently Asked Questions About Mood Disorders

1. *Are mood disorders inherited or caused by something in the environment?* Major Depression, Dysthymic Disorder, and Bipolar Disorder all have genetic components. Teens with parents or other family members with mood disorders are at *higher risk* of developing these disorders than are youth without a family history. The closer the family member with the illness, the greater the increase in risk. However, family history is only one risk factor. Environmental factors also play a significant role. Some teenagers develop a mood-related illness after experiencing a traumatic event or chronic stress. For most teens, mood disorders appear to be caused by a combination of genetics, stressful events, and the teen's coping skills.

2. *If my teen suffers from a mood disorder, will he or she outgrow it?* Even after a teen's mood returns to normal, episodes of depression or mania frequently reappear, after several months or years, in youth with Major Depression, Dysthymic Disorder, and Bipolar Disorder. Therefore, these illnesses are often viewed as lifelong illnesses that need to be managed, similar to asthma or diabetes. The good news is that teens' chances of living productive, happy, and fulfilling lives increase significantly if they comply with treatment recommendations and make healthy lifestyle modifications, including avoidance of drugs and alcohol. Untreated, teenagers with mood disorders will likely experience difficulty—in school, at home, at work, and with relationships—into adulthood; they also remain at risk for substance abuse and suicide.

3. *Are mood disorders more common in boys or girls?* During the teenage years, Major Depression occurs twice as often in girls. Bipolar Disorder and Dysthymic Disorder seem to affect both genders equally during adolescence.

4. *Is it possible my teen could have another emotional or behavioral condition in addition to a mood disorder?* Unfortunately, it is the rule—not the exception—for teens with mood disorders to suffer from one or more *additional* emotional or behavioral difficulties. Anxiety Disorders, Attention-Deficit/Hyperactivity Disorder (ADHD), Conduct Disorder, Oppositional Defiant Disorder, Substance-Use Disorders, and Eating Disorders most frequently co-occur with mood disorders. Each of these conditions can impact and worsen an adolescent's mood-related symptoms.

5. *Are there any cultural factors to be aware of with mood disorders?* Although mood disorders occur among adolescents from all cultures, the ways in which symptoms are experienced and displayed can differ depending on a teen's cultural background. Depression is expressed primarily in feelings of sadness, irritability, loss of pleasure, and hopelessness in North America and Europe. However, depression occurs largely as physical ailments (headache, abdominal pain, fatigue, or vague body complaints) in many other cultures. In addition, adolescents from certain cultures may adamantly deny mood changes despite obvious signs that they are depressed, because discussing sadness, fear, or agitation can bring embarrassment or shame to their family. Seeking care for physical health-related issues (rather than mental health-related issues) is more socially acceptable in nearly all cultures. And boys from backgrounds that encourage resilient, strong, "macho" behavior in men commonly express their depressed mood in anger, aggression, and irritability.

How You Can Help Teens Who Have Problems with Their Moods

If you recognized your teen from one of the *sets* of worry signs in this chapter, it is time to seek professional assistance. Your teen may or may not be suffering from a mood disorder. However, discovering what is underlying his or her emotional and behavior changes is important—and will provide a clearer direction on how to best help your child.

The following strategies are helpful for all teens but are *essential* when raising an adolescent suffering from a mood disorder:

- *Keep teens involved in their normal routine. It is more important than you think.* Encourage them to shower, dress, and eat, even if they are reluctant. Do not allow them to watch television or sleep all day. Unless they have a severe form of depression, encourage teens attend school or work, with modifications if necessary.

- *Help teens develop a consistent sleep schedule, going to bed at the same time each night and waking at the same time each morning.* Lack of sleep can trigger an intense shift in mood. "Catching up" by oversleeping on the weekend does not help teens with a mood disorder.

- *Modify teens' lifestyle to reduce stress and pressure.* Significant stress can trigger an episode of depression or mania. Teens with classes, teachers, or after-school jobs that are too demanding may need to switch to something less demanding. Relationships full of crisis and drama need to change or come to an end. Everyone in your home should work together to create a peaceful home environment.

- *Exercise with teens or help them develop an exercise program.* Regular fitness activities lift a depressed mood, improve sleep, and help counteract weight gained from mood-stabilizing medication.

- *Challenge teens' negative beliefs and overgeneralizations.* Question teens nonjudgmentally about what evidence exists to support their beliefs, to slowly whittle away their pessimism.

- *Help teens cut down on "mood-altering" foods and beverages,* including caffeinated beverages (sodas, coffee, iced tea) and food or drink with high concentrations of sugar.

- *Be persuasive and vigilant about the importance of teens not using cigarettes, alcohol, and other drugs.* Alcohol is a depressant, nicotine withdrawal can cause symptoms of depression, and a significant emotional "crash" can result after the intense high of methamphetamine or cocaine. Several drugs can trigger a manic episode.

- *Encourage teens to find healthy ways to have fun and release stress* (hobbies, sports, talking, journaling, video games, dancing, yoga, writing) to lift low mood and reduce tension.

- *Encourage teens with depressed moods to socialize.* These teens prefer to be alone, but isolation gives them long periods to mull over the many negatives (real or imagined) in their lives. Engage with your teen one on one. Rather than *force* teens to attend group functions, help them socialize with one or two individuals they feel comfortable with.

- *Supervise (and possibly limit) teens' socialization if they become manic* because of their impulsivity, lack of judgment, and craving for high-risk activities. These youth can become obnoxious, and sometimes aggressive, when placed in large-group situations.

- *Instill hope.* Teens with mood disorders are often pessimistic about their current situation and the future. Helping your teen focus on positive upcoming events—the next day, week, or month—gives them something to look forward to. Hope provides a sense that circumstances can get better; hopelessness is strongly related to teen suicide.

- *Be on the lookout for signs of suicidal behavior.* Suffering from a mood disorder is one of the biggest risk factors for teen suicide. Parents must be alert to suicidal thoughts, threats, and any type of attempt. Having a gun in the house significantly increases the risk of a child dying by suicide; parents of teens suffering from a mood disorder should remove all guns from the family home.

Discovering that your child may have a mood disorder can be overwhelming and even frightening. However, history is filled with famous individuals who accomplished amazing achievements despite suffering from Major Depression, Dysthymic Disorder, or Bipolar Disorder. Barbara Bush, George Stephanopoulos, Tipper Gore, Dick Cavett, Ted Turner, Buzz Aldrin, Rosie O'Donnell, Tanya Tucker, Marie Osmond, Mike Wallace, Jane Pauley, James Taylor, Patty Duke, Margot Kidder, Maurice Benard, Alvin Ailey, Linda Hamilton, and Brooke Shields are reported to have suffered from a mood disorder.

Also reported to have suffered from a mood disorder are Jim Carrey, Jean-Claude Van Damme, Sheryl Crow, Ashley Judd, Drew Carey, Winona Ryder, Robert Downey, Jr., Terry Bradshaw, and the rapper DMX.

Teens with mood disorders can achieve a satisfying, good life—perhaps even greatness. Provide them with the gift of appropriate evaluation and treatment while they are still young so that they can avoid the pain and suffering these famous individuals endured throughout their journey of accomplishments.

CHAPTER THREE

Unfocused and on the Run

Teens Who Cannot Pay Attention or Have Too Much Energy

How could you lose your keys AGAIN. . . . Put that down. . . . Leave her alone. . . . You're going to break that. . . . Let's go, we are going to be late AGAIN. . . . Are you even listening to me?

Teenagers clearly have more difficulty paying attention and focusing for extended periods than do their parents or other adults. They are also usually not as organized and tidy. In addition, the teenage years are frequently filled with spontaneous, often impulsive, decisions and behavior. And, because of their high level of energy, teenagers are commonly on the go, becoming restless when forced to sit still for extended stretches of time. This is normal.

So when should you worry that your teen has serious problems with distractibility and forgetfulness? When does disorganization rise to a level of concern? At what point does carefree, energetic behavior become uncontrolled and reckless? This chapter explores whether parents need to be concerned about teens who have difficulty with (1) attention, (2) excess energy, or (3) a combination of both.

Nicole: Daydreamer or Unable to Focus?

Nicole, fifteen, has always struggled in school. The most frustrating part is that everyone (including Nicole) knows she is bright and capable of doing better. Her mistakes are careless—she does not pay attention to details. Her teachers frequently accuse her of daydreaming in class, since she does not appear to be listening. Nicole often loses her books, misplaces her backpack, and forgets to write down her assignments. Her parents are discouraged and lose more hope each

school year. Grounding her, taking away her cell phone, and even brib-
ing her with money have had no effect on her grades. In fact, Nicole
seems to be getting worse. She was fired from two different babysitting
jobs because she repeatedly arrived late (and didn't call to let her
employers know she was behind schedule). And she recently lost credi-
bility among peers in her church youth group because she didn't follow
through on three big projects she was working on with them. Because
of her shyness and difficulty making friends, Nicole's church group was
her primary source of feeling that she belonged. It now seems that the
group is annoyed with her, leaving her feeling lonely yet again.

Nicole repeatedly displays inattentive behaviors and has for
some time. In addition, her oversights interfere with her schoolwork, babysitting jobs, and relationships with peers at church.

Teens Who Cannot Pay Attention

Many distractible youths have at least average intelligence, but the
demands for constant focus in the typical classroom can be too
much. Error-filled or incomplete school work can lead to placement in special education classes or being held back a grade. Family tension and conflict over household chores or homework are
common; these activities are usually completed only after repeated
reminders from parents.

Inattentive teens are often referred to as "bright teens who
aren't applying themselves" because of their tendency to put things
off to the last minute and or a pattern of incomplete projects and
goals. Their perception of time is inaccurate, so minutes spent on
tedious tasks feel like an eternity. They also have difficulty thinking
about the future, so impending consequences or punishments mean
little. Others view these youths as lazy and unmotivated because of
their sluggish, tired appearance and lack of motivation.

Teens who have problems with attention may seem defiant and
at times incorrigible. They appear to refuse requests of authority

figures—as if deliberately being disobedient. However, most of these adolescents do not intentionally ignore parents and teachers or try to send messages about who is in control. Inattentive teens usually want to complete the task at hand, make their parents proud, earn good grades, arrive on time, and keep track of important items. However, this is extremely difficult when they do not fully understand instructions, do not remember everything they are supposed to do, and constantly misplace what is needed to complete coursework.

Not all teens with attention difficulties appear oppositional and rebellious. In fact, some are quite cooperative and accommodating. These teens pretend to understand directions and give the impression they are busily doing schoolwork, homework, and chores to avoid conflict with teachers and parents. However, their distractibility prevents them from sticking with activities for long periods and results in incomplete or inaccurate work. These teens typically respond with clever excuses or reasons for insufficient work, promising to do better next time. Unfortunately, next time is much the same.

Making and keeping friends can be challenging for these teens because they may space out or appear as if they are not listening; or they are quiet and passive, making it difficult for others to engage with them. They may hang out in the background and do not draw much attention to themselves. If they're too shy to initiate friendships, they spend a lot of time alone. It is not that kids at school do not like them; for the most part, other kids do not notice them.

Worry Signs 3.1   Is Your Teen Struggling to Pay Attention?

The following behaviors point out important worry signs of a teen struggling to *pay attention*:

- Makes careless mistakes with schoolwork, at a job, or in other activities; has difficulty paying attention to details.

- Often seems as if not listening—even when directly spoken to.

- Is always disorganized or running late.

- Has a hard time maintaining attention until a task or activity has ended.

- Regularly misplaces important items.

- Has trouble completing tasks or goals; doesn't follow directions.

- Is easily distracted by what happens around them.

- Avoids homework or any other task requiring thinking and problem-solving; hates school.

- Seems absentminded; forgets to do what he or she has committed to do.

Is It Time to Worry About Your Teen's Inattention?

Worry Signs 3.1 lists possible symptoms of Attention-Deficit/ Hyperactivity Disorder, more commonly known as ADHD. Despite the name of the disorder, teenagers suffering from ADHD do not always exhibit symptoms of "hyperactivity." A large part of the syndrome includes difficulties with attention, organization, listening to others, and follow-through. Teens struggling with these types of behaviors are often diagnosed with ADHD, *Predominantly Inattentive Type* (previously known as Attention Deficit Disorder, Without Hyperactivity).

Because teens with the Inattentive Type of ADHD do not have major problems with impulsivity or hyperactivity, they are usually not loud or disruptive at home or in the classroom. Therefore, it is easy for parents, teachers, and other authority figures to overlook their difficulties. These teens can remain undiagnosed and untreated for years (sometimes for their entire lives), left to suffer from academic or vocational failure, parental disappointment and frustration, and a negative self-image. In contrast, the diagnosis often given to teens who have significant problems with overactivity and impulsivity is ADHD, *Predominantly Hyperactive/Impulsive Type.*

Even if your teen seems preoccupied, makes hasty mistakes, and frequently appears to not listen, *there is not necessarily reason for alarm.* Most adolescents experience some of the behaviors in Worry Signs 3.1, yet most adolescents do *not* have ADHD. This label designates a mental health disorder and is very different than occasional periods of teenage carelessness, forgetfulness, and disorganization. ADHD is a chronic condition; these behaviors are seen over many years in several different settings.

Your "worry barometer" should rise if your teen has shown most of the behaviors in Worry Signs 3.1 for much of his or her life, especially if the problems negatively impact your teen's functioning and are not primarily the result of other causes.

Adolescence is filled with periods of excitement, enthusiasm, and giddiness. Teenagers can be extremely passionate about personal beliefs, music, celebrities, and the opposite sex. Emotions sometimes seem unrestrained and volatile. How do you know when a teen is too exited or emotionally uninhibited? When should parents worry?

Daniel: Boys Being Boys or Going Way Too Fast?

Daniel, fourteen, cannot sit still. He bounces from one activity to another, without completing any of them. His overly high energy and excessive talking overwhelm his parents and sister to the point where they prefer he spend time in his bedroom. Daniel has few friends because his peers at school find him annoying; he barges in on their conversations, does not wait his turn during gym, and goofs off in class. His teachers are also at their wits' end and frequently send him to detention for misbehavior. Daniel continuously gets up from his seat during class, blurts out answers before questions are finished, and becomes increasingly excited and loud during group activities. He says he is "trying to be good" but is unable to get his behavior under control.

According to his mother, Daniel has always been "rambunctious" and "a handful." However, she now worries more about his safety. For the past several months, Daniel has regularly come home with bumps, bruises, and even a broken nose resulting from forceful roughhousing with an older neighbor. He has been caught skateboarding while holding onto moving cars—pulling him twenty-five miles an hour. He and his friends regularly climb the town's water tower, although he is the only one who hangs from the side beams once they reach the top. Daniel's latest thrill is catching rides with moving trains by holding onto ladders outside the cars. His parents know their son is smart but do not understand the foolish (and scary) decisions he makes. They are terrified to think about him behind the wheel of a car.

Although teenage boys like to roughhouse, go fast, and take risks, Daniel displays dangerous behavior that has already resulted in repeated physical injuries. His long history of impulsivity and overenthusiasm negatively affect his relationships with family members and kids his own age; he also regularly gets in trouble at school. Because Daniel will soon face decisions about cigarettes, drugs, alcohol, and sex (if he has not already), Daniel's parents need to know how much control he has to make good decisions.

Teens with Too Much Energy

Family, friends, and even strangers often become annoyed with teens who have too much energy or are too impulsive, because they touch (and sometimes take) items that are not theirs or damage objects because of their quick, reckless, or clumsy movements. They seem self-centered, bossy, and demanding and become frustrated and upset when their needs are not immediately met. They intrude upon conversations and activities and then monopolize discussions. Because they often say things without thinking about the ramifications of their words, they often hurt or offend others with insensitive comments. These youths are often viewed as rude, obnoxious, or exhausting, and rejection by peers and adults is common. Hyperactive and impulsive teens often suffer from low self-esteem and depression stemming from social difficulties; unfortunately, these teens are rarely aware of how their behavior pushes people away.

In addition to difficulties regulating their behavior, teens who are hyperactive and impulsive have trouble regulating their emotions. They may quickly go from excited and happy to extremely upset—as if on an emotional roller coaster. Given their emotional expressiveness, you typically know how they feel. Their uninhibited displays of anger can be overwhelming and scary; however, their unbridled enthusiasm and friendliness are refreshing. These youth probably do not experience feelings more strongly than others; instead, they do not rein in their emotions as much, so they can appear like drama queens or hotheads.

Hastiness and a lack of planning can result in reckless and irresponsible behavior. As youth move from early to late adolescence, impulsivity can lead to progressively more dangerous situations such as delinquency, smoking, drug use, physical injuries, sexual activity, physical fights, and car accidents.

Even when these teens know the right thing to do (and want to do the right thing), their impulsivity can make it hard for them to restrain themselves. This is why many teens who are hyperactive and impulsive engage in exciting and risky activities despite negative consequences. Penalties arrive later; their focus is what feels good *now*.

This extreme focus on the current moment typically results in trouble delaying gratification to achieve long-term goals. Consequently, adults frequently view hyperactive and impulsive teens as irresponsible, unreliable, and unconcerned about their future. The combination of society's view of them and their own disappointment with themselves leaves many of these teens feeling hopeless and destined to fail.

Worry Signs 3.2   Does Your Teen Have Too Much Energy?

The following behaviors point out important worry signs of teens with *too much energy*:

- Is always moving around or fidgets a lot.
- Finds it hard to sit still for lengthy periods of time; feels like he or she has to get up.
- Is overly active at inappropriate times.
- Is frequently loud, and has difficulty relaxing quietly.
- Is always on the move and is described as "high-energy" or "full of life."
- Talks too much.
- Is impatient and always in a hurry.
- Has difficulty waiting for his or her turn.
- Frequently interrupts or intrudes on others; often viewed as a nuisance.

Is It Time to Worry About Your Teen's Excess Energy?

Worry Signs 3.2 lists possible symptoms of Attention-Deficit/ Hyperactivity Disorder, *Predominantly Hyperactive/Impulsive Type*. Unlike the condition described at the beginning of the chapter (ADHD, *Predominantly Inattentive Type*), teens with this condition do not have significant problems remaining focused, remembering things, and staying organized. Instead, teens with the Hyperactive/Impulsive form of ADHD display excessive energy, restlessness, and a complete lack of planning.

There are many reasons teenagers exhibit the worry signs just listed; *most are nothing to be concerned about.* Some teens naturally have more energy and speak louder than their siblings or friends. And adolescents are not known for patience and good judgment. So even if you recognize your teen in a few of the behaviors described, you do not automatically need to worry.

Your "worry barometer" should rise if your teen has displayed most of the behaviors in Worry Signs 3.2 for much of his or her life, especially if the problems negatively effect your child's functioning and are not solely due to other factors.

As mentioned earlier, the syndrome of ADHD is a persistent condition, so behavioral difficulties are seen in a variety of settings and with many different people. For example, teens probably do not suffer from ADHD if they are impulsive at home but their peers, teachers, or work supervisors have never seen them behave impulsively. Adolescents with this disorder do not pick and choose specific times to be loud and lively; their overactivity is always with them. Symptoms may slightly improve with different surroundings (interacting with one person versus a group, quiet versus noisy environment), but this positive change is short-lived.

As adolescents with this type of ADHD mature, blatant "hyperactivity" often disappears; instead, teens feel restless and unable to relax.

But what if you recognize your teen in both Nicole's and Daniel's examples?

Unfocused *and* on the Run: What if You Recognize Your Teen in Both Nicole and Daniel?

Brandon, sixteen, seems to be in a hurry through life, though he usually does not have anyplace special to go. He moves through tasks (chores, schoolwork, homework) quickly, just to get them done, resulting in sloppy work and careless mistakes. His grades are poor because he becomes restless in the classroom and begins goofing off with friends. He and his parents wage nightly battles to get Brandon to do even part of his homework, because Brandon repeatedly gets up from his chair to move around. Despite rarely playing in an actual game, Brandon states that the only reason he goes to school is because he is on the football team. He says school is "totally boring."

Unfortunately, Brandon is close to being dropped from the football program. He does not follow his coach's directions and frequently interrupts when the coach is talking. Brandon does not wait his turn during football drills, which annoys the coach and his teammates. He has yet to finish memorizing this year's plays due to difficulty focusing on the playbook for more than ten minutes at a time. Brandon repeatedly arrives at football practice twenty minutes late, and when on the field, he is easily distracted by loud music or comments yelled by fans. When practice wraps up, he can still be found running laps or doing drills by himself.

Dirty clothes, old school assignments, and scratched or broken CDs and DVDs cover his bedroom floor. He is on his third cell phone; he lost his first two. Several nights a week he forgets to set the table for dinner—his only required chore for his weekly allowance. To make matters worse, he only half-listens during conversations with his parents, even when his parents are talking about his need to focus!

Teens who have ADHD, Combined Type, experience difficulty with distractibility *and* overactivity. They are forgetful *and* impatient. At school they struggle academically *and* behaviorally. These teens have displayed most of the worry signs from the "inattentive" *and* "hyperactive/impulsive" lists for much of their lives, which gets them into trouble. *The "Combined Type" of ADHD is actually the most commonly occurring form of the disorder.*

Teens with this form of ADHD are usually hyperactive as children, but their symptoms change as they mature and become increasingly aware of acceptable and nonacceptable public behavior. Rather than running around and climbing on things, they display their hyperactivity during adolescence internally—as impatience and restlessness. Problems with distractibility and disorganization typically remain unchanged.

ADHD and the Brain

Years of research on ADHD (including several types of brain research) consistently demonstrate that the symptoms of this disorder result from atypical brain development. These youth appear to have subtle, but fundamental, structural differences in their brain, as well as an imbalance in brain chemistry.

The *front portion of the brain* and its connections help us control our actions so we behave appropriately in society. It helps us:

- Pay attention.
- Plan ahead.
- Solve problems.
- Think through consequences of our actions.
- Keep our impulses in check.

This "command center" of the brain works in a way similar to how air traffic controllers decide when planes should take off, when they should wait, and when planes should return to the gate. Without this type of regulation and control, chaos would ensue, and planes would take off in a haphazard and dangerous manner. Similarly, when faced with information in the environment, teens can choose to respond immediately, wait and think before responding, or not respond at all. The front part of the brain helps teens select the most effective route given the circumstances.

Studies repeatedly show youth with ADHD have less electrical activity, less blood flow, and less brain activity in the front portion of the brain and throughout its connections. This slower activity is thought to be associated with two neurotransmitters, dopamine and norephinephrine. These brain chemicals are involved in helping us stay alert, remember things, and control our behavior. Teenagers with ADHD have *less* activity in the areas of the brain responsible for helping us to slow down, think things through, and remain focused.

ADHD is not the result of laziness, low intelligence, defiance, not trying hard enough, or being spoiled. Teens with ADHD may have these issues *in addition* to their condition, but these issues are not part of ADHD.

This Sounds Like My Teen, but What Else Could It Be?

Although many adolescents are distractible and/or impulsive, most of them do NOT have ADHD. To begin with, most teens exhibit only a few symptoms of ADHD. Even when they have several symptoms of the disorder, the majority of adolescents do not exhibit them to such an extreme that the behaviors cause significant problems in important areas of their lives, and most teens were not troubled by these symptoms as young children. Instead, difficulties with inattention, restlessness, or impulsivity developed in late childhood or early adolescence. Finally, a variety of factors can also affect teens' ability to focus attention and control their behavior, including the following:

- *High Levels of Stress:* Chaotic home environment, chaotic school environment, recent death of someone close, recent parental divorce, traumatic experience(s), parental or romantic partner abuse (emotional, physical, or sexual)

- *Biological Factors:* Sleep deprivation, hearing or vision problems, medical disorder, or undetected seizures

- *Toxicity:* Alcohol or drug use, side effects from medication, or food sensitivities or allergies

- *Lack of Intellectual Challenge:* Boredom due to understimulation at school or home

- *Another Emotional or Behavioral Condition:* Anxiety, Major Depression, Bipolar Disorder, or a Learning Disability

Although these conditions are unrelated to ADHD, an evaluation (and possibly treatment) may still be necessary if one or more of these issues is present.

Frequently Asked Questions About ADHD

1. Is ADHD inherited or caused by something in the environment, like bad parenting? There are several different causes of ADHD, some environmental, some genetic. Any pre- or postnatal experience that interferes with the flow of oxygen or blood to a developing brain can later result in symptoms of ADHD. The most common environmental causes include a maternal history of smoking cigarettes or drinking alcohol during pregnancy, multiple pregnancy complications, premature birth with minor brain hemorrhaging, and a major blow or injury to the head—especially the front of the head. Only about 20 percent of teens "acquire" ADHD in one of these, or similar ways.

Close to 80 percent of youth inherit the ADHD from their family. Studies of parents, siblings, relatives, identical and fraternal twins, children who have been adopted, and molecular genetics all show that ADHD has a strong genetic link. Parents with ADHD have a 50 percent chance of having a child with the condition, and siblings of youth with ADHD have two to three times the risk of having it themselves. Not surprisingly, this risk is even higher if the siblings are twins.

There is no evidence that ADHD is caused by "bad parenting" or "stressed-out" families. However, adolescents with ADHD function more successfully when parents appropriately modify their home and use specific strategies shown to be helpful for these youth.

2. Is ADHD a condition that affects mainly boys? Absolutely not. Boys and girls both suffer from ADHD; however, boys are more frequently *diagnosed* with the condition. Boys tend to exhibit more unruly and disruptive behavior than girls, resulting in more referrals to professionals. Girls with ADHD suffer academically to the same degree as boys with the disorder, yet girls tend to go undetected because their other symptoms are less troublesome. When they are referred, girls with ADHD are often diagnosed with depression or anxiety. Girls with ADHD are underdiagnosed and undertreated, which places them at risk for a variety of problems, including low self-esteem, school failure, and substance abuse.

3. My son has almost all of the described symptoms at home and school, but not when he spends the weekend with his father. Is that possible? Teens with ADHD are greatly affected by situational factors, and, as circumstances change, so does their behavior. Because they are even more affected by the environment (places, people, activities) than most other adolescents, behavioral consistency is rare. This discrepancy commonly causes disagreement about whether or not teens really suffer from ADHD. These youth may be calm and focused while interacting one-on-one with an adult, especially when interactions are structured and behavioral expectations are clear; they are also much better behaved when engaging in fun or interesting activities. However, these same teenagers may be overexcited and disorderly when they return to a less-structured environment or a group setting—especially in the presence of siblings or peers.

4. *Are there any cultural factors to be aware of with ADHD?* Experts believe the brain differences and behavioral symptoms seen in children and adolescents with ADHD occur in young people throughout the world, regardless of culture. However, various cultures interpret the behaviors of ADHD differently, and the manner in which mental health disorders are diagnosed also varies by culture.

5. *Is it possible my teen could have another emotional or behavioral problem in addition to ADHD?* It is rare to see a teenager with ADHD who does *not* have another mental health disorder. Learning Disabilities are seen in close to half of youth with ADHD. And, because many teens with ADHD have repeatedly experienced social, academic, and behavioral problems, they also often suffer from Anxiety and Major Depression as well. More than one-third of these youth also have Oppositional Defiant Disorder, a condition characterized by disobedience, disrespect, and annoying behavior. Teens with ADHD are also at significant risk to develop Conduct Disorder, a syndrome characterized by aggression, deceit, and delinquency. Successful treatment of ADHD is unlikely unless co-existing difficulties are treated as well. (Each of the conditions mentioned here is discussed in detail in separate chapters of this book.)

6. *If my teen truly suffers from ADHD, will he or she outgrow it?* ADHD is a chronic condition. Close to 80 percent of individuals diagnosed as children continue suffering from ADHD as teenagers,

and more than 65 percent of teenagers with ADHD continue suffering from the disorder as adults. For most teens, symptoms of
hyperactivity diminish as they mature. Inattentive symptoms sometimes improve by young adulthood, but only a small subset of teens
is completely symptom-free as adults.

7. *Isn't society overmedicating children and adolescents with ADHD?*
Has there been a significant increase in the number of teens with
ADHD on medication? Absolutely. Is it possible that some teens have
been prescribed medication for ADHD when they did not truly suffer from the disorder? Very likely. But that does not mean *most* teens
on stimulant medication do not need it. There are two likely reasons
for the increase in numbers: (1) mental health and medical professionals are better at identifying ADHD, so more youth receive the diagnosis; and (2) results from an eight-year, $10 million study by the
Federal Government on youth with ADHD (in the United States
and Canada) showed that stimulant medication was very effective
treatment for improving core symptoms of the disorder. Although
not meant to be used as the *only* intervention for ADHD, medication
is a critical part of an effective treatment program.

There are likely some cities and towns throughout the country—and particular doctor's offices—where too much medication
for ADHD is prescribed. However, studies done in several states
across the nation (in schools and the community at large) show that,
in general, only about half of youth with true ADHD ever took medication for their condition.

8. *Isn't medication for ADHD addictive? Will taking it make my teen
more likely to use street drugs?* Stimulants such as Ritalin and Adderall
are not addictive for teenagers with ADHD, *when taken as prescribed*.
These pills do not cause euphoria or a sense of being "high" (although some teens say it makes them feel funny or weird) because it
is slowly absorbed into their bloodstream. New extended-release
forms of these medications make absorption even slower. However,
when teens crush these pills and sniff the powder (like cocaine or
methamphetamine), they can experience more of a drug-like "rush"
because the drug enters their bloodstream so quickly. Teens with or
without ADHD who have drug abuse histories or who suffer from

Conduct Disorder are most likely to abuse stimulants. Nonstimulant medication is often prescribed for ADHD when concerns about abuse exist.

On occasion, parents, family members, or other caretakers of teens with ADHD have been discovered "borrowing" their teen's stimulant medication to take it themselves. Some of these adults are probably attempting to get "high." But others may find that the medication helps them better control their own attention and behavior, since ADHD runs in families. As with any mental health medication, the distribution and storage of stimulants should be closely monitored.

Teens with ADHD who do not receive treatment are three times more likely to abuse alcohol/drugs than teens who receive appropriate treatment (which may include medication) for this condition. Stimulant medication does not place a teen with ADHD at risk for substance abuse; not receiving treatment does.

9. Doesn't "treatment" stifle teens with ADHD? Shouldn't we just let them be themselves? Treatment does the opposite of stifling teens with ADHD—it increases their chance of success and allows them to soar. Research on youth with ADHD shows that almost one-third fail a grade in school, almost half are suspended from school, close to one-third drop out of high school, and only a small percentage earn a college degree. Teens with ADHD have sex earlier, have more sexual partners, use contraception less often, have higher rates of teen pregnancy, and have higher rates of sexually transmitted diseases than do their peers without this condition. They also receive more speeding tickets, have more and more *serious* car accidents, and are more likely to be at fault in car accidents. Appropriate treatment of ADHD decreases the risk of all of these unfortunate—and sometimes very dangerous—outcomes.

How You Can Help Teens Who Have Problems with Inattention, Hyperactivity, or Impulsiveness

If you recognized your teen from one of the sets of worry signs in this chapter, it is time to seek professional assistance. Your teen may or may not be suffering from ADHD. However, discovering what *is* underlying his or her difficulties is important—and will provide a clearer direction on how to best help your child.

Separating from parents and developing independence and autonomy are key developmental tasks during adolescence. Unfortunately, because teens with ADHD often behave impulsively and irresponsibly, parents feel the need to hold on tight, imposing limits and restrictions. Understandably, this can lead to increasing tension and family conflict.

The goal is to help adolescents with ADHD follow through on commitments, think through consequences of their actions, and gain better control over their own behavior—steps that can then be rewarded with increased parental trust and freedom. Parents can assist their teen in developing more responsible behavior by utilizing these strategies:

Reduce Distractions

- Teach teens to turn off anything that might distract them (cell phone, e-mail, text messages) during family dinners, when doing homework, or while doing any other activity requiring focused attention.
- Have teens sit in the front of the classroom, near the teacher and away from windows, doors, and other distractions.

Help Them Organize Tasks

- Write down behavioral expectations of teens in clear, concise language.
- Break down large tasks into small, easily managed steps.
- Help teens differentiate what is important from what is not; teach them to prioritize.
- Help teens organize their bedroom with clear containers and designated areas for specific items (books, homework, keys, cell phone, backpack).

- Buy them notebooks and folders with built-in organizers and spaces to write down daily homework assignments.

Provide Extra Support

- Supply external objects to help teens with their memory (clocks, calendars, watches, schedule books, Palm Pilots, daily schedules of appointments and tasks, weekly/monthly schedules of household chores).

- Remind teens to bring items to keep them occupied (books, magazines, video game, cell phone) when long periods of waiting are required.

- Provide repeated reminders via cell phone, pager, or text message regarding curfew, calling home, and running errands.

- Supervise potentially dangerous activities (driving, dating, or parties where drugs and alcohol may be present) until trust and independence are earned.

- Hire a mentor or coach to help teens set priorities, meet goals, and offer assistance with appropriate social skills.

- Make certain your teen takes medication (if prescribed) exactly as indicated. Look into once-daily dosing.

Help Problem-Solve

- Help teens with their decision-making skills by nonjudgmentally talking through difficult situations related to relationships, school and going to college, job choices, and risk-taking activities.

- Teach teens to make lists of "pros" and "cons" of alternative decisions to help them think through tough choices.

■ Help teens think through the consequences of their behaviors by discussing their plan of action.

Encourage New Activities

■ Encourage physical activity and exercise to reduce feelings of restlessness.

■ Do not force participation in team sports. Some teens with ADHD are physically awkward and un-coordinated and therefore are teased by athletically inclined peers.

■ Encourage teens to try summer jobs that offer variety or opportunities for movement and activity rather than working at single-focused office jobs.

■ Help teens channel their excess energy into construc-tive and productive activities.

Teens with ADHD have more trouble sticking with boring, lengthy, or tedious tasks (schoolwork, homework, household duties, or any type of lesson) than do teens without the disorder. Therefore, they need the following types of support:

■ Consistent and structured home and learning environ-ments that provide clear expectations so that they know exactly what to do

■ External motivation (praise, rewards, incentives) from adults that help them to stick with and complete activities

■ Constant feedback regarding what they are doing well and what they need to do to improve their behavior

■ Frequent, brief breaks

■ Immediate consequences for their behavior (being grounded tonight rather than over the weekend, get-ting daily report cards rather than final grades at the end of the year, receiving immediate praise rather than receiving it at the end of the day)

- Consideration (do not criticize or make fun of teens' performance in front of family, friends, or strangers)

It can be upsetting for parents to discover that their teen suffers from the syndrome of ADHD, particularly if a diagnosis was never given in childhood. However, parents also usually experience a sense of relief when discovering that they (or their parenting style) are not the cause of their teen's worrisome behavior. A diagnosis of ADHD does not take anything away from a teen's natural gifts. Teens with ADHD are some of the brightest, most creative, intuitive, imaginative, passionate, and kindhearted adolescents you will meet. Effective treatment can help teens with ADHD make the most of their talents, as well as assist them in areas where they struggle.

CHAPTER FOUR

Rebels Without a Cause
Teens Who Break Rules or Laws

I feel like I've totally lost control of my teen. It's only a matter of time before something really bad happens.

As children move into adolescence, they desire ever-increasing amounts of autonomy. Teenagers want more time with friends, less supervision, and as much decision-making power as possible. Adolescents are too young to handle every privilege of full-grown adults, yet too old to be coddled like young children. Finding the balance between letting teenagers spread their wings and also keeping a close eye on their endeavors is one of the most significant challenges of parenthood.

One way teens assert their independence is by challenging their parents and breaking household rules. During the adolescent years, parents are often shocked at how frequently their once-compliant child now talks back. It is difficult not to become frustrated when a teen repeatedly questions your requests or decisions, and difficult not to become angry if he or she blatantly refuses to comply.

Your teen may "forget" to complete household chores or "lose track of time" and return home past curfew. Adolescents frequently become irritated, annoyed, and sometimes even outraged when asked where they are going or whom they will be with. Parental supervision and family responsibilities can feel like anchors weighing them down, and some teens are quite verbal about wanting to spend time away from home. Not surprisingly, many parents and teens argue about household rules, chores, and curfew.

What is the difference between adolescents' normal need for privacy and purposely lying and hiding things from their parents? When does typical disobedience cross the line? When should you worry that your teen's risky behavior is becoming delinquent or dangerous? And at what point should you seek help outside the family for an out-of-control teen? This chapter reviews two important types of disruptive behavior: one defiant, and one aggressive, destructive, and delinquent.

Monica: Typical Teenage Autonomy or Persistent Rebel?

Denise Johnson, a single parent, feels like a horrible mother. She actually dreads when her daughter, Monica, now fifteen, comes home from school. Monica's negative attitude pervades the household, and she seems to get perverse pleasure from making the rest of the family miserable. She taunts her younger sister incessantly and refuses to do anything her mother asks of her. Monica's mother lost control of her a few years before; Monica's constant challenging and arguing finally wore her down. Monica had been difficult to manage even as a young child; if she did not want to do something, there was nothing her parents or teachers could do or say to make her comply. Now that Monica is in high school, nothing has changed. Monica's refusal to take responsibility for her behavior and her constant blaming of others for her misconduct has continued. When Monica's mother tries to hold her accountable for her negative behavior, Monica becomes irate and indignant. She refuses to go to her room as directed, and throws a tantrum, spewing mean, hurtful comments. She has called her mother a "bitch," a "fat, lazy, pig," and a "selfish slut who cares about nobody but herself."

It is not unusual for teenagers to bug a younger sibling. And getting a rise out of their parents every now and then can be amusing to teenagers. The difference is that Monica never gives it a rest. Monica disrespects her mother daily, blatantly defies her requests, and disregards her attempts at discipline. In addition, her relationship with her sister suffers because of Monica's persistent ridicule.

Teens Who Are Too Defiant

Most adolescents engage in behaviors like Monica's every now and then, particularly when stressed or in a bad mood. In contrast, teens who have problems with defiance display behaviors like hers over and over again. They are opposed to any type of directive, particularly from a parent. They are stubborn, headstrong, and demanding. These teens refuse to negotiate; it is *their* way or *no* way.

Adolescents who are too defiant constantly test any limits placed upon them; they are always checking just how far they can push those around them. These teens seem to enjoy irritating others; their goal is often to push parents to the point of exasperation. One typical way they do this is by refusing to engage with others; they answer complex questions with a single word or repeatedly utter "I don't know" to simple questions with obvious answers. Or, they just disregard those around them. For example, after repeatedly asking their teen to turn down music, annoyed parents may have to physically enter their son's or daughter's room to lower the deafening volume on the CD player. Within five minutes, the teen turns the sound up again. Blatant indifference and disrespect are common among extremely defiant teens. It is as if they forget that you are the parent and they are the child; in their minds, you both have equal amounts of power and influence.

One of the most frustrating aspects of teens who are too defiant is their heightened sensitivity to fairness and justice. They are acutely aware of when they have not received an equal share of food, time, money, attention, or use of the car. However, this heightened sensitivity runs only one way. They have a complete lack of concern for seeing that others receive their fair share of anything and in fact may minimize the person's claim or justify why the individual does not deserve something. Similarly, they find it perfectly acceptable to interrupt or disturb others but become infuriated when others impose upon them. Despite their disrespectful behavior, they view any slight against them (neighbors calling the police on a loud party, siblings reporting on the teen's negative behavior) as deserving of retaliation. Unfortunately, almost everything feels like a personal slight, so much of their energy is devoted to exacting revenge and settling scores.

Not surprisingly, teens who are too defiant have an aversion to being held accountable. They may become incensed by the accusations regarding their negative behavior. They usually blatantly deny what they have done, despite evidence or facts (the hood of the car is still warm, but a young man denies taking it for a drive; a young woman's parents see her sneak in the house at midnight, but she denies she went out for the evening). These youth always have an excuse for misbehavior and fault everyone but themselves. According to them, adults are unfair, expect too much, or did not give them enough time.

Although parents (especially stepparents) take much of the brunt from defiant teens, this group of adolescents does not discriminate. Teachers (particularly substitutes), siblings, neighbors, retail shop owners, and even police officers can experience the obnoxious, rude, and unpleasant nature frequently exhibited by these oppositional youth.

Worry Signs 4.1   Is Your Teen Too Defiant?

The following behaviors are important worry signs of teens who are *too defiant*:

- Gets angry and resentful at least four times a week.
- Deliberately annoys siblings, peers, or adults four or more times a week.
- Loses his or her temper or throws temper tantrums at least twice a week.
- Talks back or argues with adults twice a week.
- Purposely ignores or refuses to follow rules or requests from adults at least twice a week.
- Is extra-sensitive and easily irritated two or more times a week.
- Has blamed others for things he or she has said or done in the past few months.

■   Has acted in a purposely mean and vindictive way in the past few months.

Is It Time to Worry About Your Teen's Defiance?

The behaviors in Worry Signs 4.1 are symptoms of Oppositional Defiant Disorder, also known as ODD. Most parents are surprised to learn that a mental health condition primarily addressing disobedience and temper tantrums in teens even exists. In fact, most parents believe that oppositional and defiant behaviors are a normal and expected part of adolescence. They are right, but it is a matter of degree.

Teens may become increasingly argumentative or suddenly appear irritable and annoyed without necessarily suffering from ODD. In fact, the majority of teens do *not* have ODD. Oppositional Defiant Disorder is distinct from intermittent flare-ups or sporadic periods of rebelliousness. ODD tends to be a chronic condition that is present for many years and that is marked by argumentative and hostile behavior directed at a variety of individuals in several different settings.

Your "worry barometer" should rise if your teen has shown several of the behaviors from Worry Signs 4.1 for more than a few months, especially if the behaviors create problems for your teen at home, school, or work. These behaviors must not be primarily a result of factors listed in the "What Else Could It Be" section of this chapter.

Most parents with a child going through adolescence will recognize their son or daughter in a few of the behaviors I have described. A few symptoms of ODD are not the same as the syndrome of ODD. If you are the parent of a child suffering from this disorder, you probably did not need a list of worry signs to tell you something is wrong. You have likely spent years trying everything from reasoning with your child to time-outs, all with little success. Most teens with Oppositional Defiant Disorder do not spontaneously develop this disorder during the teenage years; what parents usually notice is a worsening of the defiant behaviors they observed before adolescence.

What if your teen is beyond defiance and has begun engaging in aggressive or illegal behavior?

Josh: Typical Teen Mischief or the Makings of a Criminal?

Josh, sixteen, will soon have nowhere to live. Josh's mother sent him to live with his father, but, after being threatened with military school, he returned to his mother's home and now refuses to go back to his father's. Josh regularly leaves the house at night with friends, does not return home until mid-morning, and often smells of alcohol or marijuana. His mother worries herself sick, praying she does not get a call from the police or, worse, the coroner. Josh is currently on probation for breaking into his school with friends and attempting to steal computers.

Throughout elementary school, Josh was frequently caught bullying younger children and humiliating them in front of others. He would also jab pens and pencils into the rear end of the family cat because he found it "funny" to hear it shriek. Josh's parents thought these behaviors were representative of "boys being boys" and assumed he would outgrow them.

In tenth grade, Josh's parents realized this was not just a phase. Josh regularly skipped classes, hung out with a tough crowd, and barely spoke to his parents other than to criticize or argue with them. Although his mother knew Josh regularly stole money from her purse, she was caught off guard after discovering he had forged her checks. When she confronted him about this behavior, Josh became enraged. He repeatedly slammed his fist on the table and eventually punched a hole in the door. From that moment forward, Josh's mother was frightened of her own child. Josh's continual problem behavior, combined with an already unhappy marriage, resulted in tremendous marital strain for his parents and eventually led to a divorce.

Josh displays a dangerous combination of substance use, theft, involvement with the juvenile justice system, and anger. *Without intervention, Josh is at significant risk for chronic and worsening anti-social behavior,* particularly given his history of childhood antagonism.

Teens Who Are Destructive, Aggressive, or Delinquent

Looking for excitement and taking risks are normal parts of the adolescent years. In fact, teenagers who do not engage in any risk-taking behavior often end up less well-adjusted than those who do. One survey found that a significant number of adolescents said they engaged in dangerous and potentially delinquent behavior: 35 percent reported having assaulted somebody, 45 percent said they had destroyed someone's property, 50 percent reported having stolen something, and 60 percent said they had committed more than one delinquent behavior, such as vandalism, an aggressive act, arson, or use of drugs.[3] So the question for many parents is not whether their teen is going to engage in potentially dangerous behavior, but to what extent and for how long? Fortunately, most adolescents only experiment with these behaviors and do not suffer major negative consequences. However, a subset of youth continues behaving in aggressive, destructive, or delinquent ways, usually with their actions worsening throughout the teenage years.

3. A.E. Kazdin, "Interventions for aggressive and antisocial children," in L. D. Eron, J. H. Gentry, and P. Schlegel (eds.), *Reason to Hope: A Psychosocial Perspective on Violence and Youth* (Washington, D.C.: American Psychological Association, 1996), pp. 341–382.

Worry Signs 4.2   Is Your Teen Destructive, Aggressive, or Delinquent?

The following behaviors are important worry signs that teens are in the *danger zone*:

Destroying Property

- Has purposely set fires hoping to cause serious damage.
- Has intentionally damaged someone else's property (e.g., slashing car tires, breaking windows, or smashing mailboxes).

Aggression

- Often acts like a bully; often threatens or intimidates others.
- Frequently instigates physical fights.
- Has used a knife, broken bottle, bat, gun, or another type of weapon.
- Has been physically cruel to animals.
- Has been physically cruel to people.
- Has mugged, extorted, or robbed people.
- Has forced someone to engage in sexual behavior.

Lying, Cheating, or Stealing

- Has burglarized a car, home, or building.
- Often tries to avoid responsibilities by lying; frequently tries to con others.
- Has shoplifted, forged checks, or stolen other items of value without facing a victim.

Violating Major Parental or School Rules

- Stays out all night without parental permission, beginning before age thirteen.

- Has run away from home and stayed overnight on at least two occasions while living at parent's or guardian's home; has run away and stayed away for several nights at least once.

- Frequently skips school without a valid excuse, beginning before age thirteen.

The behaviors in Worry Signs 4.2 are much more serious than the earlier questions related to Oppositional Defiant Disorder. Teens with ODD are challenging because of their rudeness, hostility, and disobedience—but they rarely injure others or commit delinquent acts. But, these are the exact behaviors seen among youth who are destructive, aggressive, and delinquent. The group of teens described in this section is more dangerous than teens with ODD, and, as you will see, they suffer from a different mental health condition.

Worry Signs 4.2 lists symptoms of Conduct Disorder, a mental health condition characterized by an enduring *pattern* of breaking rules and laws or violating the basic rights of others. *Conduct Disorder is different from ODD because of the more serious (and dangerous) nature of the condition.* Teens with ODD are disobedient, angry, and rude; they are annoying and frustrating, but usually not dangerous. Those with Conduct Disorder *repeatedly* assault people and animals, cheat, steal, or destroy the belongings of others. The behaviors that characterize Conduct Disorder are profoundly different from the occasional incidents of shoplifting, fighting, or school truancy seen among a significant number of "normal" teenagers.

Teens who are destructive, aggressive, and delinquent typically have significant school difficulties, including poor grades, school suspensions, and dropping out. They also suffer tremendous social difficulties with peers, as well as family members and other adults. These teens misperceive social interactions in the following ways:

- They view others as *more* hostile and threatening than they really are.

- They feel completely justified in responding with aggression.

- They view their own behavior as *less* hostile and threatening than it really is.

- They perceive themselves as "victims," even after harming someone else.

For example, if a peer accidentally bumps one of these teens while the two are walking through a crowded cafeteria, the aggressive teen tends to think the bumping was intentional and motivated by disrespect and/or a desire to intimidate. The aggressive teen is likely to respond with profanity, verbal threats, and possibly a physical assault. Not surprisingly, the recipient is puzzled and caught off guard; if the other teen is also aggressive, a fight is possible, with both individuals at risk for injury. Parents and other authority figures are often perplexed by the inappropriate and angry responses from these teens after neutral requests are made of them.

Destructive, aggressive, and delinquent teens are often rejected by peers because of their constant bragging and boasting, as well as their vulgarity and sarcasm. Many of these teens have not learned how to socialize appropriately. They monopolize conversations, have difficulty empathizing with the feelings of others, and are usually oblivious to the effects of their destructive and violent behavior. These teens tend to be limited regarding the topics they discuss, so most conversations with peers revolve around delinquent activity or alcohol and other drug use. When uncomfortable or apprehensive, these teens rely on what they know best: manipulation, lying, and intimidation. Because they think everyone is against them, these teens live by the motto "Get them before they get me." Most truly believe that antisocial behavior is the only way to get their needs met. As a result of their social limitations and their desire to be with individuals similar to themselves, destructive, aggressive, and delinquent teens typically end up hanging out together.

High-risk behavior is very common among these teens because of their impulsivity, thrill-seeking, and disregard for safety. They are at increased risk for unprotected and promiscuous sex, sexually transmitted diseases, unplanned pregnancies, and serious physical injury from automobile or other types of accidents or from physical fights. Both genders might use manipulation to get others to engage in sexual activities; boys may also use threats and intimidation.

Anger is a large part of the identity (how they view themselves) of this group of adolescents. If they grew up feeling powerless and out of control, their anger provides them with a sense of safety, strength, authority, and power. As a result, these teens may be attached to their anger and unwilling to give it up. Their anger may even have been adaptive in the past, given their family, neighborhood, school, or community. To them, relinquishing anger sets them up for weakness and vulnerability.

Although they appear to be strong and tough, many of these adolescents have very low self-esteem. They may be confident about their delinquent activities, ability to intimidate others, and other antisocial behavior but feel inadequate with regards to pro-social activities related to school, work, family, and relationships.

Alcohol and drug use is common among destructive, aggressive, and delinquent adolescents. For some, substance use precedes their antisocial behavior; others initiate alcohol and drug use after behavior problems are in full force. For some teens, substance use and acting out develop around the same time. Substance use can lower adolescents' inhibitions, further increasing the likelihood of their engaging in antisocial activities.

Is It Time to Worry About Your Teen's Aggression, Destructiveness, and Delinquent Behavior?

Parents understandably don't want to acknowledge that their child is cruel or committing delinquent acts. This upsetting thought is even worse if parents feel responsible for not preventing their teen's destructive activities. However, it is essential that parents admit to themselves and others when their child frequently engages in these behaviors. Without appropriate intervention, aggression, destruction, and delinquent behavior can worsen—and become even more dangerous for teens, their families, and society.

Your "worry barometer" should rise if your teen has shown three or more of the behaviors in Worry Signs 4.2 within the past year, especially if any of them have occurred within the past several months.

How Do Teens Develop Oppositional Defiant Disorder and Conduct Disorder?

ODD and Conduct Disorder are extremely complex conditions, so there is no single cause underlying their development. Although these conditions usually arise from the interaction between a child and the family in which he or she is raised, peer relationships, academic achievement, and neighborhood factors can also play a role. ODD and Conduct Disorder are not necessarily due to "bad" parenting—and blaming parents is not helpful. Some parents are unable to provide what their children need for a variety of reasons.

For example, a number of teens with ODD and Conduct Disorder were moody, irritable, and stubborn from birth. Babies and toddlers with these "difficult" dispositions are often unable to feel soothed by their parents, and some may even dislike being touched or held by anyone, including their mother. Parenting this type of child can be particularly challenging and frustrating. Despite continually trying to meet their child's needs, parents are repeatedly unsuccessful. Not surprisingly, over time, these infants and toddlers can become the target of parental anger or resignation.

The interaction between parent and child flows two ways, with each party influencing the behavior of the other. Sometimes their styles are so different that they are not a good "fit," and a parent and child bring out the worst in each other. As irritable and inflexible toddlers develop into irritable and inflexible children and adolescents, parents may never acquire the necessary strategies to manage them.

Defiant, aggressive, and destructive behavior can be learned in a variety of ways. Some children discover they can avoid unpleasant tasks by engaging in temper outbursts or blatant defiance. As their parents strive to get compliance with repeated requests or even commands, the child further escalates the behavior. Eventually, parents give in, and the child escapes performing what was asked of him or her. Although this pattern is usually learned early in life, those with behavior disorders may continue using the strategy throughout childhood and adolescence. This cycle gets worse when parents threaten negative consequences for the acting-out behavior but do not follow through and hold the child accountable.

Families may unwittingly reward disobedient or hostile behavior by providing increased attention to children when they become angry or loud. In fact, these families may not pay much attention when children behave quietly or make polite requests. There are also families in which intimidation and threats are commonplace during family interactions. Parents may yell, shame, or purposely scare their child into compliance. When parents or siblings engage in verbal or physical aggression (toward each other or a child), they inadvertently model it for young people in the home and communicate that this type of behavior is acceptable. By the same token, parents who engage in manipulative or illegal behaviors are teaching their children to do the same.

Some of the learning may take place outside the family. Many youth diagnosed with Oppositional Defiant Disorder and Conduct Disorder lived in out-of-home placements (foster care, group homes, residences of extended family members) during their formative years. These children may have experienced kind and loving environments or environments that were abusive or neglectful.

Once children learn that argumentativeness and aggression are effective tactics for getting their needs met, they may never learn socially appropriate ways of interacting with others. Unfortunately, when using antagonistic or intimidating strategies in a classroom, these youth frequently receive reprimands, sanctions, and school suspensions—lowering their desire for school involvement. Furthermore, youth with ODD and Conduct Disorder are commonly rejected by nonaggressive students at school. On the other hand, some nonaggressive peers reinforce intimidating and hostile behavior by submitting to aggressive teens' demands. Teens with ODD and Conduct Disorder tend to seek out peers similar to themselves (truant, hostile, and delinquent). Their negative behavior becomes further ingrained as these youth interact with one another and support an aggressive and destructive lifestyle.

This Sounds Like My Teen, but What Else Could It Be?

Teenage defiance, aggression, and destruction can result from a host of factors other than ODD and Conduct Disorder. Therefore, when parents observe these behaviors, they should ask themselves, "What else is going on?" Although this is an essential question for all the behaviors described in this book, it is particularly important here. Destructive behaviors can be a direct (and sometimes adaptive) response to external factors, such as the following:

- Living in a chaotic home with inconsistent parenting practices
- Experiencing a traumatic incident (contentious divorce, new school or neighborhood, physical or sexual abuse, rejection or abandonment, living on the streets, death of a loved one)
- Enduring continual embarrassment, frustration, or failure at school related to a Learning Disability
- Suffering from another mental health disorder that significantly impacts mood or behavior, such as ADHD, Depression, or Bipolar Disorder
- Living in a high-crime, drug-infested neighborhood where tough behavior is a survival strategy

- Rebellion by an adolescent searching for autonomy who is reacting to a parent who is holding on too tightly

- Experiencing intense pressure from a negative peer group or a romantic partner to defy authority or engage in delinquent activities

- Using alcohol or other drugs

Parents and professionals often jump too quickly to diagnose teenagers with Oppositional Defiant Disorder and Conduct Disorder without asking themselves *why* a teen would behave this way. There is no such thing as a "bad seed." Children do not spontaneously torture animals, steal things, or physically assault others.

It is easy for a misbehaving teen to be viewed by a family as the cause of all the family's problems, leaving other important family issues unidentified and unchanged.

The conditions just presented can each trigger rebellion or delinquency in teenagers without ODD or Conduct Disorder. Because of the negative—and often dangerous—effects of defiant, aggressive, or destructive behavior, an evaluation and possibly family treatment may still be necessary when one or more of these issues is present.

Frequently Asked Questions About Oppositional Defiant Disorder and Conduct Disorder

1. *Do ODD and Conduct Disorder look different in girls?* Much less is known about girls with ODD and Conduct Disorder than about boys with these conditions. ODD appears to occur at the same rates among both genders during the teen years, while Conduct Disorder is more common in boys. Boys with Conduct Disorder tend to engage in aggressive or confrontational behaviors, such as fighting, stealing, hurting animals, setting fires, destroying property, or rebelling at school. They are more likely to display oppositional, hostile, and destructive behavior at an early age and exhibit problem behavior for lengthy periods of time.

Girls typically develop ODD and Conduct Disorder during adolescence, with girls suffering from ADHD at particularly high risk for behavior problems. Girls usually engage in less obvious and nonaggressive behaviors such as lying, school truancy, shoplifting, fraud, running away, and prostitution. Instead of physical attacks, many girls with ODD and Conduct Disorder engage in *relational* aggression—rejecting, humiliating, slandering, alienating, or threatening other girls. Girls suffering from *severe* Conduct Disorder can be as violent and destructive as boys with the condition.

2. *Are there any cultural factors to be aware of with ODD or Conduct Disorder?* Teenagers who use aggression or delinquent behavior to survive are typically not diagnosed with ODD or Conduct Disorder. For example, teenagers living in inner-city neighborhoods plagued with violence and crime may engage in antisocial activities purely as a response to their surroundings. Adolescents who have immigrated from war-torn countries may have engaged in destructive, even violent, behavior in their homeland in order to stay alive. Because ODD and Conduct Disorder should be diagnosed when aggression or destruction stems from an intrinsic desire to challenge or harm others (rather than as a reaction to one's environment), evaluators must always consider the social context in which youth reside.

3. *Is it possible my teen could have another emotional or behavioral condition in addition to ODD or Conduct Disorder?* Attention-Deficit/Hyperactivity Disorder (ADHD) commonly coexists with these conditions. Many adolescents with ODD or Conduct Disorder also suffer from Major Depression, Anxiety, Dysthymia, Post-traumatic Stress Disorder (PTSD), Learning Disabilities, or Substance Abuse. A number of teenagers with severe Conduct Disorder suffer from neurological problems, head trauma, and seizures. Assaultive adolescents have higher rates of suicide than nonassaultive youth, and the combination of Conduct Disorder and Depression places teens at significant risk for suicidal behavior.

Unfortunately, the medical, mental health, educational, and juvenile justice systems narrowly focus on the aggressive and delinquent behavior of teens with ODD and Conduct Disorder. This typically results in repeated referrals to juvenile justice, postponing access to appropriate—and much needed—mental health services.

Treatment of ODD or Conduct Disorder must include treatment of coexisting mental health conditions if one hopes for any chance of success.

4. *If my teen truly suffers from ODD or Conduct Disorder, will he or she outgrow it?* Most children with ODD outgrow their defiant and hostile behavior—particularly when parents learn and use effective management strategies. However, when the behavior of youth with ODD worsens, they may develop the more serious condition Conduct Disorder. Children with both ODD and ADHD are at particularly high risk for developing Conduct Disorder.

Before you panic, remember that a diagnosis of Conduct Disorder does not ensure a lifetime of aggression and criminal behavior. Teens with relatively problem-free childhoods, positive friendships, and adequate grades are more likely to outgrow adolescent Conduct Disorder—especially when negative behavior primarily occurs with peers rather than solo. Teenagers most at risk for long-term violence and destruction are those who displayed these behaviors before the age of ten. These youngsters tend to be more aggressive, reckless, and irresponsible; they have greater difficulties in relationships and school than those whose misconduct began at a later age. Teens with *severe* Conduct Disorder should be viewed as suffering from a *chronic* condition requiring long-term mental health treatment.

5. *Does violence on television and in movies cause ODD or Conduct Disorder? What about violent video games?* Decades of research consistently show that children exposed to violence in the media are more likely to behave aggressively, be less sensitive to the pain and suffering of others, and feel more frightened of the world they live in. Even as adults, they are more aggressive. In 2000, several prominent health and mental health associations signed a joint statement on the dangers of exposing children to violence in the media. They all agreed that more than one thousand studies overwhelmingly point to a causal connection between media violence and aggression in some children.

Video games are a more recent phenomenon, so there has been less research on their effects. Studies have found that youth who play a lot of violent video games have more aggressive thoughts, feelings, and behaviors. They are also less willing to be kind or helpful to others. Violent video games may be even more harmful to young people than TV because of their interactive nature and reinforcement for killing people, and because teens play these games over and over again.

ODD and Conduct Disorder are not caused by one factor, so watching violence on TV, movies, or video is not likely the sole cause of either condition. However, violence in the media can certainly contribute to the development of these disorders and increase a child's risk of suffering from one of them.

6. *Will having teens arrested teach them a lesson?* Sometimes the experience of being arrested, going to juvenile court, or residing for a few days in a juvenile detention center can be enough to decrease future destructive behavior. This response, however, is most common among adolescents with a mild case of Conduct Disorder. Some teens with Conduct Disorder, especially those with a moderate to severe form, may end up incarcerated for several months or years due to delinquent or violent behavior. Confinement can be beneficial when teens receive academic assistance, help for coexisting mental health and substance abuse disorders, skill-based treatment, and parental involvement, as well as support services upon release. Imposition of punishment and accountability without addressing underlying issues, teaching new skills, and reinforcing positive changes has little chance of success and usually results in teens feeling dejected and hopeless.

7. *If my teen has been arrested or spent the night in juvenile hall, does that mean he or she automatically has Conduct Disorder?* Not necessarily. Many teens who have been arrested or spend time in juvenile hall do not show the extensive pattern of antisocial behavior required for a diagnosis of Conduct Disorder. And a good number of teenagers with Conduct Disorder have never been caught and arrested for their negative behavior. Teens processed through the juvenile court system are labeled "juvenile delinquents" or "juvenile offenders." These are *legal* terms. Con-

duct Disorder is a *mental health* term and refers to youth who exhibit a pattern of behaviors that include, but are not limited to, those that are against the law.

8. *Should I be concerned if my teen is in a treatment group with other delinquents?* Parents should exercise caution when placing teens with ODD or Conduct Disorder in treatment groups or facilities where other aggressive or destructive adolescents are present. Although designed to be therapeutic, gatherings of several ODD and Conduct Disorder youth can quickly disintegrate into a breeding ground for negative and dangerous behavior as teens reinforce one another's antisocial attitudes and actions. One of the unfortunate effects of incarceration is that adolescents with mild Conduct Disorder often adopt the attitudes and behaviors of more dangerous and antisocial teens with whom they reside.

9. *What do I do if I am afraid my teen will seriously harm me or my other children?* When teens are so dangerous that they or their family members are at imminent risk of harm, parents may need to consider an out-of-home placement. This may take the form of a crisis shelter, therapeutic group home, or residential treatment facility. Even during periods when teens reside elsewhere, it is critical that family members continue to be involved with their child's treatment services.

How You Can Help Teens with Defiant, Destructive, Aggressive, or Delinquent Behavior

If you are concerned that your teen's behavior may be more severe than normal teenage rebellion and misconduct, you should seek professional assistance. A comprehensive evaluation can help determine whether your teen's behavior is within the range of "normal" adolescence, whether he or she suffers from ODD or Conduct Disorder, or whether the behavior stems from another type of difficulty.

Although most teens benefit from the parenting strategies listed here, these skills are particularly critical when managing teenagers with ODD or Conduct Disorder:

Hold Teens Accountable

- Clearly convey that you disapprove of a teen's *behavior*—not the teen as a person.

- Establish positive and negative consequences for specific behaviors. Make sure consequences are in proportion to the behavior, and deliver them without engaging in harsh, punitive, or demeaning parenting practices.

- Remove teens from situations (mealtime, family activity, attendance at church or synagogue, social function) if teens' behavior becomes hostile or destructive.

- Choose your battles. Focus your energy on adolescent behaviors with permanent negative results or those that threaten the safety of a teen or others.

Be Clear, and Present a United Front

- Communicate simple, clear, and well-defined expectations and rules. It's okay to sound like a broken record. Tell teens what *to* do rather than what *not* to do.

- Present a united front when managing teen misconduct even if you have different opinions. Because youth with ODD or Conduct Disorder often pit adults against each other, the parents' *response* to teens should be identical.

- Mental health and health professionals, teachers, mentors, and other significant adults in a teen's life should provide rewards and discipline for the same behaviors that parents are working on in the family home.

Don't take a negative attitude or negative behavior personally

- Let teens "cool off" in their bedroom or another quiet location when their behavior becomes increasingly angry, irritated, or upset.

- Respond to teens' misbehavior in an objective, matter-of fact manner. Youth with ODD and Conduct Disorder get pleasure from provoking emotional responses in others, especially authority figures.

- Be a parent to your teen—not a friend. Adolescents may not like you when you hold them accountable, but this is temporary. This also helps you gain (or regain) their respect.

Supervise Strategically

- Allow appropriate amounts of autonomy and independence so that teens do not feel the need to rebel. Set up ways for adolescents to *earn* increasing amounts of freedom and privileges after exhibiting responsible and trustworthy behavior.

- Monitor teens' friends and out-of-home activities until teens earn your trust. Prohibit conversations that glorify antisocial activities, should you overhear them.

- Do not take a lenient and "hands-off" approach to parenting, even when frustrated and resigned.

- Express care and concern for your teen's safety. Don't appear controlling and punitive.

- Obtain weekly updates from your teen's school, and meet with school personnel several times per year.

Encourage Pro-Social Behavior, While Discouraging Antisocial Behavior

- Organize opportunities for teens to interact with pro-social youth.

- Praise and reinforce teens' attempts at appropriate and pro-social behavior. Think baby steps. This is just as important as disciplining antisocial or aggressive behavior.

- Give teens hope that their aggressive behavior can be changed. When teens are demoralized and hopeless, they cling even more tightly to their destructive ways.

- Discourage association with irresponsible, rebellious, or aggressive peers.

Be a Good Role Model

- Wait until tempers calm down (yours and your teen's) before discussing a teen's behavior, attitude, or anti-social opinion. Try to understand your adolescent's position, even if you do not condone it.

- Follow through on all agreements made with teens, no matter how trivial.

- Obtain assistance for difficulties you may be experiencing (significant stress, substance abuse, anger, depression, or excessive nervousness), even if they are in response to your teen's behavior.

Utilize Community Resources

- Promote and support all positive relationships with responsible adult figures (e.g., extended family members, teachers, coaches, neighbors, mentors, spiritual leaders).

- Utilize positive programs such as churches, synagogues, Big Brothers Big Sisters, and mentor programs as needed.

- Utilize the juvenile justice system when necessary for intensive supervision, maintenance of compliance, and access to skill-building programs and special schools.

Because adolescence is a period when all teens work at separating from parents, exploring new peer groups, pushing parental limits, and experimenting with risky behavior, your teen may appear rebellious and unsafe. I hope that this chapter helped distinguish between typical teenage defiance and misbehavior and the serious and problematic clinical conditions known as Oppositional Defiant Disorder and Conduct Disorder. When these conditions are present, appropriate intervention is critical to help your teen achieve success in school, at work, in relationships, and at home.

CHAPTER FIVE

Run by Fear

Teens Who Stress, Obsess, or Are on Edge

Why are you so worried and stressed out all of the time? I wish you could just relax.

Insecurity abounds during the teenage years. Adolescents are uncertain of who they are, who they want to be, and who they want to be affiliated with. They worry about whether they are "enough": pretty enough, skinny enough, muscular enough, tough enough, popular enough, friendly enough, smart enough, cool enough, sexy enough. These concerns are normal and expected during the teenage years (and they do not necessarily magically disappear in adulthood!). However, some adolescents take these worries to the extreme. Their worries are so strong and so intense that they overtake everyday emotions and activities. This chapter reviews five of the most common ways fear and anxiety disrupt the lives of today's teenagers.

Keisha: Typical Teenage Insecurity or Excessive Worrier?

I'm not sure how much more of this I can take. My daughter Keisha woke me up again saying she heard some "noises." She's convinced burglars are going to climb through her window and steal her computer. I found hairspray under her bed—"I'm going to spray the robber in his eyes if he attacks me," she said. I've already installed locks on her windows and we live on the second floor. At fourteen, she shouldn't be scared like this, and this isn't the only thing she worries about. If I don't return her calls immediately, she panics. I've tried telling her it's difficult for me to get to the phone at work, but she becomes so upset. And her hair, she repeatedly asks if it's too short. It looks fine, which I tell her, but it doesn't make a difference. If it isn't her hair, it's her weight, the sound of her voice, how she should wear her makeup, or her short stature. She continually complains of stomachaches and headaches. And I know she hasn't slept much for months due to this burglar thing. One minute I just want to hold my baby and tell her it's going to be okay, and the next I want to tell her to grow up!

Keisha worries much of the time about a variety of different matters, several of which seem unwarranted, given her current circumstances. In addition, her excessive worrying appears to negatively impact her health and her relationship with her mother. If this behavior has gone on for several months, Keisha's mother should be concerned.

Teens Who Worry All the Time

Adolescents who worry all the time are usually easy to recognize. They take everything seriously and seem to always be concerned about *something*. It would not be unusual to hear the following comments stated by one of these teens *during a twenty-four-hour period*: "She hasn't called me back; I hope she isn't mad at me," "I didn't know two items on the test; I think I failed it," "Does this shirt look okay?" "We have to hurry, we can't be late," "It's not good enough; I need to do it again." These youth usually strive to be the best at whatever they do. They find it imperative to achieve high grades, be popular, dress stylishly, have excellent hygiene, keep a tidy and organized bedroom, return phone calls/e-mails/text messages promptly, be punctual, and be the best at whatever pursuits they undertake (sports, dance, part-time job). As much as people encourage them to "stop and smell the roses," these youth do not know how. They are determined to complete tasks "the *right* way."

Because of their high level of worry and concern, these teens typically want to make sure everyone around them is happy. They will exhaust themselves trying to meet the needs of friends, family, and romantic partners—even without being asked. Ironically, this "people-pleasing" behavior can actually wear on others, who often would rather these teens relax and just be. Their constant need for reassurance—"Are you happy?" "Does it taste okay?" "Did I do something to make you mad?" "Can I get you something?"—often irritates those closest to them.

These teens frequently have a continual fear that something tragic is about to happen. They worry excessively about natural disasters, terrorists, car accidents, diseases, and friends or family getting injured or killed. They may worry a great deal about their own physical safety and are often scared someone is going rob, attack, or rape them. Even when they know their fears are unwarranted, these teens have difficulty letting them go.

Rather than live in the here-and-now, these teens overfocus on the future. More often than not, they predict that terrible things will occur or that they will not be able to handle what lies ahead. This thinking leads to increased apprehension and self-doubt and takes a toll on their physical health, emotional wellbeing, and ability to concentrate.

Worry Signs 5.1   Does Your Teen Worry All the Time?

The following behaviors are important worry signs of teens who *worry excessively*:

- Seems nervous, fearful, or uneasy most of the time.
- Worries too much about a variety of different issues.
- Finds it difficult to stop worrying, even after making an effort.
- Finds that the excessive worrying affects emotions, thinking, or physical health.

- Frequently seems impatient and on edge.

- Easily annoyed or irritated.

- Frequently has difficulty focusing for long periods of time or maintaining a train of thought.

- Frequently has difficulty sleeping.

- Often complains of feeling tired or "worn out."

- Regularly complains of tight or sore muscles.

Is It Time to Be Concerned About Your Teen's Excessive Worrying?

Worry Signs 5.1 lists symptoms of Generalized Anxiety Disorder, also known as Generalized Anxiety or GAD. What makes GAD different from the typical fears and doubts of adolescence is how often these youth worry, the number of issues they worry about, how intensely their worry is experienced, and how out of proportion it is to the situation.

Some teens with Generalized Anxiety Disorder appear successful due to academic, athletic, social, or occupational accomplishments. However, external victories often cover up significant internal suffering, emotionally and physically. Adolescents with GAD rarely experience pleasure in life because nothing is ever good enough (they cannot stop thinking about how something could have been better, quicker, healthier, neater, kinder, or safer) or because they fear that something terrible is just around the corner.

Your "worry barometer" should rise if your teen has shown several of the behaviors in Worry Signs 5.1 for more than a few months, especially if the worrying has negatively affected your child's relationships or physical health.

Some teens do not worry all the time; instead, their fear specifically relates to being around unfamiliar people and/or speaking in front of a group.

Carlos: Typical Teen Awkwardness or Serious Social Fears?

Carlos, sixteen, cannot talk to girls. He even seems uncomfortable around his twin sister's friends, despite having known them for several years. Whenever the girls come to the house, Carlos immediately heads for his bedroom. On one occasion, they asked him to help carry in some boxes, and he stuttered and stammered, blushed uncontrollably, and started to shake. Since that day, he refuses to even wave to them at school out of embarrassment. Carlos's friends have begun to date, but just the thought of asking a girl out makes him nauseous. More often than not, he refuses to attend social events, including large family gatherings. He always finds an excuse not to join his parents at church. And he has attended only one school football game in two years. Carlos stays busy riding his bike, playing video games, and adding to his CD collection. Because his time is spent alone or with his one best friend, Carlos's parents encourage him to broaden his social circle. They are repeatedly met with resistance and sometimes a flat-out refusal to participate in the discussion.

It is normal and expected that teenage boys will be uncomfortable and awkward around girls their own age. However, Carlos's nervousness is extreme and out of proportion to the situation and does not appear to be a phase. His social avoidance significantly limits his participation in several common adolescent and family activities; although he has other interests, socially he sticks with a peer he knows well.

Teens Who Are Too Nervous Around Others

When around new people or speaking in front of a group, teens who are too nervous around others are terrified they will do something to embarrass or humiliate themselves. These youth are significantly more self-conscious than most teens and overfocus on any social slip-up they may make—regardless of how minor. Even a casual conversation with someone new can be a challenge, because they worry that their voice will be in some way unpleasant, that they may say something foolish, or that others will think they are "weird." Blushing, sweating, trembling, and experiencing a rapid heartbeat, clammy hands, nausea, and light-headedness are common. Their concern that others will notice these physical symptoms (and then view the teen negatively) makes them even *more* nervous. Not surprisingly, these youth are most comfortable around their family and closest friends; when they are around "safe" people, their symptoms may completely disappear.

Adolescents who are too nervous around others experience extreme worry, doubt, and dread weeks or months before a new social situation or public-speaking event. As the time grows closer, they do all they can to avoid participating by becoming ill, scheduling a conflicting commitment, refusing to go, sleeping through it, or "forgetting" about it. When forced to participate, they experience overwhelming feelings of panic and dread. This reinforces for them how awful these situations are and increases their anxiety the next time they are faced with a similar situation. This vicious cycle can go on for years. Even when these teens realize they are overreacting to circumstances, they cannot control their intense fear.

These adolescents frequently lack confidence and have difficulty standing up for themselves. They are extremely sensitive to negative feedback and commonly feel rejected or criticized by others. In their minds, new people especially are always judging them.

It is common for these youth to avoid parties or proms, dating, large school events, athletic activities (including physical education classes), or any type of performance situation. Because making oral presentations, working in groups, and publicly asking or answering questions are standard classroom activities, these teens frequently avoid certain classes or sometimes refuse to go to school altogether. Just knowing that teachers evaluate exams can create significant test anxiety, compromising their academic performance. As they mature, teens who are too nervous around others may avoid applying for college or seeking employment if face-to-face interviews are required. Although this is not as common, some of these youth are unable to use public restrooms when others are in close proximity, eat in front of others (e.g., in the school cafeteria or a restaurant) for fear of choking or spitting up their food, or write in front of others in case their hands start shaking. As one can imagine, this pattern of social avoidance interferes with typical teenage interests and activities. In severe cases, youth with extreme nervousness around others can end up dropping out of school, living with their parents as adults, and never finding meaningful employment.

Given twenty-first century technology, some teens conceal their intense social angst by socializing *solely* on computers through e-mail, instant messages, and online chat rooms. Although this provides a sense of belonging and acceptance by peers (critical during adolescence), the lack of in-person interactions prevents these teens from developing appropriate social skills and true intimate relationships—and continually reinforces their avoidance behavior.

Worry Signs 5.2   Is Your Teen Too Nervous Around Others?

The following behaviors are important worry signs of teens who *are too nervous around others*:

- Acts noticeably uncomfortable or anxious when meeting or interacting with someone new.

- Is terrified to speak in front of a group.

- Seems aware that the level of distress felt is excessive compared to that felt by peers.

- Avoids situations where interaction with unfamiliar people or performance in front of others will be necessary.

- If feared situations cannot be avoided, is miserable while going through them.

Is It Time to Worry About Your Teen's Nervousness Around Others?

Worry Signs 5.2 lists symptoms of Social Anxiety Disorder (previously referred to as Social Phobia), one of the most common anxiety disorders among teenagers. Because adolescents have such a high need to fit in with peers, most teens experience periods of intense self-doubt and insecurity—particularly when attending a new school, interacting with the opposite sex, or spending time in the vicinity of the "popular" crowd. Self-consciousness about one's body, abilities, or social status is *normal* during this developmental period. So the fact that your teen feels awkward or nervous in social situations does not mean that a diagnosis of Social Anxiety Disorder is necessarily justified.

Your "worry barometer" should rise if your teen has shown several of the behaviors in Worry Signs 5.2 for more than a few months, especially if these social fears get in the way of school, work, relationships, or the performance of day-to-day tasks.

Teenagers with social anxiety may exclusively be frightened of speaking in front of groups, or they may be fearful of a variety of situations where they must interact with people they do not know well. Some teens with the condition strongly dread both.

The fears of teens with social anxiety are related to interacting with others. However, another group of teens with anxiety seem controlled by repetitive thoughts or actions.

Kristin: High Maintenance, or Thoughts and Habits Beyond Her Control?

Kristin, fourteen, is terrified she is going to catch a sexually transmitted disease (STD) and constantly worries about it. Her only sexual behavior is kissing, but she hasn't kissed a boy for over a year. Over the past eight months, Kristin stopped letting boys hold her hand for fear they would pass along an STD if they did not wash up after using the toilet. In fact, she will not let any male hold her hand—including her father and her uncle. Kristin refuses to use towels in the family bathroom for fear a family member might give her an STD. After each shower, she must use a clean towel and immediately put it in the hamper. She begs her mother to do the laundry more often because she is sometimes forced to use the same towel repeatedly. Kristin refuses to use the school bathrooms for fear of STD "germs," and has never attended a same-sex sleepover due to what she thinks she could catch from others' sheets or pillowcases. Her hands are dry and chapped from repeated washings; she takes two to three showers a day.

Teenagers must be aware of sexually transmitted diseases and take precautions to protect themselves. However, Kristin is preoccupied with catching one of these conditions, despite the fact she is not sexually active. In addition, she engages in protective behaviors over and above what is necessary, even if she were at risk. Kristin's anxiety—and her ritualistic behavior to decrease that anxiety—negatively impacts her relationships and day-to-day activities.

Teens with Obsessive Thoughts or Compulsive Behavior

Although the terms "obsessive" and "compulsive" are becoming more common in everyday language, many individuals are not aware of the true definition of these terms.

Obsessions

Obsessions are continually repeating ideas, images, or thoughts that people cannot get out of their heads. They are much more than typical concerns and are extremely troubling and upsetting, particularly because people feel they cannot control them. Adolescents who experience obsessions desperately try to stop thinking about these issues, either by ignoring them or by trying to counteract them by engaging in another thought or behavior. Common obsessions include *persistent thoughts* about contamination (being "dirty," contracting germs, catching a terminal disease); wanting items in a specific order (belongings in bedroom should be in their "exact" place, food should be eaten in a particular sequence, everything should be symmetrical or balanced); and constant doubts (wondering if the door is locked, checking to make sure the dog is still alive, inspecting the toilet to make sure it was flushed). Even when youth know these concerns are unwarranted and excessive, they cannot stop worrying about them.

Compulsions

Compulsions are behaviors or mental actions that people feel driven to carry out; they are usually related to a particular obsession or to specific rules that they believe they *must* follow. Repeated hand washing, doing the same behavior over and over, arranging things in precise order, and checking to make sure something has or has not occurred are common *compulsive behaviors*. Counting things, praying, or silently repeating words can become *compulsive mental acts* when teens continually feel driven to do them. Compulsions are not enjoyable; they are strictly done to decrease anxiety and/or stop something terrible from happening. They are extreme, with no actual connection to what they are trying to prevent.

Adolescents who worry about contamination are hypersensitive to anything they perceive as "unclean." Like Kristin, they may refuse to use public restrooms because of potential germs;

even at home, they may go through excessive amounts of toilet paper to avoid accidentally tainting their hands with urine or feces. These youth might avoid restaurants, cafeterias, or any place where they are not in control of food preparation. If forced to eat in these establishments, they have specific rituals to disinfect their meal (eating only cooked foods, eating only the parts not touched by the cooks, wiping off food surfaces with a napkin). The skin on their hands may be red, extremely dry, and cracked as a result of frequent washing with harsh antibacterial soaps. Or they may constantly think they have caught an illness or disease.

Teens obsessed with symmetry and order suffer greatly when things are unbalanced or not in their "right" place. They can become overwhelmed with distress when placed in chaotic, disorganized, or cluttered environments or situations. These youth are driven to arrange, order, and organize to calm themselves and find relief. Some may need to repeat with their left hand everything they do with their right hand, in order to "balance it out." If they looked to the left for ten minutes, they then need to look right for ten minutes.

Perplexed parents wonder why teens touch the light switch four times after turning it off, walk in and out of doorways repeatedly before walking through them, redo their homework assignments three to five times, or rewrite e-mails to friends eight to ten times before sending them. Most teens explain with "I don't know, I just feel like I *have* to," "I need to do it until *it feels right*," or "If I don't, something *bad* will happen." Because teens do not want to find out what that "something bad" is, they continually engage in the compulsive behavior to keep it at bay.

Knowing their actions are unnecessary and extreme does not stop these youth from doing them. If they resist engaging in the behavior, their anxiety and stress rise to such an uncomfortable level they almost always give in to the compulsion to find relief. If the condition goes on long enough, compulsions just become a part of their everyday life.

Adolescents usually attempt to hide their compulsive rituals so as not to appear "crazy" or "weird." However, they are more likely to engage in them at home and around people who know them well. The following is a list of possible indicators of obsessions or compulsions. Because they can be indicative of a variety of issues, you should follow up only if a *pattern* exists:

Takes Too Much Time to Complete Tasks (due to distracting obsessive thoughts or time-consuming rituals)

- Takes an excessively long time to complete homework assignments.
- Is unable to finish tests or assignments in the classroom.
- Needs an excessively long time to get dressed and ready for school.
- Spends an excessively long time in the bathroom.
- Is inclined to chronic lateness, even to important events.

Displays Unusual Rigidity About Daily Routines

- Is fixated on order or symmetry.
- Is excessively neat and tidy.

Has Unusual Appearance or Behaviors

- Has red, chapped hands, regardless of the weather.
- Overfocuses on preventing illness, without just cause.
- Touches or says things over and over.
- Repeatedly checks on or continually asks for reassurance about one or two specific issues.
- Has poor school grades despite intellectual potential and an interest in school.
- Avoids touching anything "dirty"—money, car door handles, family telephone, TV remote control.

Worry Signs 5.3   Does Your Teen Have Obsessive or Compulsive Behavior?

The following behaviors are important worry signs of teens who are *obsessive or compulsive:*

- Frequently experiences "obsessive" thoughts.

- Repeatedly engages in "compulsive" behavior.

- At some point acknowledges that these obsessions or compulsions are out of the ordinary and unnecessary.

Is It Time to Worry About Your Teen's Obsessive Thoughts or Compulsive Habits?

Worry Signs 5.3 lists symptoms of Obsessive Compulsive Disorder, also known as OCD. These behaviors are much different from those of adolescents who get a song stuck in their head or doublecheck their backpack to make sure they have their cell phone. Part of what distinguishes these teens from their peers is how *time-consuming* and *restricting* their obsessive thoughts and compulsive behaviors are. Your "worry barometer" should rise if your teen's moods, academics, job, friendships, or family life are negatively impacted by the obsessions or compulsions.

Most of the fears strongly felt by teens with Obsessive Compulsive Disorder will never be realized. Another group of adolescents who experience anxiety develop their symptoms as a direct result of very real and traumatic events.

Michelle: Typical Teenage Withdrawal or Reaction to a Terrible Experience?

I am not sure how to help my sixteen-year-old daughter Michelle. She was raped last year by a young man from her school at a party. She said the last thing she remembers is drinking beer with a group of boys. Then she woke up at 4:00 A.M. without her skirt on and with a naked boy on top of her—raping her—while two other boys watched and laughed. I took her to the ER immediately after she returned home, and then she saw a counselor at the Rape Crisis Center for a few weeks. Michelle says she has "moved on" and refuses to discuss the incident. She won't go back to the counselor, and the one time I forced her, she just sat in silence. Even though she repeatedly says she's "over it," my daughter is not the same. She gave up coed soccer, never sees her friends, and rarely smiles. She flies off the handle for no reason at all and then shuts herself in her room. And I know she doesn't sleep. I hear her listening to music in her room until three or four in the morning. Now her grades are slipping, and I'm afraid she won't graduate—she won't even discuss college anymore.

A year after the event, Michelle exhibits changes in personality, hobbies, academics, relationships, sleep, and future goals. Michelle appears more shut down and angry since the incident, yet refuses to discuss it or even admit that it still bothers her.

Teens Suffering from Trauma

The use of the word "trauma" in this chapter refers to the experiencing or witnessing of the death or serious physical injury of someone else or of injury to oneself (or even the *threat* of death or serious physical injury). The situation can cause terror, shock, distress, or a feeling of extreme vulnerability.

The following are some of the most common traumas experienced by children and adolescents:

- Being in a serious car accident

- Experiencing physical or emotional abuse

- Experiencing sexual abuse, incest, molestation, or rape

- Witnessing a physical assault or shooting or being severely beaten or shot

- Being the victim of dating violence (kicking, hitting, shoving, restraining)

- Experiencing the unexpected death or suicide of a family member or close friend

- Being severely bullied

- Living with parental domestic violence

- Experiencing severe parental neglect or incarceration of a parent

- Having a miscarriage or being forced to have an abortion

- Being diagnosed with a life-threatening illness

- Living on the street or prostituting one's body

- Living through natural disasters

- Living in a refugee camp or being exposed to war atrocities

- Being in military combat

Involvement in a motor vehicle accident is one of the most common traumatizing events during the teen years. According to the Centers for Disease Control (CDC), teen drivers are the group at highest risk for car crashes, and their risk increases with the number of teen passengers riding in their car. Teens have the lowest rate of seat-belt use and are more likely to speed, run red lights, and drive while intoxicated.

Not all teenagers who experience a traumatic event develop significant problems. In fact, *after an initial period of distress, most chil-*

dren and adolescents eventually go on to lead normal lives. It is difficult to know exactly which youth will develop major problems after exposure to trauma. However, those who experience traumas that are unpredictable, that are personal assaults (rape, sexual abuse, or physical violence), and that result in pain or injury are usually at highest risk. Teens with minimal family or social support, previous trauma, poor coping skills, or a mental health disorder are also at high risk for significant difficulties.

The following effects are common after experiencing a trauma:

Reexperiencing the Trauma. Adolescents suffering from trauma *reexperience* the horrific episode. They cannot stop thinking about what happened and may frequently have nightmares about it. At times, it may feel to them as if the distressing incident is happening all over again. These teens become emotionally upset and/or physically agitated if faced with reminders or symbols of what occurred. Reminders can be as subtle as smells, sounds, particular clothing, a tone of voice, or vague images, or they can be as obvious as an "anniversary date" of the incident. Symptoms tend to increase and decrease, depending on what is happening around them.

Avoiding Reminders of What Happened. Teens *avoid* anything that reminds them of the trauma. This may take the form of intentionally avoiding thinking, feeling, or talking about the event or purposely shunning individuals, locations, and activities that remind them of it. Some teens have no memory of significant pieces of what happened. Traumatized teens are often no longer involved or interested in hobbies or activities they used to enjoy. They may feel "different" or disconnected from friends and family and may look vacant, as if their lust for life has disappeared. These teens describe a sense of being emotionally numb—as if dead inside—even toward those they care about. Not surprisingly, given the horrible event(s) they went through, these teens believe their lives will be cut short in some way. They are solely focused on the here and now and see no point in making future plans, given the unpredictable nature of tragedies.

Feeling Agitated and Tense. Adolescents suffering from trauma are usually *agitated, jumpy,* or *tense.* They have difficulty sleeping and difficulty concentrating at school. Due to high levels of tension, they may be short-tempered and display sudden (and sometimes violent) outbursts of anger. In addition, because of terrifying experience(s) in their past, these youth are extra-attentive, watchful, and prepared. They pay attention to even the most minor details ("Why are you ten minutes late?" "Why didn't you let the phone ring so many times?") in order to protect themselves from any potential harm. Their world has changed; it is now a scary place where good people get hurt. These behaviors are likely to intensify at times of increased vulnerability, such as when the teen is alone or around unfamiliar individuals and at night.

When memories or associated emotions become too overwhelming, some traumatized teens just "check out." This is referred to as *dissociation.* Their eyes may glaze over, and they emotionally shut down. They report feeling dreamlike and disconnected from their bodies, as if watching themselves from the other side of the room. Teens who have been sexually assaulted or molested frequently report intentionally trying to detach from their physical bodies at the time they were victimized due to overwhelming emotional or physical pain. They often state, "They could have my body, but I wouldn't let them have *me*." Dissociating was their mind's way of coping with such a terrifying event. Even after the event, under periods of intense stress, their body automatically copes in a similar fashion. When experiencing a dissociative episode, teens can completely lose track of time—and sometimes have no memory of what has happened during a period of minutes or hours.

Worry Signs 5.4   Is Your Teen Suffering from Trauma?

The following behaviors are important worry signs of teens suffering from *trauma*:

- Has experienced a "traumatic" incident.
- Continually reexperiences the trauma.
- Avoids reminders of the trauma or seems emotionally or physically shut down.
- Continually seems keyed up or on edge.

Is It Time to Worry About Your Teen's Exposure to Trauma?

Worry Signs 5.4 reveals the symptoms of Posttraumatic Stress Disorder, usually referred to as PTSD. Experiencing a traumatic incident does not automatically imply that teens will suffer from PTSD. In fact, *it is normal and expected for adolescents to have many of the worry signs listed here immediately after exposure to trauma.* Teens of most concern are those that *continue* to suffer from them emotionally and/or behaviorally for more than a month after the event.

Your "worry barometer" should rise if your teen experiences these worry signs for more than thirty days, especially if there is no other clear cause for these symptoms and your child is having problems at home, at school, at work, or in relationships.

Adolescents usually develop PTSD within three months of experiencing a trauma; however, PTSD can surface many months or even years after a traumatic event. Some teens initially cope well with a traumatic incident but, after exposure to *another* trauma, begin to experience symptoms of PTSD. Teens who do not suffer from the full *syndrome* of PTSD can still exhibit emotional and behavioral difficulties as a result of a traumatic incident.

Does Your Teen Experience Panic Attacks?

Panic attacks are brief periods of *intense* and *overwhelming* fear and anxiety. These attacks typically last for only a few minutes, but some adolescents experience them for ten to fifteen minutes (an attack that lasts an hour or more is rare but can occur). During this time, teens are overcome with a sense that something terrible is about to happen and feel an overpowering need to get away. All of a sudden they experience several of the following:

- Racing heart, chest discomfort, or pain
- Difficulty breathing
- Sweating
- Shaking or trembling
- Lightheadedness or faintness
- A choking sensation or a feeling that they cannot swallow
- Nausea or other stomach upset
- Physical tingling, numbness, chills, or hot flashes
- Dreamlike feeling, as if things are not real or a feel of being disconnected from their body
- Fear of losing control, going crazy, or dying

Adolescents with any of the anxiety disorders described in this chapter can suffer from panic attacks, as can youth with other mental health and medical conditions. The attacks may occur completely out of the blue, or they may be associated with particular situations (being in an elevator or movie theater, being in a car stuck in traffic, giving a speech, attending a crowded party or concert) or particular thoughts (thinking about final exams or moving away to college, believing anxiety symptoms are a sign of serious illness, worrying about having another panic attack while on a date or in a crowd).

A teen's initial panic attack may occur completely out of the blue, although low blood sugar, hot stuffy classrooms, overcrowded social gatherings, and sleep deprivation sometimes play a role in triggering the first episode. Once teens sense their heart beating rapidly, they become concerned about what might be going on, and this concern makes their heart beat even faster. Once they begin sweating and feeling faint, they become embarrassed, worrying that others around them may notice, which increases further their anxiety and physical symptoms. When they remove themselves from the situation, the symptoms typically disappear and the teens experience complete relief.

It is usually the fear of having *another* panic attack that maintains this syndrome. Next time adolescents are in a similar situation (crowded party or hot, stuffy classroom) their initial thought is likely to be, "I hope that doesn't happen to me again." The minute they have that thought, their heart starts to beat a bit faster. This worries them, and they think, "Oh no, it's starting to happen again," which increases all of the symptoms. In a matter of minutes they are again at the mercy of a full-blown panic attack, but this time solely as a result of their *fear* of having another panic attack. It is a vicious cycle that can last weeks, months, or years. When the problem is severe, teens can be diagnosed with full-blown Panic Disorder.

To avoid suffering another panic attack, many of these teens simply avoid the places and circumstances they believe trigger the frightening episodes. Or, they have parents, friends, or romantic partners accompany them in case they need help escaping a situation. Not surprisingly, this type of avoidance or dependence on others can significantly restrict teens' activities.

How Do Teens Develop Anxiety Disorders?

These conditions are thought to develop from the interplay of several different factors that develop throughout a child's life. *Genetics* play a role; teens with a parent or close relative who suffers from severe anxiety are at higher risk to develop severe anxiety themselves. *Brain functioning* (functioning of certain areas of the brain, levels of specific neurotransmitters and a stress hormone) has been identified for further study, and it has become apparent that trauma early in life can affect a child's developing brain and nervous system.

Some babies are uncomfortable with new people and situations from the very start, and these babies often grow up to be shy, reserved, and withdrawn children and adolescents. Not all chronically shy youth develop severe anxiety, but this type of *temperament* raises their risk.

As early as infancy, the level of *parent-child attachment* can increase or decrease anxiety. In addition, parents who are overprotective, controlling, highly critical, and avoidant of social situations can place developing children at higher risk of anxiety, especially if they don't encourage youth to be independent.

Some teens develop anxiety symptoms shortly after a *harmful or upsetting experience*. Once teens experience high levels of anxiety in association with something (unfamiliar people, small spaces, specific thoughts, a traumatic event), they quickly learn what decreases their anxiety (avoiding certain situations or people, engaging in ritualistic behavior). *Actions that reduce anxiety in the short term are likely to be used again.* Unfortunately, in the long term, teens' continual avoidance or ritualistic behavior places significant limitations on their activities, relationships, and opportunities to succeed.

This Sounds Like My Teen, but What Else Could It Be?

Several factors and conditions can produce physical and emotional symptoms similar to those of anxiety disorders. Therefore, if you suspect that your teen may be suffering from excessive anxiety, it is critical to make sure none of these other factors better accounts for what they are experiencing:

> *Drugs (legal and illegal).* Stimulants (methamphetamine, cocaine, diet pills, decongestants, asthma inhalers, excessive caffeine) can make teens nervous or jittery, sometimes triggering a panic attack.
>
> *Medical or Biological Issues.* Some medical conditions (hyperthyroidism, mitral valve prolapse, inner-ear and balance problems)

can cause physical symptoms that mimic anxiety, and suffering from a chronic medical illness such as diabetes or asthma can result in teens becoming overfocused on their body and physical health. Hormonal changes the week before a girl's menstrual period can result in her becoming excessively worried or jealous.

Everyday Pressures. Too many pressures or obligations can result in tension, worry, and a feeling of being overwhelmed, and typical teenage worries and fears (appearance, grades, dating, new school, bullies, sex) are viewed as excessive to some parents,

Other Mental Health Issues. The overactivity and attention and concentration difficulties of ADHD can sometimes be mistaken for anxiety. Avoiding social situations, losing interest in activities, and obsessing about negative events can be symptoms of Major Depression. Teens with Learning Disabilities may become nervous and tense in school, and some youth may avoid particular classes or skip full days of school.

Normal Response to Abnormal Situation. Excessive fears are common immediately following a traumatic event. Intense (and reality-based) worries and concerns can stem from living in a chaotic home with inconsistent parenting. Teens who have been ridiculed, tormented, or assaulted by classmates may be too scared to go to school.

Even though these issues are not representative of true anxiety disorders, many of them still need to be taken seriously and addressed without delay.

Frequently Asked Questions About Teens with Anxiety

1. *Who has more anxiety disorders, boys or girls?* In general, girls tend to worry more often than boys, and they typically worry about more issues. Girls are more likely to suffer from Generalized Anxiety Disorder, Social Phobia, and Panic Disorder. Obsessive Compulsive Disorder is slightly more common in boys. It is unclear whether boys or girls are exposed to more traumatic events;

however, once exposed to trauma, girls are six times more likely to develop PTSD.

2. *Are there any cultural factors to be aware of with anxiety disorders?* Anxiety disorders occur in countries throughout the world; however, teens' cultural background can influence the way in which they express anxiety symptoms. For example, in some Asian cultures, adolescents with Social Anxiety are excessively concerned about insulting or being rude to others in social situations. Rather than worrying about saying something that will make them look foolish, they worry that their eye contact, blushing, or body odor will be offensive. In some cultures, teens with Panic Attacks have intense fears of witchcraft or magic. Generalized Anxiety Disorder is expressed primarily through *thoughts* in some cultures; teens constantly worry that something harmful will happen to them or their loved ones, believe they must do everything "perfectly," or overfocus on germs or contamination. In contrast, teens from other cultures express fear and worry primarily through *bodily symptoms* such as stomachaches, headaches, or vague muscle aches and pains.

Adolescents' culture should always be taken into account to determine whether their concerns or fears are realistic or exaggerated and unwarranted. Adolescents (or their loved ones) may truly be in danger of serious physical harm or they may live in disease–ridden area. Some cultures discourage youth from discussing anxieties or fears, and trauma is frequently concealed in cultures where this type of experience brings shame to one's family.

3. *Is it possible my teen could have another emotional or behavioral condition in addition to an Anxiety Disorder?* Major Depression commonly coexists with Anxiety Disorders. Adolescents with anxiety may also suffer from ADHD, Eating Disorders, Learning Disabilities, Oppositional Defiant Disorder, or Conduct Disorder. These additional difficulties may develop before, during, or after the onset of the excessive anxiety. Ironically, a significant number of teens suffering from an Anxiety Disorder also suffer from one or more *additional* Anxiety Disorders, complicating their clinical picture even further.

Living with intense anxiety places adolescents at increased risk for alcohol and other drug use. Since alcohol and other drugs can increase relaxation and decrease self-consciousness, some teens become dependent on an intoxicated state to reduce their anxiety in social situations. Teens who do not receive treatment for their anxiety disorder have an increased risk of suicidal thoughts and suicide attempts.

How You Can Help Teens Who Suffer from Anxiety

If you suspect your teen may be suffering from high levels of anxiety, you should have your child evaluated by a qualified mental health professional who specializes in adolescence. A comprehensive mental health assessment can determine whether your teen suffers from one of the Anxiety Disorders reviewed in this chapter, and if that is the case, what treatment strategy is likely to be most beneficial. On the other hand, the evaluation may find that your teen's worries are within the normal range.

Parents are essential to helping adolescents feel safe and secure, as well as confident enough to fully participate in all areas of their lives. Although most teens will benefit from the parenting strategies listed here, they are particularly important for teenagers with an anxiety disorder.

For Teens with Any Type of Anxiety Disorder

- Encourage teens to ease up on themselves. Everything does not need to be "perfect"—sometimes "good enough" is just fine.
- Promote age-appropriate independence and autonomy. Overprotective parents can hamper teens' efforts to break through their worries and fears.
- Do not allow teens to continually ask for reassurance ("Did I do this right?" "Does this look okay?") Answer

them once, and then place a limit on how many times they can repeatedly ask about a concern.

- Be alert to frequent physical complaints (stomachaches, headaches, vague muscle aches and pains), and have a physician rule out medical causes.

- Take a stepwise strategy to helping teens *gradually* expose themselves to situations they fear so they can see that nothing terrible happens. Accompany them initially for support, and then progressively remove yourself from situations over time.

- Acknowledge and praise each difficult step teens take to overcome their fears. Think baby steps.

- Never tease teens about their fears or concerns, regardless of your intention. Don't let other family members do it.

- Do not expect teens to become completely worry-free. Everyone experiences anxiety at various times, and low levels of anxiety can motivate teens to work hard.

For Teens with Generalized Anxiety

- Talk with teens about their concerns and correct distorted thinking ("If I don't get straight A's, I won't get into college," "If I don't work out every day, I will lose *all* my muscle.")

- Do not hide important issues. Teens know when something is wrong and typically envision it more catastrophic than it is. Reassure them that they are safe and loved, no matter what happens.

- Do not minimize teens' fears. You can empathize with how they feel without communicating that their fears are credible.

- Encourage teens to "check out" whether their fears have any basis. If they are worried they won't graduate, have them talk to the school counselor. If they are concerned that their boss is intentionally giving them bad shifts, have them ask their boss about the schedule.

For Teens with Social Anxiety

- Don't *force* teens to socialize with new people in unfamiliar settings. If participation in an event is mandatory, help prepare them beforehand.

- Encourage teens to attend social activities or events where conversation is not the main focus.

- Challenge teens' exaggerated social fears, and help them view social situations more realistically.

- Use private time with teens (riding in the car, eating a meal) to provide subtle coaching in basic social skills. Some teens with Social Anxiety need guidance in starting conversations, ending conversations, or keeping conversations going. Provide gentle feedback and advice in a caring tone.

- Role-model friendly, outgoing behavior for teens so that they can observe how natural and rewarding it can be.

For Teens with Obsessive-Compulsive Disorder (OCD)

- Do not become too involved in teens' rituals. Do not reinforce their fears by *continually* checking, washing, or touching things to decrease their anxiety—even when they ask or demand that you do.

- Help teens find ways of distracting themselves when the obsessions become overwhelming.

■ Encourage teens to engage in hobbies or other activities. The busier they are, the less time they have to obsess and engage in compulsive rituals.

■ Help teens stop themselves from engaging in compulsive behavior, even when driven by strong urges to do so. Each time they see that nothing terrible results, their compulsive rituals will slowly diminish.

For Teens with Posttraumatic Stress Disorder (PTSD)

■ Help teens return to their normal routine as soon as possible. Keep things consistent and predictable.

■ Encourage teens to talk about what happened to them, but let them set the pace. Listen without judgment and provide support.

■ Encourage teens to express their thoughts and emotions in ways other than verbally (journaling, artwork, writing a letter, poetry, writing a song).

■ Make it clear to teens that they are not to blame for what happened to them. You may need to do this repeatedly.

■ Convince teens to hold off on making any major life decisions (college, military, relationship breakup, marriage, pregnancy, job) while dealing with traumatic issues.

■ Provide extra support when teens are exposed to anything (anniversary date, location, individuals) associated with the original traumatic event.

■ Encourage teens to engage in activities they enjoy. Intrusive memories and painful thoughts about traumatic experiences are more likely to occur when youth are alone or unoccupied.

■ Limit teens' viewing of violent or disturbing images on television, in movies, or in video games, as this can intensify their symptoms.

For Teens with Panic Attacks

- Don't underestimate the terror and fear teens experience during a panic attack.

- Encourage teens to write down when and where their panic attacks occur. Keeping track of their thoughts, feelings, and whereabouts at these times helps identify what triggers their attacks.

- Help teens switch their attention away from their bodily sensations and toward something requiring concentration (talking to someone, going for a walk, getting on the computer) if they notice increasing anxiety.

- Remind teens that no matter how frightening panic attacks are, they will not result in physical harm.

- Help teens accept their anxiety rather than constantly trying to make it stop. Fighting anxiety only makes it worse.

Anxiety disorders are among the most disabling, yet *treatable* mental health conditions—especially when services are sought sooner rather than later. Do not expect teens to conquer their fears solely by determination and self-control. If it were that easy, they would have overcome them by now. In addition to professional help, these youth need compassion, support, and patience.

Despite suffering from severe anxiety, the following individuals attained huge dreams: Aretha Franklin, Barbra Streisand, Bridget Fonda, Howie Mandel, Amanda Peet, Naomi Judd, Willard Scott, Carly Simon, Kim Basinger, Nicole Kidman, and Donny Osmond. With help, your teen can, too.

CHAPTER SIX

Under the Influence

Teens Who Use Alcohol and Other Drugs

Isn't using alcohol and other drugs just part of being a teenager?

- *David, thirteen, is too scared to try alcohol or drugs, but he and his friends like the "rush" and "funny feeling" they get when sniffing glue, markers, and paint thinner.*

- *Maria, fifteen, has drunk beer a few times. At a recent party, everyone was taking prescription pills. Maria wanted to try some to see what it would feel like but was afraid her parents would get upset if they found out.*

- *Dwayne, sixteen, is always on the couch "relaxing." His school grades have dropped, and he has been repeatedly disciplined at work for being late and not following through on commitments. Dwayne smokes marijuana with his friends several days a week. Dwayne has no desire to reduce the amount of marijuana he smokes because he believes it is "natural" and "not a drug."*

- *Lauren, fifteen, regularly drinks alcohol at parties, frequently to the point of blacking out and not remembering things. She has completely passed out twice. Despite two recent incidents of performing oral sex while drunk on boys she did not know, Lauren is not concerned about her drinking.*

- *Christopher, seventeen, uses methamphetamine, a stimulant drug, as often as he can afford to buy it. He skips school with friends to steal car stereos to support his "meth" habit. Christopher says the drug makes him feel "normal" and is more effective than the medication his doctor prescribes for him.*

Adolescence is a time of curiosity and risk-taking. Experimenting with alcohol (and sometimes other drugs) is common among teenagers. Normal adolescent feelings of insecurity and self-consciousness, combined with the desire to separate from parents, appear "grown-up," and be accepted by peers, make teenagers particularly vulnerable to try these substances. Young people are particularly at risk to use alcohol and other drugs, referred to in this chapter as alcohol/drugs, during times of transition, such as from elementary school to middle school and from middle school to high school.

Although no parent wants to imagine a son or daughter experimenting with (or regularly using) alcohol/drugs, parents cannot put their head in the sand. Regardless of how much you love and support your son or daughter, no family is immune from alcohol/drug problems. Substance abuse affects adolescents of all races and socioeconomic backgrounds, and from every part of the country.

A 2006 survey by the Centers for Disease Control and Prevention (CDC)[4] of more than 13,000 adolescents (grades 9–12) found that:

- 74 percent of teens drank alcohol.
- 38 percent of teens used marijuana.
- 12 percent of teens sniffed or inhaled paints, glue, or chemicals in aerosol spay cans to get "high."
- 9 percent of teens used prescription drugs that were not prescribed for them.[5]
- 8 percent of teens used hallucinogenic drugs like LSD, PCP, and psilocybin mushrooms.

---

4. *Youth Risk Behavior Surveillance—United States, 2005,* MMWR 2006; 55 (No. SS-5),Centers for Disease Control and Prevention.

5. *Under the Counter: The Diversion and Abuse of Controlled Prescription Drugs in the U.S., 2005,* The National Center on Addiction and Substance Abuse at Columbia University, 2005.

- 6 percent of teens used methamphetamines.

- 6 percent of teens used the drug Ecstasy.

- 4 percent of teens used illegal steroid pills or shots without a doctor's prescription.

During the month prior to the survey, the CDC researchers found that:

- 43 percent of teens had one or more alcoholic drinks.

- 25 percent of teens engaged in heavy drinking (five or more drinks in one session).

- 20 percent of teens used marijuana.

- 10 percent of teens drove a car or another type of vehicle after drinking alcohol.

- 25 percent of teens rode in a car with a driver who had been drinking alcohol.

This survey, which was conducted through schools, likely *under-estimates* adolescent substance use, because students who use the largest amounts of alcohol/drugs have higher rates of school truancy, suspensions, and dropping out and therefore may not have participated in the study.

Even though it's common for teens to experiment with these substances, this does not mean that they are safe. Car accidents, accidental injuries, homicide, and suicide are the four leading causes of death for teenagers—and alcohol/drugs are too often involved in each.

They Are Putting WHAT in Their Bodies?

Teenagers can be exposed to a variety of different types of alcohol/drugs at parties, friends' houses, and sometimes even at school. Some of these substances are quite familiar to parents, but others may be surprising. The following are some of the most commonly used substances today's teenagers use to get "high":

Alcohol (booze, brewski, juice/jooce, sauce, pimp juice). Alcohol is the most popular drug used by adolescents. Some youth experience increased relaxation, confidence, and sociability while intoxicated; others become depressed or angry and aggressive. Adolescents who drink alcohol are much more likely to use illicit drugs than their peers who do not drink. In addition, youth who begin drinking before age fifteen are four times more likely to develop alcoholism than those who begin at twenty-one. Regular drinking can result in liver damage, cancer, and strokes. Even occasional teen drinkers can get alcohol poisoning if they drink large amounts of alcohol in a short period of time.

Marijuana (weed, pot, chronic, joint, blunt, sinsemilla, Mary Jane, ganja, grass, reefer). Marijuana is the third most commonly used drug by adolescents (after alcohol and tobacco) and is more potent than when today's parents were teenagers. Marijuana is typically smoked to experience feelings of relaxation and an altered state of mind. Teens may experience euphoria, a distorted sense of time, slow reflexes, disconnected thoughts, increased appetite ("munchies"), mood changes, and difficulties paying attention or remembering things. When high, some teens are social and talkative; others become introspective. Anxiety, paranoia, and even panic attacks can occur, and large doses of marijuana can result in hallucinations.

Short-term risks of smoking marijuana are similar to those for smoking tobacco (asthma, bronchitis), although marijuana cigarettes often contain four times more tar than a tobacco cigarette. Because the smoker's perception and timing are affected, driving while high can be very dangerous. Long-term use can result in "antimotivational syndrome" (a lack of motivation, fatigue, lack of concern about the future), attention and memory problems, changes in the reproductive system, immune system damage, and serious injury to the lungs. Marijuana increases the risk of Schizophrenia, a serious mental health disorder, among teens genetically predisposed to the illness; the drug can intensify psychiatric symptoms among teens already suffering from Schizophrenia.

Marijuana is usually rolled in cigarette-like "joints" or smoked in pipes or bongs. However, some teens smoke "blunts"— cigars that have been sliced open and the tobacco inside replaced with marijuana. Stronger drugs can be sprinkled on marijuana, or joints/blunts can be dipped in embalming fluid or formaldehyde and then smoked (often known as "wet" or "wack"). Teens typically have little knowledge of the damage these chemicals can do to their brain and nervous system.

It is now believed that chronic marijuana use can cause physical and psychological dependence. The majority of teens currently admitted to drug treatment centers report marijuana as their main substance of abuse.

Prescription Medication (oxy, Orange County/O.C., vikes, barbies, benzos, bennies, zannies, clonnies, chill pills). One of the newest, most disturbing trends among teenagers today (including youth as young as twelve) is increased abuse of prescription medication that is *not* prescribed for them. The most commonly abused medications are pain relievers (OxyContin, Vicodin, Fentanyl), stimulants prescribed for Attention-Deficit/Hyperactivity Disorder (Ritalin, Adderall, Concerta), anti-anxiety medications (Xanax, Valium), muscle relaxants (Soma), and sleep medications (Halcion, Prosom). Prescription medications are the fourth most popular substance of abuse for today's teenagers.

Because these medications are in the family medicine cabinet, professionally manufactured, and safe and effective for legitimate uses, getting high from them is viewed by many adolescents as safer (and more socially acceptable) than is use of illicit drugs. Teens can easily obtain these medications from a friend's prescription, students who sell them at school, or unregulated "medication" Web sites.

Teens are having "pharm" parties (as in pharmaceuticals) where everyone brings fistfuls or baggies of prescription pills to get high. The pills may be taken orally, or crushed or melted to be snorted, smoked, or injected. Although drugs are often taken for their euphoric effects, some teens report using prescription drugs to help them sleep, decrease stress, or enhance school performance. Pain relievers and anti-anxiety medications can be psychologically and physically addicting. Inappropriate use of prescription medication is just as dangerous as taking illicit drugs and can result in emotional, social, and physical health problems. Teens who take too many pills or mix prescription medication with alcohol can experience serious side effects, including coma or death.

Inhalants (rush, glue, sniff, poppers, whippets, snappers, kick, bang). Some teenagers sniff or inhale chemical vapors (often referred to as "huffing") to get a rapid, mind-altering high. These chemicals and poisons are found in typical homes or garages: nail polish remover, correction fluid, spray paint, glue, lighter fluid, air freshener, paint thinner, markers, cleaning fluids, and gasoline. Teens sniff directly from open containers or breathe in chemicals from soaked rags. Adolescents refer to the recreational inhaling of nitrous oxide from whipped cream aerosols as "whippets." Intoxication occurs moments after the chemicals are inhaled into the lungs through the nose or mouth; users feel lightheaded, tingly, euphoric, excited, giddy, and powerful. Some youth become drowsy or agitated. Later effects include headache, nausea, dizziness, blurred vision, slurred speech, and loss of coordination. If teens want to lengthen the intoxicating effects, they repeat the process for hours—sometimes to the point of losing consciousness.

Many teens believe these chemicals are safe, but they can be habit-forming and cause serious damage to the brain, liver, and kidneys. Death can result from chronic use or from a *single incident* of huffing ("sudden sniffing death"). Inhalants are popular because they provide a cheap, legal, easily obtained high that is easy to hide from parents; they are used more often by children and young teens than by older adolescents. Inhalants are the fifth most abused substance among today's adolescents.

Over-the-Counter (OTC) Medication (dex, DXM, skittles, robo, triple C, tuss / tussin). Over-the-counter cough suppressants (Robitussin-DM, Nyquil, Triaminic-DM, Coricidin HBP, Vicks Formula 44) can be safe and effective when taken as directed. However, some teenagers are taking inappropriately large doses of these medicines to get high from the ingredient dextromethorphan. This is often referred to as "robo-tripping" or "skittling." Effects of this drug range from confusion, drowsiness, mild distortions of color or sound, and slurred speech to visual hallucinations, "out-of-body" sensations, and loss of coordination. Teens are willing to endure the common side effects of abdominal pain, nausea, and vomiting. Serious side effects such as unconsciousness, seizures, brain damage, and death are also possible with significantly large doses.

Methamphetamine (meth, ice, crystal, crank, tweek, glass, Tina, fire, chalk). Methamphetamine (meth) is a very potent, addictive stimulant drug that keeps users awake all night. Teens who smoke or inject the drug experience an intense and pleasurable "rush" or "flash"; those who swallow or snort the drug experience a euphoric high without the intense rush. Meth causes increased alertness and heart rate; feelings of well-being, confidence, and power; and insomnia, anxiety, loss of appetite, irritability, and aggression.

Some teens "binge" every few hours (not eating or sleeping) until they run out of the drug or become too confused to continue using. Following a binge, teens inevitably "crash," experiencing severe depression—and sometimes thoughts of suicide. Regular users of meth frequently experience paranoia, hallucinations, confusion, severe weight loss, depression, purposeless repetitive behavior (e.g., disassembling objects), and beliefs or the feeling that insects or parasites are crawling under their skin (scabs or sores often result from users' obsessively picking at their arms or legs). Users may develop pock marks on their face, a large number of cavities, or severe tooth decay.

Long-term use or high dosages can result in teens losing touch with reality and becoming paranoid, aggressive, and even violent. Meth can cause liver, kidney, and lung damage, as well as strokes and death. The drug is typically made in illegal "meth labs"—some large and well-organized, others makeshift labs set up in houses, barns, garages, apartments, motel rooms, and vacant buildings. The most common ingredients in meth come from over-the-counter cold medicine, antifreeze, lantern fuel, drain cleaner, and battery acid. Meth became popular in the western half of the United States but has now spread across the country.

MDMA or Ecstasy (E, X, XTC, love drug, hug, Eve, Adam, clarity, lover's speed, love potion). MDMA (3,4 methylenedioxymethamphetamine), also known by the more popular name Ecstasy, is an amphetamine-based hallucinogenic drug (pill or capsule) that produces extremely high levels of energy, sensual arousal, and heightened sensations. This type of drug is typically consumed at "raves," which are overcrowded, all-night dance parties with pulsating music and vibrant, multicolored flashing lights. The drug makes teens feel loving and affectionate, heightens all of their senses, and makes it possible for them to dance nonstop for four to six hours. Many youth taking Ecstasy suck on pacifiers or lollipops to prevent teeth grinding or clenching, a common side effect of the drug. The combination of Ecstasy with excessive physical activity increases the likelihood of dehydration, increased body temperature, kidney failure, or cardiac arrest—all of which can result in death.

Cocaine (coke, flake, C, snow, crack, coca, blanca, blow, powder). Cocaine is a powerfully addictive stimulant. Cocaine powder is usually snorted, although it can be injected or smoked. Crack cocaine is a highly addictive form of cocaine that is typically smoked. Teens who use cocaine experience increased alertness, euphoria, excess energy, increased heart rate, loss of appetite, and insomnia. Some teens report irritability, restlessness, and anxiety while high, and also between periods of use. Depression is common when regular users of cocaine stop using the drug. Long-term effects can include a hole in the septum of the nose, seizures, or heart attacks. When alcohol is mixed with cocaine, the physical effects are particularly dangerous.

Anabolic Steroids (roids, asteroids, juice, hype, gym candy, gear, pumpers). Anabolic steroids are lab-made versions of the male hormone testosterone that are taken orally or injected. Teens use these drugs illegally to enhance athletic performance, build large muscles, or sculpt their body. Side effects of steroid use can include "roid rages" (confrontation, belligerence, angry outbursts), depression, severe acne, stunted growth, liver problems, heart attacks, and strokes. Girls can experience extra body hair or growth of facial hair, deepened voice, fewer menstrual cycles, and a reduction in their breasts; boys can experience irreversible breast development, impotence, infertility, hair loss, and shrunken testicles.

Please see www.whentoworry.com for information on tobacco and additional drugs used by today's teenagers.

What Puts a Teen at Risk for Developing an Alcohol/Drug Problem?

Although many teenagers experiment with alcohol/drugs, *most do not use them on a regular basis or "abuse" them to the point of causing problems with school, work, family, or relationships.* Possessing the risk factors discussed in the paragraphs that follow raises a teen's chances of experiencing significant difficulties with alcohol/drugs. As with risk factors for heart disease or cancer, having one or more of these attributes increases the likelihood of developing a substance abuse problem but certainly does not guarantee it.

Individual Factors

- *Age at First Use of Alcohol/Drugs.* The earlier adolescents experiment with alcohol/drugs, the higher their chances of developing problems with these substances. Teenagers who begin drinking before age fourteen are much more likely to become addicted to alcohol; early drinkers who engage in binge-drinking (five or more drinks in a row for boys, four or more drinks in a row for girls) are at even higher risk.

- *Negative Life Events.* Abuse, neglect, and other traumatic life events (during childhood or adolescence) increase teenagers' chances of abusing alcohol/drugs. Teenagers with the greatest risk of developing problems with alcohol/drugs are those who have experienced both physical *and* sexual abuse.

- *Biological Makeup.* Alcohol/drug addiction runs in families, making teens of substance-abusing parents more likely (though not guaranteed) to abuse substances themselves. The biological makeup (how the body metabolizes alcohol, some aspects of brain functioning, and overall temperament) appears to be different among children born to an alcoholic parent. Even as babies, many substance-abusing teens displayed intense emotional distress, difficulty adapting to change, and withdrawal from their parents. Heredity and genetics are only part of the story; some teens with an alcohol/drug-abusing parent do not have substance abuse problems, and not all substance-abusing teens have family histories of al-cohol/drug addiction.

- *Early Childhood Behavior.* As young children, substance-abusing teens are often more impulsive, hyperactive, sensation-seeking, oppositional, easily frustrated, and aggressive than their peers. Their risk for alcohol/drug problems increases if temper tantrums, distractibility, irritability, and aggression continue as they progress from elementary school to middle school and high school. The front part of the brain (responsible for at-tention, planning, and managing one's own behavior) may be one of the areas affected in children born to parents who abuse alcohol/drugs.

- *Personality or Mental Health Characteristics.* Adolescents who feel separate from mainstream society are at higher risk for alcohol/drug abuse. These teens tend to be overly independent, rebellious, in favor of teen substance use, and not spiritual or religious. As children, many of these youth suffered from a mental health disorder, such as Attention-Deficit/Hyperactivity Disorder (ADHD), a Learning Disability, or Oppositional Defiant Disorder.

Family Factors

- *Family's Attitude Toward Alcohol/Drugs.* Lenient attitudes and parental approval of adolescent alcohol/drug use results in teenagers consuming more of these substances. Parental attitude toward substance use plays a larger role in teens' decision to drink/use drugs than the fact that these substances are illegal.

- *Family's Substance Using Behavior.* Children pay more attention to what they see their parents and siblings *do* than to what family members *say*. The greater the number of individuals (parents or siblings) in a child's household who drink/use drugs, the greater the chance the child will use these substances as a teenager. This is particularly true if the child is involved in the substance-using behavior (fetching a beer, mixing cocktails, helping count pills, watering marijuana plants). In addition, when parents rely on alcohol/drugs during times of stress, substance use is role-modeled as an acceptable and preferred coping skill. Having an alcoholic family member (especially a parent) makes a child two or more times as likely to develop a substance abuse problem—probably because of the combination of genetics and parental modeling.

■ *Parental Consistency and Monitoring.* Youth who lack clear rules and limits, receive inconsistent consequences or discipline (sometimes permissive, sometimes harsh), and have little monitoring from parents are at increased risk of substance abuse. Teens allowed to watch three or more "R" rated movies a month (via television, DVD rentals, or neighborhood theaters) are significantly more likely to abuse alcohol/drugs.[6]

■ *Relationship with Parents/Parental Involvement.* Children raised in homes plagued by hostility and arguments, constant criticism, and minimal encouragement or support are at much greater risk of substance abuse. Parents who are not involved with their children's activities also increase the chances that their teens will abuse alcohol/drugs. In addition, *untreated* mental health issues in parents also raise a child's risk of substance abuse; this is likely because these conditions can affect parental involvement, support, and consistency.

Parent-child relationships are two-way, dynamic interactions. Children with emotional or behavior problems can make it challenging for parents to remain involved and supportive. However, teenagers who do not receive encouragement and positive social experiences at home will eventually seek it from others—too often from substance-abusing peers.

School Factors

■ *Academics.* Poor grades (regardless of reason), placement in special education classes, school discipline problems, truancy, and dropping out of school all increase the

---

6. *National Survey of American Attitudes on Substance Abuse X: Teens and Parents,* The National Center on Addiction and Substance Abuse at Columbia University, 2005.

chances teens will abuse alcohol/drugs. The earlier
children exhibit these behaviors—such as elementary
school—the greater the risk of substance abuse during
adolescence.

- *Commitment to School.* Teens who do not enjoy school,
  spend much time on homework, recognize the value of
  school work, or expect to go to college are at increased
  risk for alcohol/drug abuse.

Social Factors

- *Lack of Friends.* Aggressive children and adolescents
  typically have difficulty making and keeping friends.
  They may be accepted only by other aggressive
  youth—a high-risk group for substance use. In addition, when aggressive children and adolescents do not
  have many friends, they miss out on spending time
  with youth who do not use alcohol/drugs.

- *Substance-Abusing Friends.* Spending time with friends
  (or acquaintances) who use alcohol/drugs increases
  teens' risk of developing substance abuse problems.
  Adolescents typically learn about these substances from
  friends, usually obtain alcohol/drugs from friends, and
  almost always consume these substances with friends.
  However, do not automatically assume that these
  friends are a "bad influence" on your son or daughter;
  it is just as common for substance-using teens to *choose*
  friends with similar views and behavior regarding alco-
  hol/drugs as it is for teens to be persuaded by friends
  to use substances. Not surprisingly, the more time
  substance-using teens spend together, the more
  acceptable and "normal" substance use becomes.

Teens who exhibit one *risk factor* are not destined to develop a
substance abuse problem. However, the combination of two, three,
or four factors raises adolescents' risk significantly. Unfortunately,
possessing several risk factors is common, as the attributes are inter-

related: difficult temperament (due to genetics or brain development) and negative childhood behavior can result in a lack of parental involvement or support, as well as rejection by kids at school. The good news is that risk factors can be lessened by *protective factors* such as close and communicative families, parents who do not abuse alcohol/drugs, non-substance-abusing peers, academic success, or another type of school participation (sports, clubs, arts).

Stages of Teen Substance Use

Although there are no absolutes when it comes to alcohol/drugs, there is a *typical* sequence of substance use that applies to most teenagers. Each progressive stage is more serious and dangerous than the one before it. Fortunately, the majority of teens never move past the first or second stage; for those who do, the risks are extremely high.

No Use. Teens use no alcohol/drugs.

Experimental Use. Teens occasionally use alcohol/drugs, primarily out of curiosity. Substances are usually obtained from friends and used socially with friends. Social groups are unchanged. No major problems result from substance use.

Substance Misuse. Teens begin to use alcohol/drugs more regularly. Substances are used with friends in social environments, usually on weekend nights (except inhalants, which are often used during the day by younger teens). Teens are typically trying to have a good time and be accepted by friends. If they drink alcohol, they "drink to get drunk," engage in *binge drinking* (five or more drinks for boys, four or more drinks for girls), and experience blackouts (cannot remember part or all of an evening's activities). Teens usually do not see anything wrong with their substances use because "all the kids do it." Social group has primarily remained the same, although a few known alcohol/drug users may be added. Teens may also lie to parents about substance use, with possible guilt feelings about their dishonesty. Minor problems are possible the day after using substances (hangover, oversleeping, irritability), but no major problems result from substance use.

Substance "Abuse." Teens regularly use alcohol/drugs. Substances are used with friends (and sometimes alone), both during the week and on the weekend. Alcohol/drug use continues despite significant problems stemming from these substances: significant conflict with parents, siblings, friends, or boyfriend/girlfriend; slipping school grades; discipline problems at home, school, or work; unplanned pregnancy; sexually transmitted disease (STD); sexual or physical assault; or bike, skateboard, motorcycle, or car accident. Increased irritability and a short temper are common, and teens may be using substances to cope with emotional issues or stressful events. Teens who "abuse" alcohol/drugs often put themselves in risky and dangerous situations while obtaining or using alcohol/drugs; legal issues can occur due to behavior while intoxicated or theft to support their substance use. These youth are in denial about how negatively alcohol/drugs affect their lives and are adamant about their right to use them. They spend more time with other substance users and less time with "straight" friends. These teens compare themselves to peers who use larger amounts of alcohol/drugs to convince themselves and others they do not have a problem. Their participation in previously enjoyed activities (sports, youth groups, artistic endeavors, volunteer efforts, spiritual/religious worship) slowly wanes.

Substance "Dependency/Addiction." Teens lose control over alcohol/drug use. Teens' lives revolve around obtaining, using, and recovering from substances. No longer a social experience, alcohol/drug use frequently occurs when the teen is alone. *Addiction* is a medical condition with physical and psychological effects. Because of heavy substance use, teens' brains change, and teens process alcohol/drugs differently in this stage. They may develop symptoms of *tolerance* (needing to consume larger quantities of a substance to achieve the desired effect) and *with-*

drawal (horrible psychological or physical symptoms when they stop using substances). Once dependent on a substance, teens frequently suffer from depression and hopelessness and sometimes engage in suicidal thoughts or behavior. These youth become a shell of who they once were, and alcohol/drugs become more important than family, friends, school, work, and their health. Families may need to remove teens from the home due to disruptive, aggressive, or illegal behavior. Most addicted teens can acknowledge that substances are harming them, but they either do not care or are unable to stop, even if they want to. At this stage, teens usually use substances to avoid withdrawal symptoms and to feel "normal," rather than to get drunk or high.

The downward slope of drug use, abuse, and addiction is a slippery one. Parents need to be on the lookout for drug problems before they progress to advanced stages. There is no way to accurately predict which teens will experiment with alcohol/drugs and which will use substances to the point of self-destruction. Some teens do not like how alcohol/drugs make them feel, whereas others say that "everything finally felt okay" after trying these substances. Most adolescents experience something in the middle. Teens who continue to move through the progressively more serious and dangerous stages of substance use typically possess a combination of factors that places them at higher risk for substance abuse and dependency.

Is It Time to Worry About Your Teen's Use of Alcohol or Other Drugs?

Parents of adolescents often dismiss signs of substance abuse because they assume the changes in their son or daughter's behavior are solely due to "being a teenager." Exhibiting the following behaviors on an occasional basis does not automatically imply that your teen is using alcohol/drugs. However, observing a *pattern* of the following clues should raise your suspicion.

Because many of the worry signs of substance use described here can also indicate mental health (or physical health) problems, they must be addressed. Adolescents can be creative when concealing substance use, so parents need to pay close attention to teens' *Appearance, Behavior, Mood or Mental State, Socialization, Scent* (yes, you have to smell your teen), and *Other Clues* of alcohol/drug use.

Worry Signs 6.1   Worry Signs of Alcohol/Drug Use

Appearance

- Showing changes in eating habits or significant weight loss
- Having red and watery eyes, dark circles under eyes; wearing sunglasses inside and at night
- Having a runny nose, red and raw nostrils, frequent nosebleeds
- Having paint or stains on fingers, face, or clothing; spots or sores around mouth
- Having burns or soot on fingers or lips
- Feeling queasy, sickly, unwell or weak in the morning
- Exhibiting poor balance, being uncoordinated, feeling slow and sluggish
- Feeling sick frequently or having sores on body that do not heal
- Feeling dazed and confused
- Having shaky hands or twitching
- Frequently getting hurt, several accidental injuries
- Having poor hygiene
- Making drastic changes in hairstyle and/or clothing

Worry Signs 6.2   Worry Signs of Alcohol/Drug Use

Behavior

- Exhibiting slipping grades, irregular school attendance, discipline problems

- Losing interest in hobbies, sports, extracurricular activities

- Sleeping at inappropriate times (school); staying awake all night

- Making the bedroom absolutely off-limits; taking a long time to answer the bedroom door after a knock

- Being secretive (whispering on phone, seeming evasive or defensive when asked about plans or activities, disappearing for long periods)

- Repeatedly borrowing money, yet showing no evidence of purchases

- Exhibiting rapid, rambling, or slurred, garbled speech

- Committing acts of aggression or violent outbursts

- Breaking household rules (especially curfew)

- Being hyperactive, restless, unable to sit still

- Vomiting frequently

- Wanting to go out *every* night

- Continually scratching or picking at skin

Worry Signs 6.3   Worry Signs of Alcohol/Drug Use

Mood or Mental State

- Being agitated, irritable, hostile, uncooperative
- Seeming depressed, despondent
- Acting overly happy and excited, giggling or laughing hysterically at nothing
- Being anxious, nervous, jumpy
- Showing dramatic personality change
- Being fascinated with everyone and everything—no matter how trivial
- Appearing lethargic, unmotivated
- Being distractible, unable to focus
- Having an exaggerated sense of importance or power
- Having difficulty remembering things
- Exhiting paranoid behavior (being afraid to leave the house, believing people are out to get them)

Worry Signs 6.4   Worry Signs of Alcohol/Drug Use

Socialization

- Suddenly stopping associating with usual group of friends
- Hanging around new peer group (usually older, less supervised, less school-oriented, or known to be

alcohol/drug-users); may avoid introducing new friends to parents

- Weakening or breaking relationships with family members
- Avoiding family events and activities
- Acting withdrawn, isolated

Worry Signs 6.5   Worry Signs of Alcohol/Drug Use

Scent

- Having the odor of alcohol on breath or in sweat
- Having a chemical odor (paint, gasoline, nail polish remover) on clothing or on breath
- Having a pungent sweet-and-sour odor of marijuana on clothing or in hair
- Smelling strange odors in teen's room or car or in the garage or barn
- Frequently using mint mouthwash or breath mints
- Frequently using incense, air fresheners, or perfume

Worry Signs 6.6   Worry Signs of Alcohol/Drug Use

Other Clues

- Decrease in parents' stock of alcoholic beverages (bottles or cans are missing, or hard alcohol is diluted with water)

- Several empty boxes or bottles of cold medicine (especially extra-strength) in trash cans or teen's rooms

- Disappearance of money or checks (from purses, wallets, checkbooks, ATM accounts)

- Disappearance of jewelry or other valuable items

- Disappearance of household chemicals (glues, paints, paint thinner, correction fluid, gasoline, aerosol chemicals)

- Disappearance of prescription drugs or over-the-counter medications from the medicine cabinet

- Use of "vitamins" or "herbs," without being able to tell you anything about them

- Drug symbols on posters, tattoos, jewelry, or notebooks

- Drug paraphernalia (rolling papers, glass pipe, bong, razor blade); homemade pipe made from soda cans or empty toilet paper rolls and aluminum foil (look for black residue and pungent smell)

- Finding eye drops used to cure bloodshot eyes

- Questions from neighbors, friends, or family members about whether teen is using alcohol/drugs

- Adamant assertion by teen that using alcohol and drugs is "just part of being a teenager"

Is It Time To Worry That Your Teen Is Using Alcohol or Other Drugs?

One behavior from Worry Signs 6.1–6.6 is not proof of alcohol/drug use, but your worry barometer should rise if you repeatedly observe several signs. Adolescence is a time of exploration and discovery, so *experimentation should not cause panic.* Spending time with your teenager is the key to recognizing a pattern of substance use. Most parents are convinced they would "know" if their teen was involved with alcohol/drugs. However, most clues occur gradually and subtly, so parents looking for neon warnings and obvious evidence typically wait too long to intervene. Trust your gut—if you think there is reason for concern, follow your suspicions and investigate. Your teen's well-being is on the line.

Adolescents do not use alcohol/drugs because they are "bad kids." For most teenagers, these substances meet important needs or are tools to have a good time. Teens say being drunk or high feels good, helps them fit in, reduces worries or depression, and makes them more outgoing. This is why some teens do not understand why adults want to restrict these substances. Tragically, many teenagers do not understand the potential negative consequences of alcohol/drug use (unplanned pregnancies, physical fights, car accidents, alcohol poisoning, addiction, and the multiple ways their brains, livers, hearts, and other organs can be damaged, sometimes resulting in death).

Asking *why* your teen consumes alcohol/drugs is critical to helping him or her stop. For example, despite engaging in the same drug-using behavior, a thirteen-year-old girl taking Vicodin to "stop thinking about the uncle who molested me" is very different from a seventeen-year-old boy who takes the same prescription pain-relieving pills with his buddies because "it's fun when we're bored."

This Sounds Like My Teen, But What Else Could It Be?

Identifying signs of substance abuse in teenagers is challenging because symptoms may reflect a mental health or medical disorder, or the symptoms may be harmless. Before automatically assuming your teen is using alcohol/drugs, rule out these other possible explanations:

Physical or Medical Issues

- Runny noses, weight loss, nausea and vomiting, repeated illnesses or sores, and fatigue can all have legitimate medical causes.

- Colds and upper-respiratory infections may necessitate large amounts of cough and cold medicine (though you should monitor this and talk to a doctor about it).

Mental Health Disorder

- Agitation, irritability, sadness, distractibility, aggression, social withdrawal, and lethargy are symptoms of Major Depression. Hyperactivity, distractibility, restlessness, and rapid speech are symptoms of ADHD. Mood swings, elation, overexcitement, rapid speech, and a false sense of power are symptoms of Bipolar Disorder.

- Frequent accidents can result from impulsive risk-taking behavior, particularly if teens suffer from ADHD or Bipolar Disorder.

Injury or "Growing Pains"

- Lack of coordination and poor balance can be caused by a head injury or be the natural response of teenagers adjusting to bodies going through extreme growth and change.

Hobbies or Art Projects

- Paint stains and chemical smells can be caused by materials for art projects or other creative activities (working on cars, building model airplanes).

Sleep Deprivation

■   Overscheduled teens or those up all night text-messaging or talking on the phone to their friends or love interest may fall asleep at inappropriate times.

Innocent Uses

■   Teens may load up on mouthwash or mints to freshen their breath or simply enjoy the smell of incense and perfume.

When several worry signs of alcohol/drug use are present, an evaluation by a qualified mental health or substance abuse professional is often needed to distinguish whether symptoms are due to substances, a medical or mental health disorder, or "just being a teenager." Whether or not treatment is needed, and specifically what it is needed for, will depend on the results of the assessment.

Double Trouble: Teens Who Have Mental Health and Substance Abuse Problems

A significant number of adolescent substance abusers suffer from a "co-occurring" mental health disorder; they experience both problems at the same time. Alcohol/drug abuse most commonly co-occurs with Attention-Deficit/Hyperactivity Disorder (ADHD), Learning Disabilities, Conduct Disorder, Major Depression, Bipolar Disorder, Bulimia, Schizophrenia, and Anxiety Disorders such as Posttraumatic Stress Disorder (PTSD) and Social Phobia. Evaluating and treating adolescents with both mental health and substance use disorders is considerably more complicated and challenging than treating teens with only one disorder.

Alcohol/drug use can affect mental health symptoms in a variety of ways:

Substance use can "set off" a mental health disorder. Substance use can *set off* a mental health disorder in teens who are biologically or genetically predisposed to mental illness. Some teens with family histories of Bipolar Disorder do not experience symptoms of "mania" until they try methamphetamine, cocaine, or another type of drug.

Substance use can "produce" psychiatric symptoms. Alcohol is a depressant. When teenagers consume large amounts of alcohol or ingest alcohol for long enough periods, they can become depressed.

Substance use can "worsen" the symptoms of mental health problems. Teenagers with suicidal thoughts may actually take action to end their lives while drunk or high. Alcohol/drugs can intensify feelings of depression, lower inhibitions, and increase feelings of courage. Cocaine and methamphetamine can increase anxiety.

Substance use can "imitate" mental health symptoms. Alcohol/drug use can result in irritability, apathy, and changes in sleep—which look identical to the symptoms of Major Depression. Teens high on cocaine or methamphetamine can appear to have Attention-Deficit/Hyperactivity Disorder (ADHD). Large amounts of methamphetamine can result in bizarre and paranoid beliefs (similar to those seen in Schizophrenia). The mood swings and erratic behavior resulting from anabolic steroids or prescription pills can be mistaken for Bipolar Disorder.

Substance use can "cover up" mental health symptoms. Teens truly suffering from Attention-Deficit/Hyperactivity Disorder (ADHD) may be better able to focus when using methamphetamine, or may seem calmer when stoned on marijuana.

Substance use can be "unrelated" to mental health symptoms. Adolescents may suffer from both a mental health and a substance use disorder, even though the two are *unrelated*. In these cases, a common factor may underlie both problems. For example, teens' genetic makeup or experience of a traumatic incident can raise their risk of developing both mental health difficulties and problems with alcohol/drugs. Some mentally ill teens may be self-medicating with alcohol/drugs to *reduce* irritability, depression, distractibility, or anxiety—including severe uneasiness in social situations. On the other hand, the use of substances *increases* the chances that teens will develop mental health symptoms such as depression, anxiety, and irritability. At this time, the *exact* relationship between the two disorders is uncertain. One thing is clear, however: adolescents with co-occurring mental health and substance use disorders have significant difficulties and are at risk for continued suffering. *Teens with co-occurring disorders are more likely than teens with only one type of problem to have histories of physical and sexual abuse, be involved with the juvenile justice system, and to die by suicide.*

Adolescents with co-occurring disorders are often more willing to address one problem than the other. Some teens readily admit to abusing alcohol/drugs but refuse to acknowledge mental health symptoms. Teenagers usually perceive substance abuse as cooler than being "crazy" or "messed up in the head." On the other hand, some adolescents with co-occurring disorders readily acknowledge mental health symptoms, but are unwilling to decrease or stop their substance use. Adolescents with co-occurring disorders need to understand the nature of *both* their mental health and their substance use difficulties, the relationship between these problems, and the effect both conditions have on their lives.

Physicians must remain vigilant whenever teens who abuse substances are prescribed medication that alters their thinking, mood, or mental state. Because some of these medications can be abused, parents should ensure that teens take the medicine exactly as prescribed.

Frequently Asked Questions About Teen Alcohol/Drug Use

1. *Do boys and girls differ in their use of alcohol/drugs?* For years, boys used alcohol/drugs more frequently than girls, but now girls

are catching up. More girls than boys use prescription pills. The increasing numbers of girls using substances is particularly bad news because they are more vulnerable to the negative psychological and physical effects.

2. *Are there cultural differences in alcohol/drug use?* Although there is much variation within groups, Native American teenagers, particularly those living on reservations, report the highest levels of alcohol/drug use. African American and Asian American teens have the lowest levels of substance use (seems either they all should have hyphens or none). Caucasian and Hispanic American adolescents are somewhere in the middle. (Hispanic American teens born in the United States typically have higher rates of substance use than those born outside the United States.) Both Caucasian and minority substance abusers have high rates of co-occurring mental health disorders that need to be addressed.

Internationally, teenagers in Europe appear to drink more alcohol than those in America. However, American teens are more likely to use marijuana and other illicit drugs.

3. *Is it okay to look through my teen's stuff?* There is no clear-cut answer to this question, and it is certainly a personal decision. Regardless of your intentions, teens perceive "snooping" as an invasion of privacy, stemming from your distrust of them. Ask yourself *why* you feel the need to snoop at this particular time. If potential signs of substance use are present and your intuition is telling you your teen may be using alcohol/drugs, it is probably worth risking your teen's anger or hurt to investigate. If you are "just curious," you may want to think carefully about your decision.

Parents have different views on how much snooping is acceptable. Some casually glance around teens' bedrooms for a quick look at the tops of desks, dressers, and trash cans. Others open desk and dresser drawers, mill through trash cans, and go through backpacks, purses, or clothes pockets. Some parents inspect their teenagers' letters, journals or diaries, or their online communities (such as MySpace.com, Facebook.com, and LiveJournal.com). A tremendous amount of information can be found while searching through your teenager's private belongings. Prepare yourself for what you might find, but know that you may find nothing at all. Whatever you do, be clear about your motivation to snoop, and be prepared to communicate it to your child.

4. *How can I tell if I have found something in my daughter's room that could be drugs?* Several of the Alcohol/Drug resources listed in the back of this book have telephone numbers you can call to talk with someone about what you have found. Their Web sites also contain descriptions of various drugs, and some even contain pictures.

5. *What do parents need to know about urine drug tests?* Urine drug tests are designed to detect alcohol/drugs in the urine. Substance use can also be detected in an adolescent's saliva, blood, hair, or breath. The accuracy of these tests depends upon (1) how long ago a teen used the substance, (2) which substance was used, and (3) which method of drug testing is utilized. Many substance-abusing teens know how to affect urine tests to lower the possibility that substances will be detected: consume large quantities of water, drink "detoxifying" drinks to rid their bodies of toxins, or add chemicals to their urine sample to destroy unwanted substances. Today's adolescents can actually purchase "clean urine" to substitute for their own during alcohol/drug testing. All of these products can be easily found and ordered on the Internet.

Drug tests are usually given when there is reasonable suspicion of substance use (although they may be given routinely prior to teens being hired for a job). You should provide advanced warning to adolescents if you plan to use any type of drug testing and clearly state why you are concerned about possible alcohol/drug use. *The exact date and time of the test should be a surprise to the teen.*

A negative alcohol/drug test does not necessarily mean that adolescents are *not* using alcohol/drugs; most substances remain in the body only a short time and are difficult to detect. Or the sample could have intentionally been contaminated by the teen. A positive alcohol/drug test does not necessarily mean an adolescent is a frequent user or has a substance abuse "problem"—just that alcohol/drugs have recently been used. However, a positive result should lead to a substance abuse evaluation to explore the extent of use. If your teen refuses to take a drug test, assume that he or she has used alcohol/drugs and respond as if you had found a positive result. Have a specific plan of action in place *before* having teens take a test.

6. *What is a substance abuse "intervention," and when do teens need one?* A formal substance abuse "intervention" is typically a pre-arranged conversation with a teen in which individuals closest to him or her express how the teen's alcohol/drug use is hurting them and negatively affecting their lives. The goals of an intervention are for teens to (1) understand the breadth and depth of their substance abuse and (2) agree to get help for their problem. Help could consist of an alcohol/drug evaluation but usually also includes attending outpatient or residential substance abuse treatment. Professionals trained to lead "interventions" supervise the meeting after teaching participants how to express their concern in a caring and nonjudgmental manner. Significant members of an adolescent's life also clearly communicate what major consequences will occur if the teen does not choose to get help immediately. Interventions typically occur after adolescents repeatedly refuse assistance for their alcohol/drug use.

How You Can Help Teens Who Use or Abuse Alcohol or Other Drugs

Even if you do everything right as a parent, there is no guarantee your son or daughter will not get involved with alcohol/drugs. Substance abuse occurs in homes with stay-at-home-moms and working moms, in families with two parents, single parents, and stepparents, and in homes that are spiritual or religious and those that are not spiritual or religious. The key is doing all you can to prevent your teen from using these substances, and, if the teen does use them, to act quickly so that the use does not progress.

It bears repeating: adolescents who exhibit a pattern of worry signs that indicate possible alcohol/drug use need a professional evaluation by a qualified professional with training and experience in teen substance abuse. Communicate your concerns and be forth-coming about your suspicions. A comprehensive evaluation can help determine whether or not your child is using alcohol/drugs (and if so, what type, how often, how much, and whether negative consequences have resulted), whether a mental health disorder is present, and what else may be causing the mood and behavior changes you have observed.

Even if your teen has never touched these substances, it does not mean he or she never will.

You have a great deal of power in helping prevent your child from developing a substance abuse problem. Parents are one of biggest reasons teens report they do not use alcohol/drugs.

Strategies to Help Teens Remain Alcohol/Drug Free

- Talk with teens about their views on substance use. Use news stories, neighborhood, or family-related alcohol/drug incidents to open the conversation. Listen closely and nonjudgmentally, without interrupting them.

- Be clear you do not want teens using alcohol/drugs, and say how disappointed you would be if they started using these substances. Be specific about the risks and dangers of alcohol/drugs.

- Help teens resist offers from friends or acquaintances to try alcohol/drugs (you may need to give suggestions or role-play situations). Help them become comfortable refusing substances so they communicate their position in a confident, friendly way.

- Parent as an authority figure rather than as a friend.

- Learn everything you can about the dangers of alcohol/drugs (including inhalants and prescription or over-the-counter medications).

- Pay attention to what you model to your child about alcohol/drug use—they learn from what you do rather than from what you say.

- Be adamant about not riding in a car with a driver who has been using alcohol/drugs, and make it easy for teens to *leave* environments where these substances are present. Encourage them to call you, no matter how late in the evening, for a ride home.

- If they *do* drink or take drugs, consider allowing teens to call you for help. Communicate that you are not condoning alcohol/drug use and that you disapprove of teen substance use. Follow up the next day to discuss the situation.

- Keep an eye on teens. This is one of the most critical ways to protect them from alcohol/drug use. Know *where* they are, *who* they are with, and *what* they are doing.

- Be awake and interact with teens (even if briefly) when they return home late at night. This provides them with accountability, and it enables you to examine their appearance and behavior for signs of substance use.

- Allow teens to attend only parties supervised by adults. Check to make sure adults will be present and that alcohol/drugs will not. Do not allow them to go without both these assurances.

- Listen for street or slang terms for alcohol/drugs. Being intoxicated or high is often referred to as being *amped, loaded, baked, wasted, booted, blazing, trippin', stoned, ripped, skied, riding the wave, coasting, hopped up, leaping,* or *lit.*

- Treat teenage alcohol/drug use as a health and safety issue rather than as a moral issue.

Strategies if You Suspect Teens Are Using Alcohol/Other Drugs

- Write down suspicious behaviors you observe; you may need them to confront teens or to share with professionals.

- Explain to teens why you have your suspicions (without accusing them), by listing the specific "worry signs" you have observed. Allow them to give alternative explanations and *really listen.* If their stories are vague or farfetched, let them know you are not convinced. If your suspicions are wrong, at least they know you care and are monitoring their behavior.

- Do not be upset if teens storm off, respond angrily, or just glare at you in silence when you voice your suspicions. Wait until everyone calms down and attempt the conversation another time. If multiple attempts meet with a similar response, move forward with a substance abuse evaluation, and inform teens that their lack of discourse left you with no other choice.

- Have teens call you to briefly "check in" while they are out. This may affect their decision to use substances, and it gives you a chance to monitor their state of mind.

- If teens have just begun experimenting, your strong stance against substance use and enforcement of consequences for negative behavior may be enough to stop them from continuing.

- If nobody occupies your home during the day, have neighbors call you immediately if teens return home when they should be in school; this is how some teens hide substance use from parents.

Strategies if You Have Evidence Teens Are Using Alcohol/Drugs

- Feelings of guilt, shame, sadness, anger, helplessness, and fear are natural reactions of parents after discovering their teen is using alcohol/drugs. Experience your emotions, but do not get stuck in them. Focus your energy on figuring out the necessary actions to help your child.

- Even if teens have used alcohol/drugs, they do not necessarily need to be whisked into treatment. Experimenting out of curiosity is very different from using substances regularly. Find out how much and how often they have used these substances.

- Seek assistance from trusted professionals to learn effective ways to approach, engage, and communicate with teens regarding substance use. Contact substance abuse hotlines listed in the resource section of this book.

- Continue to be clear that alcohol/drug use is unacceptable. *Require* teens to inform you of where, when, and with whom they are going, and monitor extra-closely on weekend nights.

- Do not argue with teens when they minimize their alcohol/drug use and adamantly deny they have a "problem." Instead, have them show you that there is not a problem by not using any substances for a specified period of time. If they continue alcohol/drug use, obtain an evaluation.

- Attend community support groups specifically for parents or family members of substance abusers, such as Al-Anon or Families Anonymous, for guidance and encouragement in dealing with your teen. This is critical to your child's well-being, as well as your own.

- If teens have goals and aspirations (college, dream job, athletics, military), explain how alcohol/drugs can prevent them from ever achieving these goals.

- Share your concerns with parents of your teen's friends, and ask about your child's behavior while at their home. Collaborate on how to monitor teen activities, including possible restrictions.

- Do not allow flippant, rude, hostile, confrontational, or aggressive reactions or behaviors deter your attempts to obtain a substance abuse evaluation (or treatment) for teens. Youth who refuse to attend appointments should be told that decisions regarding next steps will be made without them.

■ Discreetly verify teens' activities and whereabouts. Drop by wherever they said they would be. Inform them this is a consequence of their substance-using behavior and that it will lessen once they earn your trust back.

■ Consider requiring teens to take urine drug screens to check for substances in their system, depending on the extent of substance use.

■ Do not rescue teens from negative consequences resulting from alcohol/drug use (hiding their substance use from your spouse, providing excuses to their teachers or boss, paying for their DUI ticket, not allowing them to be arrested). Experiencing the cost or penalties may motivate them to quit using.

■ Catch yourself if you start to judge, lecture, or moralize to teens regarding their substance use. Reiterate your love and concern, and continue to treat alcohol/drug use as a "safety" issue.

■ Restrict privileges until their substance use is under control. Praise and reward teens for not using alcohol/drugs and for avoiding or leaving situations where substances are present.

■ Whenever teens get angry at your watchfulness or expressions of concern, consistently repeat a simple message, such as "We care about you and will not accept this behavior" or "We care about you and want you to get help." Sound like a broken record. Reiterate the specific behaviors that make you uneasy.

You are your child's most important protector. Be prepared to make complicated, tough, and often gut-wrenching decisions if he or she continues using alcohol/drugs and refuses to comply with your requests. Even when your teen is unresponsive (or hostile) to your overtures—he or she still needs your guidance during this difficult time. Taking action can be frightening, but thinking about what could happen if you do not should scare you more.

The decision to use alcohol and other drugs is complex and multifaceted—and so is the decision to stop. It may take many conversations and several actions on your part before you see changes in your teen's substance-using behavior. Although a significant number of adolescents experiment with alcohol/drugs, the good news is that most never develop a problem. For those who have developed a problem, substance abuse evaluations and treatment services are more advanced today than ever before. Every day, around the country, teenagers recover from alcohol/drug abuse and regain their lives. The sooner parents take the first (and most difficult) step to get help for their teen, the quicker their son or daughter begins the journey of recovery.

CHAPTER SEVEN

Hungry for Help

Teens Too Concerned About Body Image, Weight, and Food

Why can't you just eat like a normal person?

Our culture bombards us with messages that our lives would be more exciting, happier, and more successful if we just looked the right way. Even when you teach your children "inner beauty" is more important than "outer beauty," every magazine they read and every movie, television show, or music video they watch conveys the opposite message.

A national survey of teenagers found 15 percent of adolescents were at risk for becoming overweight. Yet, 31 percent described themselves as overweight, and 45 percent were trying to lose weight.[7] The survey also found the following:

- 40 percent had cut their intake of food or calories or eaten low-fat foods to lose weight or to keep from gaining weight, one month before the survey.

- 12 percent had gone without eating for twenty-four hours or more to lose weight or keep from gaining weight, the month prior to the survey.

- 6 percent took diet pills, powders, or liquids without a doctor's advice to lose weight or to keep from gaining weight, the month before the survey.

- 4 percent vomited or took laxatives to lose weight or keep to from gaining weight, the month before the survey.

---

7. *Youth Risk Behavior Surveillance—United States, 2005,* MMWR 2006; 55 (No. SS-5), Centers for Disease Control and Prevention.

Teenage girls were more heavily represented than boys in every category.

So how do parents differentiate typical teenage concerns about food, weight, and wanting a good body from the intense preoccupation and dangerous behaviors seen among teens suffering from mental heath conditions related to eating and weight loss?

This chapter focuses on two forms of serious eating problems seen among adolescents: Anorexia Nervosa and Bulimia Nervosa. Teens with Anorexia Nervosa are *underweight* and continually strive to become even thinner. Teens with Bulimia Nervosa *overeat* and then compensate by *ridding their bodies* of calories they consume. Because problems with food and weight are significantly more common among teenage girls than boys, this chapter will primarily reference girls. The ways in which boys tend to suffer from these conditions are addressed near the end of the chapter in the "Frequently Asked Questions" section.

Emily: Typical Teenage Dieting or Dangerous Undereating?

Emily, fourteen, gets irate when her mother tells her to eat. She is finally content with her "totally flat" stomach and arms that don't "jiggle," but she cannot stop thinking about how to reduce the size of her thighs. Her goal each day is not to eat until noon, at which time she allows herself two pieces of fruit for lunch. Because her mother forces her to eat dinner, Emily has become a vegetarian and will eat only salads with fat-free dressing. Emily's father begs her to have a bite of pizza or steak, but she is terrified she would "gain five pounds" if she did. She regularly gets dizzy and lightheaded, and a boy at school told her she looked like she had AIDS because of how thin she is. Emily viewed the boy's comments as a compliment and confirmation that her diet was working. She runs before school and rollerblades with friends after school; she also flexes her stomach in class and does sit-ups in her room. At five feet five inches tall and ninety-seven pounds, all Emily thinks about is wanting to lose more weight. She is obsessed with celebrities and fashion magazines and says, "I just want to be pretty, and skinny, and perfect like they are." Emily once told her mother, "If I weighed over a hundred pounds, I would kill myself."

Many teenage girls desperately want to be thin. However, Emily is already *significantly* underweight, not eating enough food for healthy development and experiencing negative physical symptoms—yet she wants to be thinner. Her association between gaining weight and a desire to be dead is clearly problematic.

Teens Trying to Be Too Thin

Teens trying to be too thin remain underweight primarily by restricting how much they eat (often no more than 300 to 800 calories a day) and limiting their foods to those that are low-fat or low in calories. They are terrified of gaining weight and becoming fat. Yet, no matter how much weight they lose, their goal is to be even thinner. Despite being underweight, some of these teens still view themselves as flabby and disgusting; others realize they are thin but remain preoccupied with specific body parts (stomach, face, thighs) they believe are still "fat." These youth constantly comment on how fat they are and repeatedly ask others if they are skinnier than so and so. Teens trying to be too thin do not lose their appetites; instead, they override them. They feel empowered with each meal they skip, believing themselves superior to friends and family who eat due to "weak wills" and "lack of self-control."

These adolescents can become emaciated and malnourished. They frequently complain of being cold, and they bruise easily because they have a low percentage of body fat. Negative comments from others about their skeletal bodies and gaunt faces are viewed by these teens as compliments, often strengthening their resolve. Family members plead with them to eat more food and gain weight—even a little. But these teens cannot understand why someone would force them to eat; in their minds, this would cause them to become overweight, or even obese. Gaining weight is a sign of failure and weakness, and they believe they must be in control at all times. Regardless of how thin they are, these teens will do whatever it takes to lose just one more pound. Although sometimes competing to be skinnier than others, most of these teens also compete with themselves to achieve the absolute lowest weight possible. In their minds, to be anything else signifies that they are fat. Teens trying to be too thin are commonly goal oriented, high achieving, and perfectionists—traits that help keep them entrenched in their mission to be thin.

Because they often view food as an "enemy," eating can cause tremendous anxiety and distress for these teens. They prefer to eat alone and may eat only once a day. They often develop meticulous routines at mealtime to calm themselves down enough to eat. The following are examples of eating rituals:

- Limiting themselves to eating the exact same food every day

- Cutting their food into a precise number of tiny pieces

- Avoiding touching any food with their hands

- Eating their food in a specific order

- Allow themselves only a brief amount of time to complete a meal

- Not allowing their lips to touch the prongs of forks

- Weighing their food; using a different fork or spoon for each type of food consumed

- Arranging food on a plate in very precise order

- Drinking a sip of water after each and every bite

The rigid and controlling attitudes and behaviors of teens trying to be too thin can also be seen in several areas of their lives. These youth attempt to manipulate others to do things their way, and when things do not go as they have planned, they become extremely upset and angry. They are run by how and what they "should" be doing. Because they also have rigid beliefs and rules for how *others* should behave, these teens can be difficult to live with or even be friends with. Their daily schedules are usually set in stone, so unplanned events or happenings are met with resistance, frustration, and sometimes anger.

Teens who are significantly underweight may exhibit some of the following physical symptoms: lightheadedness or fainting, extreme energy levels (feeling tired all of the time or having continuous, frenetic energy), always feeling cold, thinning hair, dry skin and nails, and languo (fine, silky hair that keeps a body or face warm when there is not enough fat).

Maintaining control is a primary way of making sure their adversary (food) does not tempt or dominate them. So they meticulously keep track of everything that passes their lips—whether chewing gum, diet soda, a grape, a salad, or one bite of chicken. It all must be tabulated so these teens can assess how "good" or "bad" they are each day. This evaluation directly impacts how they feel about themselves, as well as how much (or how little) they will eat and/or exercise the following day.

Worry Signs 7.1   Is Your Teen Trying to Be Too Thin?

The following behaviors point out important worry signs of teens who are trying to be *too thin*:

- Is significantly underweight, weighing 15 percent less than what is considered normal for teens of the same height and age.

- Is too thin because she *refuses* to gain weight.

- Is terrified of becoming of becoming fat, even though she is clearly underweight.

- Sees herself as much heavier than she really is.

- Bases her confidence and self-esteem on her weight or the shape of her body.

- Is in denial about the seriousness of being so thin.

■   If menstruating, misses three menstrual cycles in a
    row; if menstruation has not yet begun, the physician
    indicates she is behind schedule.

Is It Time to Worry About Your Teen Being Too Thin?

The behavior in Worry Signs 7.1 describes symptoms of Anorexia
Nervosa. Most parents of teens with Anorexia Nervosa suspect
something is amiss as they watch their child lose increasing amounts
of weight. However, sometimes it is difficult to know when a
teenager is *too* thin. Our culture worships slender bodies; magazines,
celebrities, and fashion runways all feature individuals significantly
skinnier than the average woman. In addition, parents may be unaware of the enormous amount of time and energy their teen
spends striving to be thin. Just because teens think they are fat
when they are not, or are preoccupied with losing weight, does not
necessarily indicate they are suffering from Anorexia Nervosa. It is
a matter of degree.

Your "worry barometer" should rise if your teen refuses to put
on weight, despite being much thinner than what is expected for
her height, especially if she is obsessed with her body size or sees
herself as bigger than she is or her moods are dictated by how much
she weighs each day.

For the most part, teenagers with Anorexia Nervosa *restrict* the
amount of food they eat to attain their overly thin bodies. However, in order to lose weight, they may also exercise excessively;
purposely vomit their food; or abuse diet pills, laxatives, diuretics,
or enemas.

Anorexia Nervosa is very different from typical teenage dieting
and concerns about weight. It is a serious and debilitating illness that
can result in a range of medical problems. Unfortunately, teenagers
with Anorexia Nervosa usually deny to themselves and others that

they have a problem, making it difficult to provide these youth with the help they desperately need.

Restricting food, as teenagers with Anorexia do, is one form of dangerous dieting. There is another form of harmful weight control practiced by many of today's teens.

Christina: Typical Teen Weight Control or Binging and Purging?

Christina, seventeen, is a walking diet book, constantly commenting on how many calories, fat grams, and carbs are in every piece of food any-one places in her mouth. All she ever talks about is food, food, food—what's in foods, and what shouldn't be in foods. Yet, her family never sees her eat. She usually tells her parents she ate at school or with friends. But recently her mother found a mound of junk food wrappers under her bed. There was also a shopping bag with chips, cupcakes, cookies, and a whole pie in her closet. As her mother looked around, she found two empty packs of laxatives in Christina's wastebasket. What was a sixteen-year-old doing with laxatives, she wondered. She knew Christina constantly weighed herself and that her daughter's day was ruined if she gained more than a pound. And Christina's "twice a day, every day" workouts wreaked havoc with family activities. But, her mother assumed it was all just a phase, because "My daughter's body looks normal—she isn't too heavy or too thin." Her mother was perplexed.

The majority of teenage girls worry about their weight—some more than others. It is not uncommon for them to weigh them-selves or go on a "diet." But, clearly there is something more go-ing on here. Christina's mood is determined each day by a number on the scale, her inflexible (and excessive) exercise routine affects her entire family, and the presence of laxatives and large amounts of junk food—all these can indicate a problem.

Teens Who Binge and Purge

One of the biggest differences between teens like Christina and those described earlier in the chapter is that these youth *do not appear half-starved* like those suffering from Anorexia Nervosa. In addition, this group of teens manages weight primarily by engaging in frequent episodes of *binge eating* and *compensatory purging behaviors,* rather than by restricting their calories. However, both groups of teens share an extreme preoccupation with food and an intense fear of gaining weight. Like teens with Anorexia, this group of teens also bases self-worth on physical appearance.

Binge Eating

Binge eating typically refers to the consumption of an exceptionally large amount of food in a brief amount of time (usually less than two hours). Most people eat much more than normal at large holiday dinners or big buffets. Who has not eaten a meal so huge we wished our pants had an elastic waistband? However, these times of indulgence usually happen only a few times a year. In contrast, the youth described in this section eat huge meals—usually thousands of calories—on a regular basis. These teens typically consume foods high in sugar, salt, fat, and carbohydrates, and they usually binge alone.

It would not be unusual for one of these teens to eat half a gallon of ice cream, six cookies, four slices of pizza, three candy bars, and a milkshake in one meal. It is the sheer *amount* of food eaten in less than a few hours that characterizes these youth. While binging, they typically eat very rapidly, practically shoving the food into their mouths—often not fully chewing before swallowing. Teens describe feeling numb or "in a trance" while binge eating. They often report feeling frantic, out of control, and unable to stop putting food into their mouths. Some have said, "It feels like the food has this power over me" or "I get so full like I am going to explode, but I just keep eating."

Binges can occur spontaneously or be meticulously planned

(where, when, what foods). Some teens go to one fast-food restaurant, eat, throw up their meal, and then go to another restaurant and do the same. Others just go to one all-you-can-eat restaurant, consume huge portions, throw it up, then go back to reload their plates. Some teens who binge purchase large amounts of food from grocery stores and bring everything home when they know their family is not around.

Teens typically consume between 1,000 and 30,000 calories during an episode of binge eating. Because their meals are so immense, the end of a binge typically occurs when their overexpanded stomach becomes painful, someone is about to discover them, they are too exhausted and drained to continue eating, or their body begins to regurgitate some of the food from their stomach into their throat.

Binge eating is often the direct result of *deprivation*. To manage their weight, these teens restrict their food in ways similar to those practiced by people with Anorexia Nervosa; they may skip meals and/or limit themselves to "low-fat" or "low-calorie" foods. However, the repeated denial of food eventually leads to splurging on large quantities at one time.

Episodes of binge eating may also be triggered by feeling overwhelmed, relationship difficulties, or despair over the size of their body. The rapid eating of high-sugar and high-fat foods helps them forget their troubles and can even produce feelings of euphoria. Unfortunately, these emotions are short-lived and are typically replaced with guilt and shame over their loss of control.

Parents can look for the following clues to identify teens who may possibly binge eat:

- Large quantities of food "disappear" from refrigerator or kitchen shelves.
- The teen has frequent fluctuations in weight.
- Eats extremely quickly, as if shoveling food.
- Eats huge quantities of food at mealtimes, even in front of others.

■ Continues eating despite complaints of being uncomfortably full or sincerely stating she "cannot stop"
   eating.

■ Refuses to eat with the family or needs to eat "in
   private."

■ Disappears into her bedroom carrying large amounts
   of food.

■ Hides food or acts embarrassed if you walk in on her
   eating.

■ Eats particularly large portions of food when
   emotionally upset.

■ Hides junk food or junk food wrappers under beds or
   in closets.

Because of a desperate fear of gaining weight, these teens panic
immediately after engaging in a binge. They feel disgustingly full and
experience an irresistible urge to rid themselves of the mass amount
of calories. They must "counteract" the binge, so they purge.

Purging

Teenagers who *purge* usually vomit to undo the damage of their
binge. They stick their finger down their throat or use utensils to
stimulate their gag reflex. Adolescents who repeatedly binge and
purge often get to the point of being able to vomit by contracting their stomach muscles. It may be difficult to understand why
anyone would want to throw up. However, for these teens, vomiting is effective on two counts: it relieves their physical sense of
fullness and discomfort after a binge, and it prevents them from
gaining weight.

Teens who purge work hard to keep the behavior secret; therefore parents need to look for clues, including these:

■ Has calluses on knuckles from repeatedly sticking a
   finger down the throat.

- Develops "chipmunk cheeks" as face and cheeks become puffy from repeated vomiting.

- Develops broken blood vessels in the eyes from strenuous vomiting.

- Has the odor of vomit on breath or in hair.

- Brushes teeth much more often than siblings or peers or is always chewing gum.

- The presence of tiny pieces of food in the toilet that did not get flushed with vomit.

- Develops dry skin on lips and the area around the mouth.

- Repeated loosening of braces on teeth as stomach acid weakens the bonding agent.

Teens who purposely vomit often have specific systems and rules regarding their purging behavior. Some intentionally drink colored beverages (orange soda, grape juice) before binging so that when the colored liquid appears in their vomit, they know their stomach is empty. Other teens force themselves to vomit until they see blood. A number of teens allow themselves only one or two heaves because vomiting is so unpleasant. Most teens who deliberately throw up their food got the idea from someone else, know the behavior is abnormal, know the behavior is harmful to their body, feel ashamed of and embarrassed about the behavior, vow to never do it again—to themselves, and anyone else who is aware of it—and will throw up again if they binge eat. Toilets are the most common places teens force themselves to vomit. However, they may also vomit into showers, sinks, trash cans, plastic bags, or dirt holes in the backyard.

A number of teens who binge find vomiting too disgusting, too hard to conceal, or too difficult to accomplish. Instead, they *counteract their binges by overexercising, fasting, or taking laxatives, diuretics, or diet pills.* Many adolescents who force themselves to throw up engage in these behaviors *in addition* to vomiting.

Worry Signs 7.2   Is Your Teen Binging and Purging?

The following behaviors point out important worry signs of teens who *binge and purge*:

- Repeatedly engages in binge eating.
- Frequently uses unhealthy behaviors to prevent weight gain: purposely vomiting. food; misusing diet pills, laxatives, or diuretics; fasting or overexercising.
- Bases self-image primarily on body shape or weight.
- Is not considered significantly underweight.

Is It Time to Worry That Your Teen May Be Binging and Purging?

Worry Signs 7.2 indicates symptoms of Bulimia Nervosa, usually referred to as Bulimia. It is disturbing to imagine any adolescent engaging in these unhealthy weight-related behaviors, let alone one's own child. However, teens can conceal these activities from their parents for months, even years. Every additional day these teens go without treatment, the further entrenched they become in this very dangerous disorder. Therefore, it is critical for parents to closely monitor teens' eating, exercise, and *all* weight-loss efforts.

Your "worry barometer" should rise if your teen exhibits suspicious behavior related to binging or purging. Teens typically receive a formal diagnosis of Bulimia if they binge and purge at least twice a week for several months. However, you do not need to wait until your child has a full-fledged eating disorder. Take action if you believe she has engaged in binging or purging more than a few times, to prevent these behaviors from progressing.

A significant number of adolescents with Anorexia Nervosa eventually develop Bulimia; therefore, the distinction between the two disorders is not absolute.

Eating Disorders: Major Danger Ahead

The destructive food and weight–related behaviors seen in Anorexia Nervosa and Bulimia are very dangerous. The longer an eating disorder continues, the greater the possibility of medical problems. A great deal of physical development occurs during adolescence; a lack of food and nutrients during this critical period can delay the onset of menstruation, inhibit growth, and make bones weak and brittle. Vital organs such as a teen's heart can be affected, resulting in low blood pressure, a slowed or irregular heartbeat, or even heart failure. Eating disorders can affect hormones, resulting in irregular periods, the complete loss of periods, or infertility later in life. Abdominal pain, bloating, and constipation are common; food may start leaving the stomach more slowly, leaving teens feeling uncomfortably full after a tiny meal.

Teenagers with eating disorders can develop anemia, swollen joints, severe dehydration, an electrolyte imbalance, and impaired kidney function. The stomach acid associated with frequent vomiting can result in permanent loss of tooth enamel, cavities, and a chronically irritated and sore throat. Some teens who continually throw up their food eventually develop "spontaneous vomiting." After eating, their body automatically and involuntarily vomits what has been ingested, making it difficult for them to eat in front of others. Anorexia Nervosa has one of the highest death rates of any mental health condition; one in ten individuals with Anorexia Nervosa dies from starvation, suicide, or serious medical problems.

How Do Teens Develop Anorexia Nervosa and Bulimia?

Anorexia Nervosa and Bulimia are complex illnesses caused by a multitude of different factors. Once they take hold, eating disorders can create a vicious cycle that negatively affects every area of teens' lives. Heredity and genetics play a role in the development of both Anorexia Nervosa and Bulimia. However, it is likely that environmental and social factors that trigger the disorder in teens who are biologically vulnerable because of their family history. The following are common triggers.

Relationships. Many teens with eating disorders have experienced difficulties in relationships prior to developing Anorexia Nervosa or Bulimia and believe their relationships with others would magically change if only they lost weight. Some teens blame their weight for feelings of rejection ("If only I were thinner, he wouldn't have left me" or "If I lost weight, I know he would ask me out"). Some may have suffered ridicule from peers or family members for their weight or size.

Major Life Changes. Change can be particularly stressful and overwhelming during adolescence, as everything seems to be shifting at once. Going through the physical changes of puberty, adjusting to parental divorce and stepparents, entering high school, starting a first job, graduating from high school, going to college, mourning the death of a loved one, and experiencing the end of romantic relationships or best friendships can be confusing, scary, and upsetting. When teens believe they cannot control or predict the events in their lives, they find something that provides them with a sense of control. Restricting food, counting calories, exercising compulsively, and other behaviors typical of Anorexia Nervosa and Bulimia can give teens a sense of control and power over their bodies—regardless of the changing nature of the events in their lives.

Family Factors. Teenagers with eating disorders often come from families that fall into one of two extremes. On one end of the continuum are families that tend to be overattentive and/or overcontrolling of their child; teens have little to no privacy or autonomy. Adolescents in these types of families often develop eating disorders because their body and what they do with it is something of their own—and something their family cannot control. On the other end of the continuum are families that are distant, disengaged, and/or chaotic. Adolescents from these types of families frequently develop eating disorders as a way to fill up feelings of emptiness or to distract themselves from problems at home.

Individual Qualities. Low self-esteem, feelings of never being "good enough," and loneliness are common among teens who develop eating disorders. Many of them have histories of sexual abuse or other types of trauma. They tend to be overachievers and perfectionists and have difficulty expressing emotions such as anger, sadness, and fear. A significant number suffer from obsessive thinking and compulsive behavior. For many of these teens, obtaining the perfect body is viewed as a way of improving themselves, making them feel more acceptable and worthy. They typically receive compliments and praise from others once they start losing weight, which further validates their belief that weight loss is an effective way to better oneself. The thorough and goal-oriented nature of these teens makes it more likely they will grab hold of extreme weight-loss behaviors and never let go. Research is currently focusing on the connection between an individual's brain functioning and the development of an eating disorder.

Cultural Issues. Growing up in a culture that worships thin and toned bodies affects impressionable teenagers. Adolescence is a time for figuring out who one is, and teens are surrounded by messages from the media that outward beauty and physical shape are much more important and valuable than intelligence, integrity, or unique personality traits. Teens who participate in pursuits that highly value slender bodies—actresses, models, dancers—are under extreme social pressure.

Dieting. The physical effects of dieting can trigger eating disorders. If you have ever severely restricted your food on a diet, you may have noticed that you thought about food *all the time*—especially the particular food(s) you were not supposed to eat. In time, most people who seriously restrict their calories cheat by eating a "forbidden" food, especially when stressed. You may actually binge and eat much more than you usually would. People usually feel guilty and ashamed after this type of overeating, which they consider a sign that they lack self-control. So they resolve to restrict their food again, and the cycle continues. Eventually, some dieters begin to purge in order to avoid weight gain from binging on their forbidden foods.

Athletics. The following groups of athletes are at particular risk for developing an eating disorder because their sport has weight restrictions or values a lean body: runners, swimmers, wrestlers, gymnasts, ice skaters, rowers, jockeys, cheerleaders, and bodybuilders.

This Sounds Like My Teen, but What Else Could It Be?

Adolescence is a time of significant physical growth and development, including changes in weight. Therefore, even if your child is losing weight, binge eating, or increasing her exercise, it does not necessarily mean she is suffering from an eating disorder. Instead, the following factors may be responsible for her changes in eating and exercise habits:

■ Medical illnesses (gastrointestinal disorders, diabetes, thyroid disease, neurological disorders) can cause significant weight loss or repeated vomiting.

- Major Depression and Dysthymia can cause teens to eat less or more than usual.

- Puberty, as well as some prescription medications, can cause significant weight gain in girls, so they may attempt to eat less or exercise more to compensate.

- Teens who discover a new sport, exercise, or other type of physical activity may enjoy it so much that they devote an excessive amount of time to it. Teens involved with athletics may intensify exercise programs to become stronger competitors.

- Some teenage boys experiencing growth spurts eat significantly more than they used to.

- Some teens experiment with new ways of eating (vegetarian, no junk food, no longer eating kosher) as they attempt to figure out who they are and what works for them.

- Teens may try odd diets or exercise programs because their friends are doing it.

What distinguishes teens with these issues from adolescents with eating disorders is the lack of *obsessing* about food and the absence of an *intense fear* of getting "fat." If these two features are present in addition to the behaviors listed here, the possibility of an eating disorder should be considered.

Frequently Asked Questions About Eating Disorders

1. *I thought only girls suffered from eating disorders. Do boys get them too?* While close to 90 percent of cases of Anorexia Nervosa and Bulimia involve girls, boys can suffer from both of these illnesses, as well. Most girls who suffer from food and weight issues focus purely on being thin. However, boys with eating disorders typically want to be lean, muscular, and toned. The rate of eating disorders among boys has increased in recent years, which is not surprising given the rise in pressure from the media for boys to have the "perfect" body. Many magazines feature young tan men with "six-

pack" stomachs and bulging muscles on the cover. Boys who are homosexual are at greater risk of developing eating disorders; this may be partially a result of the extreme focus on physical appearance (especially being thin) in many circles of the gay community.

Boys who fall prey to eating disorders display most of the same food and weight-related attitudes and behaviors as girls with these illnesses; the course of these disorders is also very similar. Unfortunately, the majority of boys suffering from Anorexia or Bulimia go undiagnosed, because these disorders are thought to affect only young women and girls. This stereotype also makes it more difficult for boys to reach out for help, since they also view these conditions as a "girl's problem."

Most teenage boys are much more comfortable with their weight and body than are girls of the same age. In fact, most boys are concerned with *gaining* weight and getting "bigger." A new problem is developing as boys take muscle-enhancing powders and supplements in record numbers; one in ten boys admits to using anabolic steroids, which are illegal and dangerous. In addition, many young men are exercising and body-building to excess.

2. *Do teens of other races or in other countries suffer from eating disorders?* Most of what is known about Anorexia Nervosa and Bulimia is based on studies of Caucasian girls and young women. Much less is written about minority females with these conditions. However, it appears that teenage girls (and boys) from all racial groups can suffer from eating disorders. It is now believed that Hispanic American and Asian American girls experience levels of unhappiness with their weight or shape similar to those of Caucasian girls.

Although African American girls tend to be more accepting of their body size and shape, the percentage of these girls who engage in binge eating and purging is the same as for Caucasians. When clinicians rely on stereotypes of minority females (Asian American girls are naturally thin, or African American girls are naturally heavy), they can fail to recognize a teenager suffering from Anorexia Nervosa or Bulimia. Furthermore, individuals from certain ethnic backgrounds may be reluctant to seek help for their difficulties, particularly from someone outside their family or place of worship.

Sometimes girls of minority backgrounds receive treatment for mental health conditions that coexist with eating disorders, such as depression, substance use, or anxiety—rather than for an eating disorder itself. By the time their eating disorder is identified, it has often progressed to a more serious stage.

From an international standpoint, eating disorders occur most frequently in modern and developed societies that have a high regard for slender bodies, such as Europe, Japan, Australia, New Zealand, South Africa, Canada, and Argentina. Although the exact rates of Anorexia Nervosa and Bulimia are not known for these areas, the numbers appear to be increasing.

3. *If my teen suffers from Anorexia or Bulimia, will she outgrow it?* Eating disorders usually begin in adolescence or early adulthood; they rarely begin before puberty or after the age of forty. The course of these disorders is unpredictable and highly dependent on the unique traits of teens suffering from the conditions. Some adolescents develop an eating disorder to cope with a particularly stressful event or phase in their lives. Once the situation resolves, their eating disorder completely remits. Other teens may cycle between healthy food and weight behaviors and eating-disordered thoughts and activities. They may take proper care of themselves for days, weeks, months, or years before relapsing to destructive weight-loss behaviors. For a small percentage of teens, eating disorders are persistent and unremitting, worsening with each year that passes. Even when teens recover from an eating disorder, they may still focus on food, weight, and exercise more than most others, but not to such an extreme and dangerous level. For many of these adolescents, the fear of getting fat never fully goes away.

4. *Is it possible my teen could have another mental health condition in addition to Anorexia or Bulimia?* Teenagers with eating disorders frequently suffer from one or more additional mental health conditions. Mood Disorders (particularly Major Depression and Dysthymic Disorder) are common. The depressive symptoms can begin around the same time as the eating disorder, as a consequence of living with such a difficult illness. A small group of teens

are depressed even before an eating disorder takes hold. Many adolescents with Bulimia abuse alcohol and other drugs; stimulants
such as diet pills, methamphetamine, or cocaine may initially be
used to lose weight or maintain weight loss, but teens eventually
become addicted. Some adolescents with eating disorders suffer
from Anxiety Disorders, including Posttraumatic Stress Disorder
(PTSD) and Obsessive-Compulsive Disorder (OCD). These disorders frequently precede the onset of Anorexia Nervosa or Bulimia.

5. *How do I know if my teen is exercising too much?* Although parents want their teens to exercise for good health, overexercising can
do more harm than good. The 2005 *Dietary Guidelines for Americans*
(a joint effort between the U.S. Department of Health and the U.S.
Department of Agriculture) recommend that teenagers participate
in "at least sixty minutes of physical activity on most, preferably all,
days of the week." Just because teenagers exercise more than this
does not necessarily indicate they have gone overboard. Compulsive
exercising has to do with a teenager's mindset and is not just a function of the amount of time spent in physical activity.

Teens who compulsively exercise no longer enjoy it but feel
compelled to exercise. Their self-esteem and confidence are based
on how much and how hard they are training, yet they are never
satisfied with their effort. Because they are ridden with feelings of
guilt and depression if they miss a workout, these teens exercise
despite exhaustion, illness, cold weather, or physical injury. Their
exercise routine takes priority over social invitations, time with
loved ones, school, or work. If they have to miss a workout, they
typically exercise twice as hard or as long during the following
workout. Exercising and how their body looks and performs are
constantly on their mind; they try to schedule their life around
their physical activity.

Although not all teens who compulsively exercise have an eating disorder, many of them do. Others use exercise as a way to cope
with stress or overwhelming emotions, in a manner reminiscent of
teens who use alcohol or other drugs. Workout routines are predictable and completely under a teen's control, which can be em-

powering when adolescents feel lost, unsafe, or unstable in the midst of major change. Some teens exercise excessively because of a need to surpass their peers in athletics or another type of competitive event. These teens do not realize that their muscles need to rest in order to benefit from intense workouts. Too much exercise can actually damage joints, tendons, and ligaments, which can prevent teens from exercising at all down the road.

6. *Is it helpful or harmful for my daughter to spend time with others who suffer from an eating disorder?* Receiving support from another teen who suffers from an eating disorder can be invaluable. Your daughter may be relieved to know others share her struggle, and this can decrease her feelings of isolation and separateness. There are therapy groups, 12-step programs, Internet chat rooms, Web sites, support groups, and residential treatment programs specifically designed for individuals with Anorexia Nervosa and Bulimia. That being said, parents must be cautious about the type of "support" teens with eating disorders receive from other teens with similar conditions. Some adolescents with eating disorders share secrets with one another about how to maintain their illnesses and how to keep their illnesses hidden from others.

There are Pro-Anorexia Web sites and chat rooms that provide workout tips, excuses to avoid eating, creative ways to hide food, and encouraging words to reinforce the drive for thinness and perfection. Some teenagers with eating disorders wear bracelets to identify themselves (red for Anorexia Nervosa and purple for Bulimia) to one another, as well as to have a concrete reminder to reflect on if their will to not eat begins to dwindle. Sometimes teenagers with eating disorders compete with one another, striving to go the longest without eating or attaining the lowest number on the scale. If teens participate in supportive environments for individuals with eating disorders, great care should be taken to ensure that no "tips" are provided, eating disorders are not glorified, and the focus remains on teens' thoughts, feelings, and ability to make healthy choices.

7. *Are there only two kinds of eating disorders?* Although we know the most about Anorexia Nervosa and Bulimia, there is a third condition known as *Eating Disorder, Not Otherwise Specified (NOS).* Teens

with this condition are just as preoccupied and compulsive about food and weight as those diagnosed with Anorexia or Bulimia, but they do not exhibit all of the signs of these conditions. *Eating Disorder, NOS, can be just as psychologically debilitating and physically dangerous.*

A fourth type of eating disorder, *Binge-Eating Disorder*, is currently being reviewed and researched and has yet to be approved as an official mental health condition. Adolescents engage in frequent binge-eating episodes as described in the section on Bulimia, but these teens do not engage in any purging behavior. This condition is sometimes referred to as "compulsive overeating." Teens with this condition usually use food to comfort and nurture themselves and to push down negative emotions. They usually end up feeling guilty, ashamed, and depressed after binge eating. This condition can result in medical problems such as obesity, diabetes, and heart disease.

How You Can Help Teens with an Eating Disorder

If you are concerned that your teen may be suffering from an eating disorder, have her evaluated by a qualified mental health professional specializing in these types of difficulties. Experts can differentiate typical teenage concerns about appearance and diet from the intense preoccupation and dangerous behavior seen among teens with Anorexia or Bulimia. They can also guide you toward effective treatment approaches that match the unique needs of your child.

The following parenting strategies are important in the prevention of eating disorders. They are also crucial for helping teens already suffering from Anorexia or Bulimia, to prevent the condition from getting worse and to increase the chances for a full recovery.

Promote Healthy Eating and Weight-Control Strategies

- Stock your kitchen with a variety of wholesome, healthy foods and snacks.
- Help teens understand that body weight, shape, and size are partially due to heredity/genetics and partially

due to eating/exercise habits. Only the latter can be modified, and the most effective way to do so is by consuming healthy foods and engaging in moderate physical activity.

■ Educate adolescent girls that it is normal to gain twenty pounds or so during puberty.

■ Be straight with teens regarding the serious dangers associated with changing one's body through fad diets, fasting, overexercising, vomiting, or using laxatives, diet pills, and diuretics.

■ Encourage adolescents to talk to a nutritionist, dietician, or mental health professional who specializes in eating disorders if they seem overly concerned about food and losing weight.

Help Teens Love and Accept Themselves Just as They Are

■ Avoid criticizing your teen's weight, shape, or size— even if it is said with the best of intentions. If teens criticize their own weight, shape, or size, listen carefully and engage in a conversation to better understand their concerns. Don't minimize or make light of their worries or fears.

■ Regularly compliment teens' efforts, achievements, personality traits, and unique qualities. Focus on inner beauty rather than outer appearance.

■ Verbally express appreciation for all body sizes and shapes. Teach teens there is no such thing as the "perfect" body shape, and make sure you don't admire only thin celebrities. Don't make negative comments about friends, family members, or strangers' weight or physical appearance.

■ Encourage teens to communicate when they are upset. The more they use their words, the less they need to express themselves through food. Expect teens to be annoyed, angry, defensive, or even offended when you express your concern about their negative food- and weight-related behaviors. Reiterate your commitment to their health and happiness.

Take the Focus off Food

- Eat together as a family as often as possible. Serve balanced meals and *focus on a teen's day* during mealtime.

- Do not continually comment or control what or how much teens are or are not eating, unless instructed by a physician for medical reasons. When feeling under surveillance, they will hide their eating behavior from you.

- Plan activities with teenagers that have nothing to do with eating or food.

Support Independence

- Be open-minded if teens want to experiment with food choices (vegetarian, low-carbohydrate), as long as they eat healthy amounts and get enough nutrients. Discourage skipping meals or rigid diets.

- Respect teens' privacy. Do not walk in on them while they are dressing or force them to show their bodies.

- Give teens the freedom and autonomy to make their own decisions in life where appropriate so that they do not need to rely on food- and weight-related behaviors to assert their control.

Monitor Your Own Behavior

- Teens learn more from your behavior than from what you say. Eat regular meals that are healthy and balanced, exercise moderately, and accept your body. Don't criticize your own weight or body shape, or judge yourself by how you ate or exercised.

- Eating disorders are complex, so refrain from giving teens simple solutions, such as "Just eat" or "Everything would be okay if you would stop focusing on your weight."

- Do not blame yourself. Even if you believe you contributed to a teen's eating disorder, focus on what you can do now to help her recover. Families play a valuable role in helping adolescents heal from eating disorders.

- Be honest with yourself regarding your hopes and dreams for teens. Are you emphasizing physical appearance, weight, or body shape? If so, broaden your goals for them.

- Learn all you can about eating disorders by reading books, using the Internet, contacting eating disorders organizations, and calling eating disorders hotlines. See the Resource Section in the back of this book.

Teenagers today model themselves after young, thin actresses and pop stars, many of whom suffer from eating disorders. Although it may feel like an uphill battle, educate your daughter that celebrities do not really look like the "image" we see in magazine photos, music videos, television shows, or movies. Emphasize how much help celebrities receive from professional stylists, makeup artists, special lighting, and even airbrushing. Many celebrities spend thousands of dollars on private personal trainers and specially prepared foods; some rely on drugs such as nicotine, caffeine, and cocaine to keep from gaining weight. The dangerous food- and weight-related practices of some young female celebrities are slowly destroying healthy bodies and minds—their own, and those of the teens who attempt to emulate them. Many celebrities are encouraged to remain underweight by those who make money from them. Recently, some celebrities have rebelled against the accepted standard and allowed their bodies to look as nature intended. Most are normal weight and look beautiful and healthy; not surprisingly, they are viewed as "overweight" by the media and the majority of teens.

The following celebrities have all suffered from Anorexia Nervosa or Bulimia and recovered: Sally Field, Elton John, Jane Fonda, Paula Abdul, Felicity Huffman, and Richard Simmons. These individuals have gone on to achieve amazing accomplishments and serve as positive role models for young people. If your teen suffers from an eating disorder, she too can recover and realize her greatest goals. She just needs to take the first step toward treatment.

CHAPTER EIGHT

Secret Pain

Teens Who Cut or Burn Themselves

Why would she do this? What's wrong with her?
Is she trying to kill herself?

Teenagers are currently decorating their bodies with tattoos and piercings in record numbers. Almost every classroom in any middle school or high school has at least one student with pierced ears, a belly-button ring, or an eyebrow or tongue stud—not to mention other pierced body parts. The current popularity of adolescent piercings and tattoos is mostly related to teenagers' wanting to look a certain way (attractive, sexy, tough, trendy, cool), express their identity, rebel against their parents, or fit in with a group, gang, clique, or crowd.

In general, parents have no reason to be concerned about one or two tattoos or piercings—particularly if the motivation was one of those just stated. This type of "injury" to the body is usually performed by someone else and is socially acceptable. In some groups of teens, tattoos and piercings are actually encouraged.

In contrast, a number of teens secretly cut, scratch, or burn their skin in an attempt to "feel better." The damage to their skin is done purposely and voluntarily by the teens to themselves as a way of coping with overwhelming emotions. This is typically referred to as "cutting," "burning," or the more formal "self-injury." Although these teens are harming themselves, they typically do not want to die. Self-injury is perplexing and even sad to outside observers. However, to a parent, discovering that your teen deliberately hurts his or her own body repeatedly can be alarming and frightening.

Despite the fact that self-injury is dramatically increasing among adolescents, most teens purposely hide this behavior from family members, and parents are often completely unaware of it—even when it is happening in the very next room.

> ### Brittany and Ryan—Different Personalities, Similar Secrets
>
> Brittany, fifteen, is beautiful. She always looks perfectly put together—neatly styled hair, flawless makeup, and outfits reflecting the latest trends. Brittany is a cheerleader, hangs out with the popular girls, and does well academically. Her boyfriend, a star player on the basketball team, is sought after by most girls at school. Brittany has a huge heart and is kind to everyone she meets, making it difficult for other girls to hate her. However, they are envious of her "perfect" life—inside and out. She seems to have what they all want. What nobody knows is that Brittany cuts her arms with razor blades until she bleeds.
>
> Ryan, sixteen, is angry and rebellious. His parents have struggled to have a meaningful conversation with him for close to a year. Whenever they ask him questions about his friends or school, Ryan becomes annoyed and accuses them of prying into his personal life. At home he regularly storms out of rooms and slams his bedroom door—often not resurfacing until the next morning. Ryan was recently caught shoplifting CDs from a local music shop. Because of his increased isolation and intense need for privacy, Ryan's parents suspected he had started smoking marijuana, although they had no evidence to prove it. What they never suspected was that Ryan was burning his ankles and legs with matches and lighters.

So when should you worry that your teen may be intentionally harming him or herself? What clues can help parents identify a self-injuring teen in their family?

Adolescents who secretly cut or burn themselves may or may not experience difficulty in school, at work, or at home. They may appear "just fine." Given the hectic and demanding schedules of today's teens and their families, the warning signs of teens who self-injure can be easily overlooked or disregarded—even by loving, caring parents.

Worry Signs 8.1   Does Your Teen Secretly Self-Injure?

The following behaviors are important worry signs of teens who *cut or burn themselves*:

- Wears long-sleeved shirts, turtlenecks, or long skirts and pants when it is warm or hot outside; always wears dark tights or pantyhose.

- Acts vague and evasive when asked about cuts, scratches, burns, or scabs, and explanations seem phony.

- Becomes angry and defensive when asked about cut, scratches, burns, or scabs.

- Covers wrists with excessive number of bracelets, wide leather bands, or sweat bands.

- Wears an orange or orange-and-white beaded bracelet or plastic band (to identify self as current or past self-injurer).

- Refuses to wear a bathing suit in the summer, despite having no significant body image issues.

- Presence of razor blades, knives, or broken glass in teens' room.

- Presence of ordinary household objects (paper clips, thumbtacks, forks) with dried blood on the tip.

- Presence of bloody tissues in teens' bedroom or bathroom trash can.

- Presence of scar-healing medication in teens' room; concealer makeup found in boys' room.

- Presence of blood stains on the inside of teens' clothing.

- Seems more secretive than most teens their age; withdraw from friends and family members.

- Is close friends with someone who cuts or burns himself or herself.
- Is suspected of deliberately self-injuring by anyone.

Is It Time to Worry That Your Teen May Be Cutting or Burning Himself or Herself?

Teenagers can be careless and even reckless—particularly teenage boys. They can get cuts, scratches, bruises, and burns from animals, accidents, horseplay, and sports. Therefore, you should look for a *pattern* of behavior. If teens exhibit one or more of the behaviors in Worry Signs 8.1, they are not necessarily intentionally hurting themselves. However, you should investigate if any of the other worry signs are also present; if they are, your worry barometer should rise. If teens indicate that their cuts are associated with attempts to kill themselves, you should take action immediately.

Although this behavior is on the rise among teenagers, the good news is that most teens do *not* engage in deliberate self-harm. That being said, just because you have not *noticed* any of the above warning signs does not mean your teen has never engaged in self-injury. Some adolescents are incredibly skillful at hiding their self-harm.

Each self-injuring teen is unique. Some teens have cut or burned themselves once or twice just to see what it was like and have no interest in continuing the behavior. Others self-injure for years. Some teens have the desire to cut or burn every day—sometimes more than once a day. Others cut or burn once a week, once a month, or even once a year.

It can be helpful to ask your teens if they have ever heard of cutting or self-injury, known anyone who has engaged in this behavior, or ever cut or deliberately injured themselves. Then ask them for their thoughts about this behavior. And just listen. What you hear may be upsetting, but it is essential for you to know if they are harming themselves in order to get them the help they need.

Other Ways That Teens Purposely Injure Themselves

Although cutting and burning are the most common way teenagers deliberately harm themselves, some adolescents engage in different methods of self-injury, such as punching themselves, hitting their fists against cement walls, biting themselves, pulling out their hair, banging their heads against doors, continuously picking at tattoos or piercings, repeatedly rubbing their skin with erasers, and interfering with the healing of scabs or wounds. Parents may notice that their teen has all of a sudden become "accident prone"; with frequent unexplained bruises or physical injuries. Parents may find matches or lighters in their teen's room, even though he or she does not smoke. Or their teen's sores, tattoos, or piercings always seem to be infected.

Items Teens Use to Self-Injure   Some of the most common objects used by teens who self-injure (although they can use almost *anything* to cut, scratch, slice, or poke themselves) include razor blades, thumb-tacks, forks, knives, sewing needles, staples, scissors, pen caps, eye glasses, fingernails, teeth, paper clips, broken glass, safety pins, pencils, combs, brush bristles, barrettes, earrings, and nose rings. Adolescents typically use matches, lighters, cigarettes, and marijuana pipes to burn themselves.

When access to these items is restricted, teens become creative in finding tools to harm themselves, relying on such items as the pull-top from a soda can, a metal zipper on clothing, corn chips, pieces of floor tile, dried chicken bones, playing cards, the metal clasp on ace bandages, belt buckles, dried apple cores or orange peels, paint chips, sandpaper, or the edge of plastic CD covers.

Fortunately, most adolescents who self-injure cut or burn the surface of their skin, so there is only minor damage. However, a small subset engages in very dangerous and severe forms of the behavior. These teens carve deeply into their skin, causing considerable bleeding and sometimes requiring stitches or other medical care. Others have tried to break their bones, inserted sharp pencils deep into healing wounds, held toxic cleaning agents in their mouths to experience the burning sensation, aggressively ripped out medical stitches, or inserted sharp or pointed objects into their genitals. This type of self-injurer typically begins with superficial wounding but engages in more severe forms of self-injury over time. These teens usually need to make deeper and larger cuts, or experience more intense levels of pain, to experience the positive effects of self-harm behavior.

Marks or Scars from Self-Injury　The forearm is one of the most common places teenagers intentionally harm themselves—most likely because the area is fairly easy to reach. However, a number of teens injure themselves on their hands, thighs, calves, ankles, chest, breasts, upper arms, stomach, or wrists or between their toes.

The majority of teens hide their self-injury from others, so they try to cut or burn areas where others will not see marks or scars. If they injure a highly visible area, such as arms or legs, teens typically wear long sleeves or long pants to conceal any indication of self-harm. Injuries on the torso are the most easily hidden, and some teens cut only in areas covered by a bathing suit. To avoid being caught off-guard, most self-injuring teens invent excuses for their cuts or scars before anyone asks.

In contrast, some teenagers are not at all concerned about physical markings; to them, scars signify emotional crises they have survived or life experiences they want to memorialize.

Superficial cuts or scars do not necessarily indicate less distress. All self-injurious behavior should be taken seriously.

Are Self-Injury and Suicide Attempts the Same Thing?

Unfortunately, many youth who have engaged in self-injurious behavior have been identified and treated as if they were suicidal. Although teenagers who self-injure are *at risk* for suicide, their repeated self-harm is usually not an attempt to kill themselves. In fact, most adolescents who self-injure become upset and offended if you refer to their harming behavior as "suicidal."

If you notice cuts, bruises, or burns on your teen's body, do not panic and automatically think your teen is suicidal. This will only make the situation worse.

The following are some general guidelines regarding the differences between self-injury and suicidal behavior:

Intent. Teens who self-injure view their harming behavior as "life sustaining," not life ending. These youth report that cutting or burning keeps them alive. Without it, they would be overwhelmed and unable to cope and would likely become suicidal. They do not injure their bodies to bring an end to their lives; they engage in this behavior to continue living.

Frequency. Most teenagers do not attempt suicide. For those who do engage in this heartbreaking behavior, they rarely do so repeatedly. On the other hand, teens who self-injure may do so twenty, thirty, even 200 times. They may cut themselves every day, every week, every month, or every year, and their behavior may continue for years.

If you know of a teen who has "attempted suicide" more than fifteen times, it is likely that he or she self-injures and has been misunderstood and mischaracterized.

Method Used. Teenagers who are suicidal tend to use different methods when harming themselves than those who self-injure. Adolescents with a desire to die tend to use pills, guns, razor blades, belts or sheets, cars, trains, and bridges during their attempts at self-harm. Other than razor blades, teens would not use any of these other methods to self-injure. And even with razor blades, self-injuring teens usually do not cut as deep as teens trying to end their lives. Teenagers who self-injure are likely to use other items mentioned earlier in this chapter.

Dangerousness. Teens who self-injure are likely to superficially cut, scratch, poke, or burn their skin. They may hit themselves, rub their skin with erasers, or interfere with the healing of wounds. Even if done repeatedly, the damage caused by the typical self-injurer is not life-threatening and tends to result in much less damage to the body than serious suicide attempts. *Most teens who deliberately harm themselves know exactly where and how deep to cut in order to keep themselves safe.*

Co-Occurrence. Although self-injury and suicide are two different and distinct behaviors, they can occur simultaneously. Some self-injuring teens develop thoughts of suicide and may even try to kill themselves. If the suicidal crisis can be resolved, most self-injuring teens will no longer want to die, but they are likely to return to self-injury to cope with everyday emotions and stress.

However, adolescents who engage in self-injury are at higher risk to kill themselves than adolescents who do not self-injure. This is likely due to several factors: they lack good coping skills, they are accustomed to harming their bodies during times of distress, their self-injury may accidentally go too far, or they may feel desperate and hopeless over their inability to stop cutting or burning.

Why Would Teenagers Want to Cut or Burn Themselves?

Self-injuring behavior is not only confusing and upsetting, but it also requires the complete opposite of what most people think of their bodies—that it is something to protect. The following are some of the most common reasons adolescents give for engaging in self-injuring behavior:

Tension. Many of these teens report feeling "pent up" and tense much of the time; they often feel as if they are going to "explode." Cutting or burning leaves them feeling relaxed; it is like a release valve reducing the pressure.

Feelings of Depression. Some teens who self-injure believe they deserve to be punished; they view "badness" flowing out of them with blood from their cuts or fluid from their burns. Some of these youth smack or punch themselves or carve derogatory words such as "ugly," "slut," or "bitch" into their skin.

Anger. These teens frequently feel out of control when angry. Because they do not want to view themselves as mean or violent, they would rather take their aggression out on their own bodies rather on than someone else's.

Anxiety. Many adolescents who self-injure experience high levels of worry, anxiety, and fear, sometimes to the point of being unable to function due to overwhelming panic or dread. Cutting or burning themselves provides a distraction, as well as a physical sensation of relief and calm.

Depersonalization/Dissociation. When teens become severely anxious, they may experience episodes of depersonalization or dissociation, in which they feel "unreal." Adolescents describe the sensation of not being in their bodies and feeling as if watching themselves from the outside. This can be terrifying, and teens may feel as if they are going crazy. Teens may cut or burn to jolt themselves back to a tangible sense of their bodies. This is likely why self-injury is often described as "grounding" and is seen as helpful in enabling the teen to feel "clear-headed" and "whole."

Zoning Out. When some teens feel overwhelmed and stressed, cutting or burning themselves provides a trance-like effect. They can zone out and escape their worries or problems.

Pain. Physical pain validates the emotional pain of these youth. Some self-injurers enjoy the sensation of pain and feel "high" while cutting or burning. Others describe feeling little or no pain during the act but say the pain comes later, as wounds begin to heal. Another group feels emotionally numb, empty, or "dead inside." Cutting or burning helps them *feel* something; pain ensures that they are alive.

Comfort and Nurturance. For some teens who self-injure, nursing their cuts and wounds often represents nurturing their emotional hurt. In addition, adolescents may associate nurturance with pain if they experienced childhood abuse by individuals who took care of them or said they loved them.

Communication. Some teenagers use self-injury to communicate to family members, friends, or romantic partners when they feel hurt, criticized, abandoned, or rejected. Although this strategy usually works, occasionally the behavior pushes people away; some individuals find it disgusting, weird, or too much to handle.

Belonging/Being Accepted. Some teenagers cut or burn themselves solely to be accepted by a certain crowd or clique at school who approve of this behavior. There are currently numerous Web sites, online chat rooms, and message boards exclusively dedicated to self-injury. Many are educational, but a number of sites allow teens to trade suggestions and secrets about how and where to cut, the best tools to use, new ways to hide scars, and first-aid advice. Sharing intimate thoughts and feelings with others who self-injure can create a sense of belonging and bonding, as well as identifying oneself as a "cutter."

In one of the newest and scariest forms of self-injury, two or more teens get together and cut themselves. What begins as a bonding experience can escalate into a competition over who can make the most cuts or who can cut the deepest.

Control. A wide range of physical, emotional, and cognitive changes occur during adolescence. Parents may divorce, peers may reject them, and romantic relationships break up. Some teens who self-injure say self-injury is one thing they can control; during the act, they feel empowered and in charge. Unfortunately, as their cutting or burning intensifies, these youth often feel powerless and out of control.

Attention Seeking/Rewards. Although the decision to hurt themselves may *initially* be driven by one of the other motives mentioned, it can subsequently be maintained by rewards from the environment, such as attention and support from others. People typically provide increased care and concern if they discover that teens are deliberately harming themselves—whether superficial scratches or more serious self-injury. A small subset of teens deliberately harms themselves for the shock factor. They may thrive on crisis and drama, or they may use their wounds and scars to intimidate or frighten others. Some adolescents harm themselves after observing self-injuring peers obtain rewards (attention, affection, special treatment, exemption from responsibilities, lowered expectations). Their self-harm is strictly a way to obtain similar goodies. As one might expect, this behavior can easily spread through a classroom, school, or afterschool program.

Most teenagers who engage in self-injury are *not* doing so for attention; hiding marks and scars is the norm. Self-injury is a coping mechanism for strong and overwhelming emotions; emotional pain is vague and evasive, whereas physical pain is tangible and can be managed. For the small subset of teens who harm their bodies solely as a strategy to solicit attention, their behavior should still be taken seriously. There are a variety of ways to obtain extra support from others, and cutting one's skin is not a normal way for adolescents to accomplish this.

The Cycle of Self-Injury

Most adolescents who self-injure go through a predictable series of steps before harming their bodies. Typically, something happens (an event, an interpersonal exchange), and these teens feel angry, disappointed, sad, frustrated, anxious, embarrassed, scared, insecure, envious, or annoyed. This is followed by an irresistible urge to cut or burn themselves. As their negative feelings intensify, their emotions seem overwhelming and out of control, which is unbearable to them.

Thinking clearly and logically and coming up with healthy coping responses is difficult when teens are this upset, so they rely on what has worked in the past. After an act of self-harm, these teens almost always experience immediate (though temporary) relief. All feels right with the world. When this peaceful feeling fades, however, it is usually replaced with guilt and shame over the harm they have caused their own bodies.

Then, as happens in everyone's life, something occurs days,

weeks, or months later that triggers negative feelings. This starts the cycle all over again. Self-injury may be effective only for the short term, but it works. Most acts of self-injury are done impulsively as a response to overwhelming emotions, but some youth consciously plan their self-harm, hours or days in advance.

Many teens who self-injure want to stop. Scars and physical markings can be embarrassing, and continuously trying to cover them up is exhausting. Teens who self-injure know they are emotionally hurting those around them. However, these teens describe intense and overpowering urges to cut or burn that they feel incapable of resisting. Most teens who cut or burn are terrified to stop this behavior because of the emotional and psychological pain they will feel. These youth have little faith that alternative coping strategies will be as effective.

Frequently Asked Questions About Self-Injury

1. *Which teens are most at risk for self-injury?* Self-injury is likely due to the interaction between a teen's genetic make-up and his or her life experiences. Trauma (especially physical or sexual abuse as children), parental neglect, and family environments that discourage emotional expression are often in the history of teens who self-injure.

Adolescents who appear most vulnerable to self-injury include those who are isolated, impulsive, abusing alcohol or other drugs, disgusted by their bodies, confused over sexuality, raised in domestically violent households, or highly perfectionistic. In addition, the loss of a parent, the experience of childhood illnesses or surgeries, or difficulty expressing or handling feelings also appears to put teens at risk for this behavior.

2. *Do boys self-injure? I've heard it's mostly a problem among girls.* Although not enough research has been done to say for sure, it does appear that teenage girls are more likely to engage in self-injury than teenage boys. However, a significant number of adolescent boys cut, burn, and hit themselves. Studies of young adults have shown that equal numbers of men and women engage in this behavior.

3. *What other mental health conditions commonly occur with self-injury?* Many teenagers who hurt themselves have eating disorders such as Anorexia Nervosa or Bulimia. They may also have problems with alcohol and other drugs. Depression is common among teens who self-injure, as are Obsessive-Compulsive Disorder and Posttraumatic Stress Disorder (PTSD)—both of which are anxiety disorders. Some teens who self-injure just have difficulty dealing with strong emotions and stressful situations in a socially appropriate manner.

4. *What about cultural factors and self-injury?* Teenagers in some cultures around the world use cutting, burning, and other ways of modifying their bodies as part of a "rite of passage ritual" or some other cultural tradition. This does not fit the definition of self-injury as defined in this chapter. The same is true for adolescents who burn or tattoo themselves as part of initiation into or identification with a certain group or street gang.

Self-injury refers to deliberate, non–life-threatening, self-inflicted damage that is not socially acceptable (not part of any culturally sanctioned ritual). It is seen among girls and boys from middle-class, upper-class, and poor backgrounds; deliberate self-harm is seen among adolescents from all racial backgrounds countries throughout the world.

5. *How do teens start self-injuring?* Many adolescents get the idea after hearing about someone at school, including a close friend, who deliberately hurts himself or herself. Of those who experiment out of curiosity, only a small subset continues the behavior repeatedly.

Some teens describe feeling a sense of calm or release after accidentally cutting or burning themselves or after getting a tattoo or piercing. These youth then deliberately try to recreate the feeling by intentionally inflicting injuries. Other teens initially cut or burn themselves superficially to shock parents or friends. After a while, they may begin to enjoy the sensation or the relief they experience.

Self-injury has been popularized by magazines, television, and the movies; celebrities such as Johnny Depp, Colin Farrell, and Angelina Jolie have all said they self-injured. Although media depictions and celebrity disclosures can help shed light on this secretive behavior and are not meant to encourage young people to try it, they do sometimes have that unfortunate effect.

Teens with healthy coping skills and good support systems are not likely to fall prey to this behavior after hearing or reading about it. Those who are most at risk are isolated teens who have difficulty handling strong emotions.

6. *My teen has been self-injuring for more than six months; will she ever outgrow it?* The majority of self-injurers begin cutting or burning around thirteen or fourteen years old (although a number of teens first injure themselves before the age of twelve). For some adolescents, self-harm is done out of curiosity, occurs only once or twice, and is never repeated. Others may rely on the behavior to cope with intense emotions for weeks, months, or even a year. It can be a temporary solution to help teens through a particularly stressful period. Or it can become a long-term solution to dealing with life's difficulties. Fortunately, only a small percentage of adolescents fit this latter category and continue cutting or using other forms of self-injury into adulthood.

7. *My daughter does not hide her scars. Does that mean she is hurting herself for attention?* Some teens who cut or burn themselves primarily to cope also enjoy the attention they receive afterward. Others see no need to hide markings and may even be proud of what they view as "battle scars." Although attention is not the primary aim of most adolescents who cut or burn, these youth still need attention. Self-injury is usually a sign that something is wrong and teens need help.

8. *My son's friend has homemade burns and tattoos on his upper arms and neck. Is that self-injury?* If your son's friend burned himself and gave himself tattoos as a way to deal with stress, loss, or intense emotions, they are forms of self-injury. However, if his burns and tattoos were done to identify himself as someone who is gang affiliated or as a member of one particular gang, they are not considered a form of self-injury. These markings would likely convey his commitment to gang activity and be used to intimidate others. The

same is true for teens who burn or cut their skin during contests with peers to show who is the toughest. These teens are not injuring themselves as a way to manage emotions.

9. *What about teens who have a lot of tattoos or piercings?* Numerous tattoos or piercings do not necessarily indicate self-injury. However, you should explore adolescents' motives whenever they intend to obtain additional piercings or tattoos. A major difference exists between teenagers who express themselves and those who experience a sense of "release" or a "high" from the pain. Self-injurers may become preoccupied with getting more and more piercings or tattoos; the behavior becomes compulsive instead of a preference or choice.

How You Can Help Teens Who Self-Injure

If you suspect your teen may be intentionally harming himself or herself, express your concern and ask your teen. Some adolescents answer honestly when directly asked about deliberate self-harm. Others continue to make unconvincing excuses for the marks and scars on their skin or the bloody instruments and tissues found in their room. Either way, once aware that a teenager purposely injures him or herself, you must take action.

Teens who superficially hurt themselves on one or two occasions out of curiosity are at less risk. However, when teens describe a pattern of self-injury (especially if they plan to continue harming themselves), *you should seek help from a qualified mental health professional who is knowledgeable about deliberate self-harm.* Because all self-injuring teens are unique, a comprehensive evaluation is needed to determine why a particular teen intentionally injures himself or herself and which type of assistance will most likely help him or her stop.

The following are important strategies to use with adolescents who self-injure:

Monitor Your Reaction

■   Do not ignore the behavior or assume it is just a phase; self-injury is a sign that teens need help.

- Stay calm and do not overreact. Teens who self-injure are usually not in danger of serious harm or death.

- Try not to take it personally. It may feel as though teens are trying to manipulate you with self-harm, but this behavior almost always stems from emotional factors.

- Be honest about your confusion over their self-injurious behavior, but never display disgust or anger or try to make them feel guilty.

- Believe teens if they say they do not know why they purposely hurt themselves; many of them are confused by it as well. All they know is that it makes them feel better.

- If teens seriously injure themselves, get medical help immediately.

Do Not Reinforce Self-Injury

- Make sure teens are not receiving *extra* attention, resources, or goodies after incidents of self-injury, since this can further reinforce the behavior. Show lots of attention and care when teens are *not* self-injuring so that they won't need to engage in this behavior to obtain these.

- After an incident of self-injury, help teens identify what events and feelings triggered the incident rather than focus on the act itself.

Teach Teens Effective Coping Skills

- Help teens learn alternative ways to cope, such as talking to friends, exercising, drawing, journaling, engaging in physical activity, taking a bath or shower, playing videogames, listening to or playing music, crying, talking to supportive adults.

- Help teens communicate verbally their thoughts and feelings ("That hurt my feelings," "Don't leave me alone," "I need you to pay attention to me") in relationships rather than relying on self-injury to convey their messages.

- Help teens realize they *can* tolerate negative emotions without exploding or falling apart by talking them through stressful times or periods of loss.

- Help teens find ways to distract themselves when the urge to cut or burn arises; waiting even five minutes can be enough time for the urge to pass.

- Provide plenty of praise and attention when self-injuring teens use appropriate coping skills in place of harming themselves.

Decrease Risk Factors for Self-Injury

- Try to understand why teens are hurting themselves rather than focusing only on getting them to stop. Self-injury is a symptom of a broader psychological problem.

- Discourage teens from hanging around other youth who self-injure.

Help Teens Develop a Positive Self-Image

- Emphasize teens' strengths, interests, and talents to help them create an identity away from being a "cutter."

- Allow teens to make decisions and personal choices, no matter how small. Many teens who harm themselves feel they have no control over anything except injuring their bodies.

- Tell teens they are not alone and that others have suffered from self-injury and recovered.

Helping teens identify adults to talk with (parents, school counselor, mental health professional, family member, or family friend)
when urges to cut or burn arise is essential. Adults should provide
a great deal of support *before* adolescents self-injure. When care and
concern come mainly *after* an incident of self-harm, teens begin to
rely on this method to solicit support from those around them.

Do know that most teens who self-injure do not continue cutting or burning into adulthood. Once adolescents understand the
reason(s) they hurt themselves, obtain treatment for underlying issues, and learn adaptive coping skills, they can begin to break free
from the cycle of self-injury. Talk with teens about this behavior;
continued stigma and secrecy around self-harming keeps teens from
getting the help they desperately need.

CHAPTER NINE

Ending It All

Teens Who Think About Dying

This could never happen to my child. I would know if he or she were in that much pain. Wouldn't I?

- *Brooke, fifteen, keeps to herself, wears black lipstick, listens to music about death and destruction, and thinks school is a waste of her time and talent. She often talks about "wanting to go to sleep and never waking up."*

- *Robert, sixteen, is a straight-A student, varsity baseball and basketball player, and one of the most popular boys at school. When his girlfriend revealed she was pregnant with another boy's child, he was devastated and humiliated. Within a month, Robert became profoundly depressed, dropped out of all athletics, and seriously contemplated killing himself.*

- *John, seventeen, had repeatedly been involved in physical fights, regularly used alcohol and other drugs, and eventually dropped out of high school. After an arrest for drug possession, he searched his family's home for a gun and took his own life.*

Teen suicide is tragic. It is a parent's worst nightmare come true. Just imagining your son or daughter thinking about suicide can be distressing and frightening. But, you must educate yourself about this heartbreaking behavior, because no family is immune.

Suicide is the third leading cause of death for teenagers. More than eleven young people die by suicide each day, which translates into a death by teen suicide every two hours. Because suicides among youth are sometimes mistakenly recorded as "accidental" (motor vehicle accident, drug overdose, train accident, drowning), this number is probably an underestimate.

In 2005, the largest national survey of high school teens, the Youth Risk Behavior Surveillance (YRBS),[8] found that in the twelve months preceding the survey:

- 28 percent felt so sad or hopeless every day (for at least two weeks) that they stopped doing some of their usual activities.

- 16 percent seriously considered attempting suicide.

- 16 percent made a plan as to how they would kill themselves.

- 8 percent tried to kill themselves (with some attempts requiring medical attention).

Dropping out of school (or being suspended or expelled) increases a teen's risk of suicidal behavior; if the survey had included these teens, the numbers would likely have been even higher.

Adolescent girls suffer from depression at higher rates than boys; they also *think about* suicide and *attempt* suicide (usually with pills) more often than boys. However, boys *die* by suicide six times more often than girls—partly because they use more lethal methods (guns, hanging, car crash). Girls may also be more willing than boys to seek and accept help when suffering from depression and hopelessness.

---

8. *Youth Risk Behavior Surveillance—United States, 2005*, MMWR 2006; 55 (No. SS-5), Centers for Disease Control and Prevention.

Worry Signs 9.1   Which Teens Are at Risk for Suicide?

The following risk factors make teens more vulnerable to suicidal thoughts and behaviors:

- Mental health disorder
- Use of alcohol and other drugs
- Negative life events and stressors
- Exposure to suicide
- Access to guns
- Disruptive behavior or aggression
- Lack of connection to school
- Lack of close relationships
- Poor coping skills
- Conflict-filled family relationships or chaotic home environment
- Previous suicide attempt
- Poor impulse control
- High expectations or "all-or-none" thinking
- Involvement with the juvenile justice system
- Family history of suicide

Which Teens Are at Risk for Suicide?

A number of issues place adolescents at *higher risk* of attempting or dying by suicide. Many of these factors overlap and are interrelated. Presence of these risk factors does not mean teens will attempt to kill themselves; however, it makes teens more vulnerable and raises the likelihood they may do so. Recognizing the following risk factors for suicide is an essential step in keeping your son or daughter safe.

Mental Health Condition

A teen's mental heath is one of the strongest predictors of suicidal thoughts and behavior. The vast majority of teens who die by suicide suffer from one or more mental health disorders. Major Depression is the most common mental health condition associated with the death of young people by their own hands. As detailed in Chapter 2, depressed adolescents frequently appear irritable and agitated. They lose interest in people and activities they used to enjoy and may experience physical symptoms, changes in their eating and sleeping patterns, and difficulties concentrating. Teens who are depressed often feel helpless, worthless, and pessimistic about their lives and future. They view themselves negatively and commonly believe no one cares about them. Depression during adolescence can manifest in sadness, crying, and isolation—but just as often appears as declining grades, defiance, delinquency, aggression, sexual acting out, and even running away.

Too often parents—as well as teachers, coaches, and physicians—do not recognize signs of depression in adolescent children, because they attribute symptoms to "typical teenage behavior." *A critical step in preventing the tragedy of teen suicide is for parents to educate themselves on the signs and symptoms of Major Depression and to obtain help for their children if these behaviors become apparent.* Teens with Bipolar Disorder, Conduct Disorder, Panic Attacks (particularly teenage girls), and Schizophrenia are also at increased risk for killing themselves.

Though most mental health disorders during adolescence can be successfully treated (particularly Major Depression), most teens who die by suicide are never referred for mental health services. Of those who are referred, only a small proportion receive mental health treatment at the time of their death.

Alcohol and Other Drugs

A significant number of teens are intoxicated at the moment they take their own lives. The mind-altering effects of alcohol and other drugs provide adolescents with a false sense of courage to *act* on self-destructive thoughts or feelings. In addition, some teens abuse alcohol and other drugs to "self-medicate" mental health disorders or to cope with problems such as family troubles, relationship difficulties, or struggles at school. Although intoxication temporarily helps them forget these problems, substance use eventually makes each of these problems worse. Alcohol and other drugs deplete the brain of chemicals that control one's *mood*. A number of adolescent substance users report trying to kill themselves by overdosing on drugs or getting alcohol poisoning. It is not clear how many "accidental" drug overdoses are actually intentional suicides.

Conflict-Filled Family Interaction or Chaotic Home Environment

Family relationships characterized by high levels of arguing and tension, poor communication, and a lack of support significantly increase a child's risk of suicide. Parents who are unpredictable, abusive, overly rigid, or hostile also heighten the chance that their teen will die by suicide. Adolescents who kill themselves frequently come from homes with inconsistent rules, a lack of structure and supervision, parental mental illness or substance abuse, domestic violence, or a lack of family connectedness. These teens may run away from home or be forced to leave by parents.

Some degree of conflict is normal and expected during the teenage years, but parents must address *continual* fighting between themselves and their adolescent children. Parents may not realize when the home environment causes teens to feel rejected, humiliated, devalued, or "tolerated." Too often this can lead to deep feelings of isolation, helplessness, and wanting to die.

Negative Life Events and Stressors

Teen suicide is rarely caused by one particular incident, no matter how terrible the experience. For some youth, negative events or stressors build up over the years until teens reach a point where they can no longer cope. For others, a very specific incident can serve as "the final straw" for adolescents already upset or struggling. Childhood physical abuse or childhood sexual abuse (including unwanted sexual touching) are common events in the *histories* of teens who die by suicide.

Common triggers in the *present* include situations associated with loss, humiliation, rejection, or failure: break-up of a romantic relationship; victimization by a bully; sexual assault; parental death, divorce, or separation; unexpected pregnancy; a bad grade on a test or assignment; school suspension or expulsion; a forced change in schools; arrest or legal issues; anniversary of a loss; holidays after a loss; and rejection by peers.

Teenagers suffering from mental health disorders may have more difficulty coping with stressful events than their peers, and many actually have more challenges to handle. Even with the help of a close and supportive family, stressful events can be difficult for adolescents to manage. Struggling with them in the context of an argumentative, chaotic, or alcoholic home can be overwhelming.

Exposure to Suicide

Exposure to the suicide of a friend, classmate, or family member can increase a teenager's risk of dying by suicide, especially in the weeks immediately following the other's death. This is often referred to as *contagion* and is a very real and tragic phenomenon. Contagion refers to "clusters" of teen suicide attempts and deaths that occur close together in time or location and follow the suicide of another teen. Adolescents are particularly vulnerable to suicide contagion, and this risk is increased when teens feel responsible for the suicide of another (did not see warning signs, failed to take suicide talk seriously, mistreated the victim, argued with the victim, made a suicide pact with the victim, encouraged the victim). However, contagion can affect teens who have never met the suicide victim, particularly if they identify with him or her (that is, believe they share similar characteristics or struggles or viewed the victim as a role model). Exposure to a family member who has died by suicide can be a double risk factor—the terrible loss of a loved one coupled with potentially inherited depression.

Contagion also occurs after exposure to the reporting of suicide in the media. This effect is heightened when the suicide victim is a celebrity or the story is recycled again and again.

Exposure to suicide in and of itself is not enough to cause adolescents to take their own lives. However, teens already suffering from mental health or substance abuse problems, and other types of vulnerable youth, are more likely to be affected by contagion.

Access to Guns

Close to half of all teenagers who kill themselves use a gun. In most cases, the gun belongs to a family member and is found within the teen's home. The likelihood of a young person dying by suicide is several times greater in homes with a gun, regardless of whether the firearm is locked up or loaded. In addition, adolescents who use guns to take their own lives tend to exhibit fewer risk factors than teens who use other methods; these deaths tend to be more impulsive and often include the consumption of alcohol.

Disruptive or Aggressive Behavior

Many adults are surprised to discover the strong connection between suicide and aggression, or "acting-out" behavior. Teens who attempt or die by suicide are not always sad, lonely, and isolated. They are also the loud, destructive rebels who repeatedly find themselves in trouble. Students who attempt to kill themselves are four times more likely than their peers to report involvement in physical fights the year before their suicidal behavior. And one in four youth who die by suicide have injured or killed someone at some point before taking his or her own life. Depressed teens sometimes express their emotions through hostility, destruction, and violence. When these young people feel they have nowhere to turn, they may end up taking their own lives.

Lack of Connection to School

Teenagers spend the majority of their time at school. Therefore, the experience of feeling connected there is crucial to teens feeling good about themselves and their abilities. Adolescents can derive a sense of belonging at school from achievement in academics or participation in sports, school clubs, school leadership, other school-related activities, or the social scene. Teens who are not engaged at any of these levels are at increased risk for suicide—as are teens who are repeatedly bullied. Adolescents who drop out of school are also at greater risk, particularly if they do not have a job. Parents should closely monitor teens' school activities and further explore if their child's behavior goes through a sudden downward change: declining grades, quitting a sports team, failure to complete assignments, unexcused absences, lack of interest in friends, or withdrawal from school clubs.

Lack of Close Relationships

Social relationships are of the utmost importance during adolescence. Many teens who die by suicide have few friends and feel very alone. These youth may have intentionally withdrawn from peers, or they may have been blatantly rejected or simply not noticed by peers. Many of these teens lack important social skills and can be perceived as shy and introverted, irritable and angry, impulsive and irresponsible, or just plain "weird." They have few people to turn to during difficult times; and if they do attempt to get help from peers, they are usually not skilled in doing so. These teens often develop unhealthy (and sometimes harmful) friendships and romantic relationships in order to experience a sense of belonging. Or they may join fringe groups (satanic cults, white supremacy groups, unconventional religions) with other teens who do not fit in with mainstream peers.

Poor Coping Skills

Teens who have difficulty coping with stress and difficult situations are at higher risk to take their own lives. They may continually blame others for their problems, lack the ability to control their emotions, or not know how to problem-solve when in conflict with others. Other at-risk youth habitually see the negative in any situation and blame themselves for everything that does not go well (regardless of whether they were responsible). These types of coping styles make it difficult for teens to manage stressful incidents, and often make difficult situations worse.

Family History of Suicide

A family history of suicide attempts or death by suicide also increases teens' risk. This may be due partly to the influence of inherited genes and partly to the effects of modeling, in which teens learn coping skills and other behaviors by watching their parents.

Previous Suicide Attempt

Past behavior is one of the best predictors of future behavior. A significant number of teens who take their own lives have made a known suicide attempt prior to their death. However, some teens attempt suicide once and never attempt again, and other teens die by suicide without any history of prior attempts. That being said, a previous suicide attempt is a significant risk-factor for eventual death by suicide.

Juvenile Justice Involvement

Many teenagers who die by suicide have been involved with juvenile justice; the more contact they have with the system, the greater their risk of taking their own lives. Serious delinquent behavior, aggression, and thoughts of killing others are all risk factors for suicide during adolescence. Unfortunately, youth who exhibit these characteristics are rarely referred for mental health treatment; instead, they are referred to juvenile justice. If teens are incarcerated, their risk of dying by suicide becomes even greater.

A national study of teens behind bars who died by suicide found that most were Caucasian males between the ages of fifteen and seventeen, were locked up for nonviolent offenses, had histories of abusing alcohol or drugs, and had histories of a mental health disorders (most were thought to be suffering from depression).[9]

Poor Impulse Control

Teens who take action without thinking through the consequences of their behavior are at higher risk for taking their own lives. Adolescents with Attention-Deficit/Hyperactivity Disorder (ADHD) are often impulsive and reckless. Teens with ADHD are at particularly high risk for suicide if they suffer from an additional mental heath disorder, such as Major Depression, Bipolar Disorder, or Conduct Disorder. Impulsive adolescents who are suicidal may intentionally engage in risky and dangerous behavior, such as running into traffic, ingesting large amounts of drugs or alcohol, outrunning trains, or playing with knives or guns.

High Expectations or "All-or-None" Thinking

Some teens who die by suicide are high achievers and appear to "have it all," but underneath their successes are teens who place tremendous burdens upon themselves. Parents and teachers often add to this pressure with high expectations. These youth strive to be "perfect" and stop at nothing to attain their goals. "All-or-none"

---

9. L. Hayes, "Juvenile Suicide in Confinement: A National Survey," National Center on Institutions and Alternatives. Alexandria, Va., 2005.

thinking is common among these teens; if they do not complete something the way they believe it *should* be done, they view themselves as failures. This attitude can apply to any area of life: academic achievement, sports performance, relationships with friends or romantic interests, success in the performing arts, or any other involvement. Because of the unrealistically high expectations they hold, these adolescents are constantly evaluating and criticizing themselves. Even minor events (failing a test, getting into a car accident, embarrassing themselves in front of an ex-boyfriend or ex-girlfriend) can significantly impact their self-esteem and send them into a state of deep depression. For these young people, the desire to die usually stems from feeling like a failure or fearing that they are a disappointment to those around them—especially their family.

Exhibiting these risk factors increases the likelihood that an adolescent is in danger. In general (although there are exceptions), the more risk factors teens have, the higher their risk.

What Are the Most Common Ways Teenagers Try to Kill Themselves?

In the United States, 60 percent of teenagers who die by suicide use a gun; hanging and poisoning (pills, toxic chemicals, or alcohol/drugs) are the next most common methods used. A small number of teens jump from high places, jump in front of trains or cars, intentionally drown, cut their wrists, or purposely crash their car. Suicide among youth ages 10–14 occurs more often by hanging than by guns.

Although guns are the primary way teens *die* by suicide, taking pills (pain medication, mental health medication) is the most common way teens make suicide *attempts*—sometimes resulting in hospitalization.

Some adolescents (particularly non-Caucasian teens) die by *victim-precipitated* suicide, also known as "suicide by cop." These teens strategically and intentionally provoke police officers, gang members, or other weapon–carrying individuals in hopes of being shot and killed.

Worry Signs 9.2   Is Your Teen Thinking About Ending His or Her Life?

The following behaviors are important worry signs of teens who may be thinking about ending their lives:

- Makes statements about suicide, dying, or being "gone."
- Experiences a deepening of depression.
- Is curious, fascinated, or preoccupied with death.
- Talks about feeling inadequate, hopeless, or guilty.
- Gives away possessions of value.
- Becomes withdrawn and isolated.
- Exhibits abrupt personality change.
- Drops out of usual routine.
- Neglects hygiene.
- Engages in self-destructive or risky behavior.

Is It Time to Worry That Your Teen May Be Thinking of Taking His or Her Life?

Although it may be difficult to imagine, suicidal thoughts are fairly common during adolescence. However, it is *not* common for youth to think about it seriously enough to plan how they would take their life or to make verbal threats about killing themselves. Suicide is a relatively rare event, and at this point, *there is no definite way to predict exactly which teens will move from thinking about suicide to actually attempting to take their own lives.*

The behaviors listed in Worry Signs 9.2 are commonly seen among adolescents who are suicidal and should alert you to the possibility that your teen may be thinking of ending his or her life. Your worry barometer should rise with each additional worry sign you see, especially if your teen has any of the listed risk factors. Teens who end their lives typically have a combination of risk factors and worry signs.

Most suicidal adolescents give warnings to friends about the desire to take their own lives, but they may also tell parents or other adults. Warnings may be direct, clear statements about their thoughts or plans to kill themselves. Or teens may convey their intentions more subtly and indirectly, which can result in friends and family overlooking their cries for help. The following are common *indirect* statements made by suicidal youth:

- I won't be a problem for you much longer.

- I wish I were dead.

- You'd be better off without me.

- If a person did _____, would he or she die?

- You probably wish I would just die.

- It hurts so much, I just can't go on.

- I want to go to sleep and never wake up.

- Life's just not worth living.

- I wish I could disappear forever.

- Maybe if I died they would finally see how much they hurt me.

- Maybe I should just kill myself—just joking.

Suicidal teens may start asking numerous questions about what death or heaven would be like or inquire whether suicide is a sin. They may write stories, poems, or songs about death, dying, or destruction; these themes might start appearing in artwork or random doodling. Some suicidal teens are obsessed with television shows that deal with murder, forensic investigations, and gruesome deaths. They may be fascinated by guns, knives, and other weapons or listen to music with morbid and sinister lyrics.

Parents need to act *before* teens are hopeless and talking about suicide. When signs of depression are present for more than a few weeks, adolescents should be evaluated to determine whether professional help is necessary. *Teens at highest risk for suicide suffer from the combination of Major Depression (or another mental health disorder), substance abuse, and behavior problems such as aggression or delinquency.*

Why Would a Teenager Want to End His or Her Life?

We can never know the exact reason why a particular teen has taken his or her life. The answer leaves us when the child does. There is not one specific reason behind youth suicide; a complex interaction of several factors is usually at play. Teens who have survived suicide attempts frequently list the following factors as playing a role in the decision to end their lives.

> *Seeking Relief or Escape.* The majority of adolescents who die by suicide are in serious emotional pain before their deaths. They want relief from intense feelings of depression, anxiety, or rage; they do not necessarily want to die, but they want the pain to stop. When teens are extremely desperate and helpless, they are unable to see alternative solutions to their difficulties; they view suicide as the *only* answer.
>
> Suicide typically results when teens experience several significant stressors all at the same time—family conflict, loss of romantic relationship, school difficulties. Because of the cumulative effects of negative experiences over the years, teens who have repeatedly been in trouble may attempt to take their lives after what appears to be a minor incident. To suicidal teens, dying is better than living life in so much pain.

Avoiding Failure or Disappointment. In achievement-oriented societies, some adolescents experience overwhelming pressures from their families or even just from themselves to constantly achieve. This pressure may be combined with demands that they attain unrealistic and impractical goals. After what they perceive to be a "failure," some teens make a suicide attempt in response to feeling they have disappointed their family. Or, they may see suicide as a way to relieve the overwhelming pressures and stress they encounter every day of their lives.

Communicating Pain. Suicide attempts can be a way for adolescents to communicate to significant others that they are in tremendous emotional pain, cannot handle it alone, and desperately need help. Suicide typically occurs when teens *believe* they have no one to turn to (whether or not they have friends or family there for them).

Exacting Revenge or Retaliation. Some suicidal teens want to get back at an individual or particular group they believe has "wronged" them. They may fantasize about their funeral and imagine everyone feeling regret, sorrow, and guilt for how badly they treated the teen.

Seeking Reunion. When someone close to them has died, a small number of teens may take their own lives to relieve their intense loneliness and also to attempt to reunite with their loved one.

Helping Their Family. Some suicidal teens think their death will benefit their family. For example, teens who repeatedly get into trouble (e.g., arrests, substance abuse, school difficulties) may truly believe that their family would be better off without them. Others believe that their suicidal behavior will bring family members closer together (parents will stop fighting or will spend more time at home). These teens may also mirror messages they receive from their parents (a parent's life would be better without children, the family would be happier without the problems of the teen).

Most teens do not understand the finality of death. Some teenagers may not be thinking clearly at the time they take their lives; intoxication from alcohol or other drugs, severe depression, or another mental health disorder can cloud and distort their thinking. Many of these youth are ambivalent about killing themselves until moments before their death, regardless of whether the suicide is something they have thought about and planned for years or is an impulsive act.

Suicide vs. Self-Injury

You should be concerned any time you discover teens are purposely harming their bodies. However, you should not automatically panic and assume teens are trying to kill themselves. Some adolescents engage in "self-injury"—cutting, scratching, burning, or hitting their bodies—in order to feel better. These youth have no intention of dying and no desire to die. Adolescents who self-injure typically use nonlethal methods and are careful not to inflict fatal wounds. Although self-injury and suicide are two different and distinct behaviors, they can occur at the same time for a particular teen. Most self-injurers are not suicidal; however, they are at increased risk of killing themselves. This is likely a result of their lack of coping skills, their habit of harming their bodies when upset, or their desperation and hopelessness regarding their inability to stop physically hurting themselves.

Frequently Asked Questions About Teen Suicide

1. *Where in the United States is suicide most common?* Although suicide occurs across the country, it is most common in the western half of the United Sates (Wyoming, Montana, Nevada, Alaska, New Mexico, Oregon, Colorado, Idaho, Arizona).

2. *Are gay, lesbian, and bisexual teens at increased risk for suicide?* There are no national statistics on how many gay, lesbian, or bisexual adolescents have died by suicide. However, minority youth of

alternative sexual orientation frequently report higher rates of suicidal thoughts and suicide attempts than minority youth who are heterosexual. This increased risk appears to stem not from sexual orientation per se but from the prejudice, victimization, and rejection these youths experience on a daily basis; these issues are associated with several risk factors for teen suicide (Major Depression, drug and alcohol abuse, loneliness and isolation, family conflict, stressful life events, lack of connection to school, hopelessness). That being said, most sexual minority youth cope with stresses and never engage in suicidal behavior. More research is needed in this area.

3. *Does suicide only affect middle-class white teens?* Suicide affects teenagers of all races. However, recent surveys have found Hispanic teens (especially girls) *think about* and *attempt* suicide more frequently than African American and Caucasian youth. Hispanic youth born in the United States are at higher risk than those born outside this country. Caucasian adolescents *die* from suicide at higher rates than Hispanic or African American youth, although suicide rates among African American teens have increased significantly over the past two decades. Suicide rates for Native American and Alaska Native teens are higher than those for any other group, including Caucasians, although Native American tribes with better preserved traditional structures are somewhat protected. Although rates for Asian American teens are less understood, they appear to be lower than those for youth from other backgrounds.

Minority adolescents are underrepresented in all types of mental health services, so those at risk for suicide frequently do not receive the treatment they need. Regardless of ethnic or cultural background, the risk factors for teen suicide appear to be the same.

4. *How common is suicide in other countries?* Although rates vary between countries, suicide is one of the most common causes of death among adolescents worldwide. Suicidal teens in all countries appear to share similar risk factors—depression, substance abuse, family problems, acute stressors, and difficulties in romantic relationships. Sadly, only a small number of young people around the world receive quality mental health care, because of the stigma as-

sociated with mental health disorders and minimal access to appropriate treatment. Lower rates of suicide are found in cultures where religion prohibits taking one's own life, such as in Arab countries. Lithuania, Russia, Hungary, Estonia, and Sri Lanka have particularly high rates of suicide. And the rates of suicide in Japan and China have significantly increased in recent years.

Teens residing in countries with restricted access to firearms use hanging, jumping, or the ingestion of poison to end their lives. Around the world, death by suicide is more common among boys, and suicidal thoughts and attempts are more common among girls (except in rural parts of India, Pakistan, Sri Lanka, and China, where suicide attempts often result in death for teenage girls who ingest lethal pesticides).

5. *What role does religion play in teen suicide?* For some adolescents, strong religious beliefs can be protective against suicidal thoughts and attempts. Religion and spirituality are complex issues and difficult to measure; researchers typically look at such things as attendance at religious services, frequency of prayer, participation in religious activities, belief in something bigger than oneself, acceptance of traditional doctrine, and a personal sense of the importance of religion or God. Religious beliefs and practice may lower suicide risk because of the sense of belonging and social support that religion brings to some teens or because of the strong message that suicide is socially and religiously unacceptable. Much more work needs to be done in this area before we fully understand the relationship between religiosity and suicide among young people.

6. *Do "no suicide" or "safety" contracts prevent suicide?* Mental health and medical professionals often ask suicidal teenagers to sign "no suicide" or "safety" contracts. Adolescents typically agree, in writing, to keep themselves safe for a specified period of time (the next twenty-four hours or until the next meeting with the therapist) and to contact a responsible adult if they feel unable to keep themselves safe. Unfortunately, suicide and safety contracts do not prevent suicide. Adolescents may genuinely commit to the conditions of these contracts and wholeheartedly believe they will abide by them.

However, when faced with overwhelming painful emotions, unresolved stresses, or strong suicidal impulses, teens may find that the contract is the last thing on their mind.

Despite this limitation, and despite the fact that there is no way to enforce these contracts, written agreements can still be helpful. Adolescents' risk of dying goes up significantly when they are *unwilling* to agree not to kill themselves or to alert an adult when suicidal urges arise. Refusal to sign no-suicide or safety contracts can be an indication of how serious teens are about taking their lives and should give rise to a more cautious safety plan.

7. *I keep hearing about the "choking game." Is it the same as suicide?* The Choking Game (also known as the Pass-Out Game, Tingling Game, or Space Monkey) is an activity in which children and adolescents cut off a friend's circulation by choking, strangling, or suffocating the individual until he or she passes out. Once the victim passes out, the friend lets go and releases the pressure, which results in tingling and euphoria as the victim regains consciousness. When airflow has been restricted for too long, some teens have suffered brain damage from playing the Choking Game, and others have died. Some of these deaths have been mistakenly classified as suicides, though the teens were not trying to kill themselves. Please see www.whentoworry.com for additional details, including warning signs of this dangerous behavior.

8. *My neighbor's son died by suicide, but they said he was masturbating. I'm confused.* A small number of teenage boys (as well as adult men) engage in a practice called *autoerotic asphyxiation*. While masturbating, these boys attempt to cut off blood flow and oxygen to their brain in order to heighten the intensity of sexual pleasure, particularly at the point of orgasm. Many of them place ropes, belts, or ties around their necks and attach them to a fixed object, usually above their head. This extremely dangerous behavior has resulted in many accidental deaths that are often misclassified as suicides.

9. *If my teen is now in college, do I still need to worry about suicide?* Although suicide is the third leading cause of death among teens,

it is the *second* leading cause of death among college students. Attending college brings about many changes: living away from home (even college commuters gain a new level of independence), spending time with new friends unknown to parents, having increased opportunities to experiment with alcohol and other drugs, and facing increased academic expectations. College students are notorious for inconsistent and unhealthy eating habits and erratic sleeping patterns. Major mental health disorders such as Major Depression, Bipolar Disorder, and Schizophrenia often do not manifest until late adolescence or early adulthood, and the stress of college can increase psychiatric symptoms. For young people with mental health disorders to successfully participate and graduate from college, their emotions and behaviors should be stabilized and appropriately treated. Unfortunately, most college counseling centers have limited resources and are designed for handling short-term mental health issues.

How You Can Help Teens with Suicidal Thoughts or Behaviors

Adolescents who talk about wanting to die or who a make suicide attempt must be attended to *immediately.* These teens need a comprehensive evaluation by a qualified mental health professional who is knowledgeable about teen suicide. The evaluation should determine your teen's level of risk, whether he or she suffers from a mental health or substance abuse disorder, what current stressors are present, and which strategies need to be in place to ensure his or her safety.

When teens present an imminent risk of suicide, they may need to be hospitalized for a brief period to ensure their safety and stabilize their behavior. Hospitalization offers the time to evaluate teens and keeps them safe; the underlying issues that triggered the suicidal thoughts and behavior are typically not resolved. Therefore, follow-up with outpatient therapy immediately following discharge from a hospital is required.

Parents play a crucial role in the management of suicidal adolescents. If they can provide stability, hope, and support, parents can significantly decrease teens' emotional distress and suicidal feelings. Although a complete guide to managing suicidal teens is beyond the scope of this chapter, the following points are important to keep in mind when interacting with suicidal youth:

Ask About Suicide

- When worried that teens are thinking about suicide, ask about it directly. Being open about the topic shows teens that you understand their despair. Help them clarify what is upsetting them.

- Ask suicidal teens, "What has changed?" if they exhibit an abrupt and unexpected improvement in mood or lack of suicidal thought. Teens may suddenly be in good spirits because they have made the decision to kill themselves.

Get Immediate Help in a Crisis

- Do not leave suicidal teens alone if they have an *immediate plan* and *access* to a gun or another potentially lethal method.

- Get help immediately by calling 911 or take teens to a psychiatric hospital or the emergency room of a local hospital.

Validate Teens' Pain

- Do not underestimate adolescents' pain and distress. You may think their problems are trivial, but teens' may be so overwhelmed by them that suicide seems their only solution.

- Listen. And then listen some more. Venting anger, frustration, or sadness can significantly reduce teens' distress and help them feel less alone. Lecturing suici-

dal teens on the value of life is not helpful. Silences
are okay.

Be Aware of Your Behavior

- Do not act shocked, angry, or panicked when talking
  with teens who are suicidal. To feel safe, suicidal teens
  need to know you can handle their painful emotions
  and destructive impulses.

- Never promise to keep suicidal talk or behaviors
  secret; instead, promise help and discretion. Teens may
  get angry at you in the moment, but it will not last.

- Do not ever say to a teenager, "You're the cause of
  this family's problems," "My life would be better
  without you," or "You cause us so much pain."

- Without guilt and self-criticism, look to see what
  changes in family interactions will help teens. Suicide
  attempts affect the entire family, and the entire family
  can positively affect a suicidal youth.

Take Appropriate Precautions

- If teenagers are actively suicidal, guns should be
  removed from the family home; alcohol and medication should be locked up.

- Provide extra supervision, but do not ask suicidal teens'
  friends or siblings to monitor behavior. This is too
  much responsibility and can be traumatizing if they are
  unable to stop something terrible from happening.

- Identify what triggers suicidal thinking and urges for
  your teen, and get professional help for these issues.

Help Teens See Options

- Point out that "suicide is a permanent solution to
  temporary problems." Repeatedly emphasize that

things can and will get better. Help teens think of safer solutions.

■ If teens hold cultural and religious beliefs that discourage suicide, use that to help keep them safe.

Take All Suicidal Behavior Seriously

■ View suicidal teens as individuals who lack coping skills, rather than as manipulative, attention-seeking, or needy. If these teens had the skills to get their needs met more appropriately, they would use them.

■ Even if teens are using suicide as a way to obtain attention, this method of gaining attention is not normal; it is dangerous, and it calls for an immediate evaluation.

Help adolescents identify trusted and responsible adults to talk with (parents, mental health professional, school counselor, teacher, coach, spiritual leader, extended family, or family friend) when thoughts of suicide arise. Efforts should be made to provide support and assistance *before* adolescents threaten or make a suicide attempt. When attention and connection primarily come *after* suicidal talk or behavior, some teens begin to view suicide as an effective way to acquire comfort and care from significant others.

What to Do if Your Teen Knows Someone Who Has Died by Suicide

Teens are likely to experience a variety of emotions, including numbness, shock, or overwhelming grief, if someone they know attempts or dies by suicide. Guilt, anger, and confusion are also common. Adolescents exposed to others' serious suicide attempts or suicide deaths are at increased risk of suicidal thoughts and behavior themselves. This is especially true for teens who abuse alcohol/drugs or who suffer from anxiety, depression, or previous suicidal thoughts or behavior. Adolescents who are particularly close to the victim, had a conversation with the victim within twenty-four hours of the suicide attempt or death, or witnessed the attempt or death are also at increased risk of emotional and behavioral difficulties. Make sure your teen understands that he or she is never to blame for someone else's death, provide support during this difficult time, and keep daily routines in place. If your teen's schoolwork, relationships, or health are negatively affected for more than a few weeks, obtain an evaluation by a professional experienced in grief and loss. If a suicide victim survives an attempt, your teen may want to avoid this individual out of fear, discomfort, or guilt. However, your teen's support can play an essential role in helping this individual feel less isolated and alone.

Although the thought of teen suicide is upsetting, it is important to remember that many adolescents experience suicidal thoughts and feelings at some point—yet most do not make a suicide attempt. Even fewer die by suicide. The majority of teenagers who seriously think about killing themselves are suicidal for only a limited period of time. They are typically seeking a solution for a problem and see no other way out. Getting teens treatment for underlying mental health and/or substance abuse disorders, teaching them effective coping skills, and decreasing the stress in their lives can help prevent suicidal thoughts and urges. Even teens who have already made a suicide attempt can go on to live successful and fulfilling lives if they receive appropriate professional help and the continual love and support of their parents.

CHAPTER TEN

Not Making the Connection

Teens Who Have a Hard Time "Getting It"

*How could you have done that? What were you
thinking? We've gone over this so many times!*

This chapter covers four different conditions that appear similar, yet
have their own unique characteristics. A common feature among all
adolescents with these conditions is that they have more difficulty
understanding things than their peers. *Do not spend too much time
trying to decide exactly which description best fits your teen, if any. If you
recognize your child in this chapter, the important thing is to let a professional identify exactly what's going on.* The various conditions can require different approaches to treatment, so clinicians must take the
necessary time to differentiate the disorders so that your teen is not
misdiagnosed and given ineffective treatment.

Teens Who Perform Academically Below Their Potential

> Ryan, fourteen, can't take it anymore. As he does his homework, his
> mother hounds him with questions and comments such as, "Are you done
> yet?" "Stop wasting time," "You're going to miss your favorite TV shows."
> Rereading the same paragraph six times is awful enough, but with his
> mother standing over his shoulder, it's unbearable. Ryan has never liked
> school, but now that it's getting harder, he hates it. He daydreams and
> doodles while doing his homework, which makes his mother furious.

Parents of smart teens expect their children to do well in school.
Yet, sometimes they don't. After several years of watching their chil-

dren fail to perform up to their potential, the parents of intelligent teens typically believe that their son or daughter is not trying hard enough, is too focused on nonschool activities (sports, music, friends, the opposite sex), or is just plain lazy. Laziness, apathy, and nonacademic interests are fairly accurate explanations for poor grades among a small percentage of teenagers. However, *most* smart adolescents who perform poorly at school have a very real and valid reason for their academic problems.

Worry Signs 10.1   Is Your Teen's Academic Performance Below His or Her Potential?

The following behaviors are important worry signs of teens who have problems with "processing information" and learning:

- *Trouble in School.* Performs poorly on assignments or tests; receives report cards with grades lower than is capable of; has repeated a grade, or has been recommended for retention.

- *Avoidance of Schoolwork.* Procrastinates or completely avoids activities requiring reading, writing, or mathematics; hates reading anything out loud.

- *Poor Writing Skills.* Has very messy handwriting, as if still in elementary school; holds pens and pencils awkwardly, usually grasping them too tightly.

- *Takes a Long Time to Complete Tasks.* Spends longer on homework than should be necessary; often needs a lengthy amount of time to respond when you ask a question.

- *Unorganized.* Seems excessively unorganized with homework (sometimes loses the directions or lacks the necessary book or papers to complete the

assignment); experiences difficulty planning what
steps need to be taken to accomplish a task.

■   *Frequently Forgets or Does Not Understand.* Repeatedly
forgets to turn in homework; often does only part of
what you ask or repeatedly has difficulty following
your directions; appears "spacey," especially during
discussions or activities involving complex thought;
struggles to adjust to new situations.

If your teen frequently displays these traits *and* is struggling in
school, your teen may be suffering from a Learning Disability (also
known as a Learning Disorder or LD). Teens can have learning disabilities in reading, mathematics, and writing.

Types of Learning Disabilities

There are various kinds of learning disabilities; a teen may have one
or all of them. The most common are these:

Reading. This is the most common of the learning disabilities
and is often referred to as *dyslexia.* Any aspect of adolescents'
reading ability can be affected—accuracy, speed (slow), com-
prehension. These teens may add or omit certain letters or
complete words. They may also have difficulty connecting the
letters of the alphabet with specific sounds, making it hard to
sound out words they do not immediately recognize.

Mathematics. A disability in mathematics can mean problems
with numbers, arithmetic, and calculation skills. These teens
may have difficulty understanding mathematical concepts or
translating arithmetic word problems into numerical symbols.
These teens may struggle to remember which steps are necessary
to solve math problems, even simple steps such as addition, sub-
traction, multiplication, or division. They may forget—or never
learn—the multiplication tables.

Writing. Adolescents with a learning disability in written expression tend to have significant difficulty with grammar, punctuation, and spelling. And their handwriting skills are usually terrible. They often make a number of errors when asked to copy down what is being said or when asked to spontaneously write a story.

Learning disabilities tend to occur in clusters, so if your teen has one of these three challenges, there is a good chance he or she may suffer from one of the others, as well.

Learning Disabilities and School Performance   Teens' school performance is assumed to match up with their intellectual ability. Adolescents with high intellectual potential should do very well in school, while those with low intellectual potential should have poorer school performance. The key to Learning Disorders is that, whether the teen has superior or average intelligence, there is a major gap between the teen's *potential* to learn and what is *actually* being learned in school.

Although adolescents with LD frequently feel "stupid" or "slow" because of their school performance, this is far from the truth. Most teenagers with LD are of average or above-average intelligence. In fact, some are even intellectually "gifted," even though they perform below their potential.

Learning Disorders are neurological conditions that can affect how adolescents listen, understand, remember, and produce information. These teens typically have original and creative ideas. However, transferring what is in their brains onto a piece of paper can be difficult and trying—particularly when they are given short time periods to complete assignments. Some teens with LD have difficulty learning information solely by hearing it aloud and need to see it in written form. Others have problems translating their thoughts into language; they know what they want to communicate, but when they speak, what comes out is not exactly what they intended. Adolescents with LD can repeat what they hear but may not comprehend the message the way the speaker intended. When the brains of these teens modify or translate what is communicated, frustration can abound for the youth and the adults interacting with them. Miscommunication is sometimes an everyday occurrence.

Because they have problems integrating all of the information in their brains, learning-disabled teens may find school (and any other type of learning experience) challenging, overwhelming, and anxiety provoking. Over the years, adults may have accused them of being "lazy" or of "not applying themselves." By the time they reach adolescence, many of these youth are tired of struggling academically and give up trying to do well. They may avoid schoolwork by pretending to be ill, skipping specific classes, or "acting up" so that teachers remove them from the classroom.

Unfortunately, the more time teens spend outside the classroom, the more they miss learning critical information. This typically causes teens with LD to fall even further behind in their schoolwork and to experience more anxiety and frustration when they return to the classroom. Some teens with LD may eventually avoid school altogether, skipping classes for days or weeks at a time. These youth typically hang out with other teens who have left school without permission (and who also probably have Learning Disabilities). The combination of unoccupied time, a lack of supervision, and low self-esteem places teens with LD at significant risk for delinquency and alcohol/drug use. School suspensions are not uncommon, and a significant percentage of these youth drop out before graduation, further fueling their feelings of failure and shame.

Learning Disabilities and Social Behavior   Communicating one's thoughts and listening to others is key to making and keeping friends; these abilities are often negatively impacted among teens with LD because they have difficulty processing information. Poor social skills, such as standing in someone's personal space, talking too loudly, not empathizing with another's feelings, and difficulty picking up subtle social cues are common among these youth. Adolescents with LD commonly misinterpret what others say and may interpret others as unfriendly, antagonistic, or even hostile when they aren't. Needless to say, these teens' interpersonal style can inadvertently irritate or offend peers or adults—which only reinforces the negative view they already hold of themselves.

Because they fear rejection or embarrassment, teens with LD don't like to put themselves out on a limb. They are often found spending endless hours playing video games or on the computer. They usually want their life consistent and predictable, so they may resist going to college, moving out of their parent's house, getting a job, or dating. They commonly avoid intellectually challenging activities and choose hands-on hobbies and careers rather than those that require a lot of reading, organization, and attention to detail. Teenagers with LD often suffer from mental health disorders in addition to their learning problems. After repeated humiliating or upsetting incidents resulting from their processing difficulties, these teens may develop anxiety, especially when placed in learning-type situations or when asked to perform in front of others. With each additional diagnosis, teens with Learning Disorders experience increased difficulties at home, at school, at work, and with peers.

Identification and Causes of Learning Disabilities   Although Learning Disabilities are usually identified early in a child's educational career, some teens remain undiagnosed into middle school or high school. This is especially true for youth who have subtle symptoms, exhibit other mental health disorders, are particularly bright, or distract adults with athletics, aggression, or "class clown" behavior. An unidentified LD typically comes to light as teens get older and the demands of school (or a job) become more complex and demanding. Even if your teen was diagnosed with a LD at a younger age, your child may still experience problems if he or she did not receive the appropriate level and type of corrective services needed.

The exact cause(s) of Learning Disorders remains unknown, although the following factors can play a role in the development of these difficulties: in utero exposure to tobacco, alcohol, or other drugs, complications during pregnancy or delivery, genetic factors, environmental toxins (lead, mercury), and incidents after birth (nutritional deficiency, harm to the head).

Brain Injury—More Than a Bump on the Head

The human brain is a wondrous organ. It is the CEO of our bodies—directing, guiding, coordinating, organizing, and integrating our speech, emotions, and actions. According to International Brain Injury Association, well over a million individuals experience an injury to the head every year in the United States. Each year in Europe, there are a million hospital admissions for head injuries, with many more victims never seeking medical care.

Given their attraction to taking risks, feelings of invulnerability, and potentially dangerous hobbies, adolescents are at highest risk of an injury to the head—and this is particularly true for adolescent boys. The leading causes of head injury among teenagers include car, motorized cycle, and bicycle accidents; being hit by a car as a pedestrian or while on a bicycle, scooter, or skateboard; sports-related injuries; hobby-related accidents; physical assaults by others or fights with peers; and falls.

If your teen has been hospitalized after a serious accident involving the head, you were probably given an explanation regarding the potential consequences of a head injury. However, some adolescents who have experienced less severe blows to the head (from falls, fights, minor crashes, sporting injuries) and who did not require hospitalization are walking around with mild head injuries that affect their day-to-day functioning—and their parents have no idea what warning signs to look for.

Marcus, seventeen, was a well-behaved young man, until getting injured in the homecoming game last year. Marcus had taken hard blows on the football field more times than he could count, and, after lying on the field for a minute or so after being hit at the homecoming game, he shook it off and kept playing. But he knew something wasn't right.

Since that time, Marcus has gotten himself into various kinds of trouble. He has received two speeding tickets, which he has forgotten to pay. He was caught trespassing with his friends and became belligerent and confrontational with the security officer who discovered him. Marcus seems unconcerned that charges will likely be filed against him. His parents don't understand this Jekyll-and-Hyde change in their son.

A mild brain injury is sometimes referred to as a "concussion." Teens who experience a concussion frequently feel disoriented and "foggy." After their head is hit or jolted, they may appear dazed and confused, slur their speech, and/or have difficulty walking. These reactions are typically short-lived, lasting a few minutes or less. They are indicators that the brain has been affected. Some teens actually lose consciousness for several minutes or have no memory of what happened immediately before or after they were hurt.

Fortunately, *the majority of teenagers who experience mild trauma to the head do not have any permanent cognitive, emotional, or behavioral difficulties.* In fact, some adolescents experience no lingering negative effects at all. However, a small percentage experience long-lasting problems.

Worry Signs 10.2   Has Your Teen Been Injured in the Head?

The following behaviors are common after teens experience *damage to the head*:

- *Physical Changes:* headaches, nausea/vomiting, sleep difficulties, blurred vision, low energy, coordination problems.

■ *Thinking Changes:* memory problems, difficulties in school, slower thinking, increased distractibility, poor judgment, difficulty problem-solving

■ *Emotional/Behavioral Changes*: irritability, mood swings, depression, anxiety, "short fuse"/angry outbursts, suspiciousness/paranoia, strong emotional reactions; may be very easily frustrated and overwhelmed and exhibit socially inappropriate behavior

■ *Interpersonal Changes*: isolation, difficulty relating to others, loss of friends because of acting "different" or "weird"

■ *Other Changes*: lack of motivation, inability to get started, sensitivity to bright lights or loud noises

Is It Time to Worry About a Possible Head Injury?

Teens should be evaluated and monitored by a physician if they experience the symptoms in Worry Signs 10.2 for several hours or days after experiencing a mild injury to the head. Some of these changes may be immediately evident; others may not show up for days or weeks after the injury.

Many of the these changes are the result of an injury to the front part of the brain—the area essential to controlling one's emotions and behavior. When this part of the brain is injured, teens can become *very* reactive. The logical, problem-solving part of the brain that helps them calm down is often damaged when the front part of the brain is injured.

These youth can be incredibly self-centered and may throw tantrums—sometimes even becoming violent. Injury to the frontal lobe makes it difficult for teens to grasp the concept of the "future," so everything must happen "right now." These teens experience significant problems at home, in school, and with relationships.

The longer the symptoms continue (over weeks, months), the more your worry barometer should rise. You should also be concerned if your teen has experienced repeated concussions or accidents or injuries involving the head. Teen athletes don't always tell coaches or team physicians about the severity of their symptoms (or, if they do tell, they may not be taken seriously), so teens may be placed back in a game before they are ready. The effects of mild head injuries are cumulative, and experiencing a second injury before the first one has healed is very dangerous. *This not only increases the chances of permanent injury but is potentially fatal.*

Adolescents recover from trauma to the head at their own pace, and much depends on the location and severity of the injury, as well as the teen's emotional and behavioral functioning before the accident (including preexisting issues related to mental health or alcohol/drug use).

What makes this type of injury so complex is that a young child can experience trauma to the head (from falling down stairs, child abuse, a bicycle accident), yet the problematic effects may not show up until the child is much older—sometimes not until adolescence. The younger a child is when an injury occurs, the higher the likelihood of long-term effects.

When mild head injuries occur in adolescence, teens typically remember everything they learned *before* the injury—but have problems learning and remembering any *new* information. Therefore, even if your teen has never had learning problems or was never involved in special education, you may still see a significant decline in grades after the teen gets hit in the head.

Nothing Seems to Work

One of the most challenging aspects of teens with mild trauma to the head is that frequently nothing helps them control their emotions or behavior. They are usually misdiagnosed with ADHD, Oppositional Defiant Disorder, Conduct Disorder, or Bipolar Disorder; not surprisingly, treatment for these conditions (medication and nonmedication options) seems to have little or no long-term effectiveness. Adolescents with head injuries can appear lazy, spoiled, and unmotivated. Creative parenting strategies that work with siblings are not helpful with them. Parents are repeatedly exhausted and at a loss as to how to deal with their overly sensitive, reactive, moody teen who continues to do poorly in school. And no one is aware of the damage to their brain.

Because they exhibit poor judgment, repeatedly make the same mistakes, do not take responsibility for their behavior, and appear to lack empathy and remorse, these teens commonly end up involved with the juvenile justice system; this is usually because society believes that after enough punishment, the teen will eventually "straighten up" and "get his or her act together." Ironically, when treated in this manner, teens with brain injury often become increasingly frustrated, angry, paranoid, and aggressive because they don't understand why they repeatedly receive punishments and restrictions. This vicious cycle can continue for years, with many of these teens "graduating" into the adult criminal justice system once they turn eighteen.

Mild brain injuries do not always show up on routine brain scans (EEGs, MRIs, CT scans). You may have to request a more advanced x-ray, such as a PET scan or SPECT scan, if you believe your teen's difficulties may stem from an injury to the head. If your teen's difficulties continue for more than a few months, I recommend you contact a *neuropsychologist* to determine whether your teen needs a *complete neuropsychological evaluation* or whether something else should be done.

Although I have discussed mild brain injury that results from a jolt or blow to the head, please keep in mind that teenagers can also experience similar damage to the brain when they do not get enough oxygen. This can be caused by a near-drowning experience, complications during birth, drug overdose, or repeated use of drugs—particularly "inhalants."

The Effects of Alcohol During Pregnancy

Alcohol during pregnancy can cause problems for an unborn child. Some pregnant women drink alcohol before they become aware of their pregnancy but discontinue drinking once they discover they are expecting a child. Tragically, for some children, the damage may already have been done.

Do not panic if you had a few drinks while pregnant with your teen. Not all children exposed to alcohol in utero have resulting problems. The amount of harm done, if any, depends on many factors, including but not limited to how much alcohol a mother drinks, during which trimester she drank the alcohol, the mother's metabolism, the child's metabolism, what part of the brain was developing when the alcohol was ingested, genetic influences, and whether the child was exposed to any other toxic substances.

You may wonder why in a book about teenagers, I am writing about pregnancy and babies. Unfortunately, the damaging effects of alcohol exposure present at birth typically remain with youth throughout adolescence and into adulthood. In fact, *thinking and behavior problems directly resulting from alcohol in utero are frequently overlooked or misdiagnosed as one of the other conditions in this book.*

Fetal Alcohol Spectrum Disorders (FASD) is the term currently used to describe the range of clinical conditions resulting from prenatal alcohol exposure. The diagnosis of Fetal Alcohol Syndrome (FAS) is given to adolescents who have a specific set of indicators, including these:

- *Facial Features.* As children, youth with FAS tend to have small heads, flat cheeks, small eyes (sometimes appearing slanted because of extra skin on the upper eyelids), high and arched eyebrows, and *very* thin upper lips. The area between the upper lip and the nostrils tends to be smoother than that of peers. These facial features usually become less obvious after puberty.

- *Body Size.* As children, many teens with FAS weigh less, and are sometimes shorter in height, than peers of the same age. Fortunately, most youth with FAS experience growth spurts during puberty, which can result in fairly normal physical growth during adolescence.

- *Central Nervous System.* Abnormal development of the brain typically causes youth with FAS to have difficulties in the following areas: speech and language, impulse control, reasoning and judgment, intelligence, academic achievement, physical coordination, and hearing or vision. Structural irregularities of their brains can often be seen with x-rays.

- *Prenatal Exposure to Alcohol.* The diagnosis of FAS is specific to *alcohol* exposure in utero. If an adolescent's mother did not consume alcohol during her pregnancy, the diagnosis of FAS is not given.

The terms Fetal Alcohol Effects (FAE) and Alcohol Related Neurodevelopmental Disorder (ARND) are sometimes used to describe conditions in which many, but not all, of the distinctive characteristics of FAS are present. Even without the entire set of FAS symptoms, teens exposed to alcohol before birth can still have significant difficulties.

Kylie, thirteen, never takes a break. She talks nonstop and bounces around with unrelenting energy. Although a sweet girl, she seems to always stir up trouble—talking to the wrong people, wandering into places she doesn't belong, or getting too loud in quiet places. After a brief interview and screening by a professional, Kylie was diagnosed with ADHD and prescribed stimulant medication. The medication did seem to help her calm down, but her poor judgment and bad choices remained. Kylie's parents didn't understand why their daughter made the same mistakes again and again, despite the restrictions and negative consequences they gave her. They wanted to give her more autonomy now that she was a teenager but were afraid of what less supervision would bring.

Adolescents with FAS usually have a variety of school-related problems. Even if their IQ is in the average range, teens with FAS have difficulty with theoretical concepts and problem-solving. They frequently have poor memories, making it difficult for them to score well on tests. They can be hyperactive and reckless in the classroom and on school grounds, frequently violating the personal space of others. Teens with FASD may feel badly in the moment when confronted with their thoughtless or unruly behavior, but they don't learn from their experiences and tend to repeatedly make the same mistakes.

Fetal Alcohol Syndrome and Social Skills

Poor social skills are common among teenagers with FAS. They are often very talkative, frequently monopolizing conversations. They may wander off topics, switch to a different subject midstream, or just go on and on about nothing. Teens with FAS have difficulty tracking what is being said, sometimes including what they themselves are saying. Parents and peers are often frustrated by their mood swings; even with little or no provocation, they may alternate between being gentle and friendly and being hostile and rude. Although many adolescents with FAS are dependent and affectionate, some are distant and rebellious.

Teens with FAS are at high risk for physical and emotional abuse by peers. Because of their poor social judgment, teens with FAS may be confused as to who is a stranger, who is a friend, and who is an enemy. Peers can easily persuade these teens to engage in delinquent behavior. In fact, some youth with FAS are attracted to gang or pseudo-gang membership because of the structure and clear social pecking order these groups offer. These teens are naïve and gullible, so peers exploit them and set them up to take the blame for inappropriate, and sometimes illegal, behavior.

Fetal Alcohol Syndrome and Day-to-Day Behavior

One of the most challenging aspects for parents of teens with FAS is the unpredictability of their child's behavior. One day, their son or daughter follows directions, completes chores and school assignments, and pleasantly interacts with family members. The next day, the same teenager can have difficulty carrying out simple tasks, does not follow any of the parents' instructions, and fights with siblings. Parents conclude their teen must be *choosing* to act negatively since he or she behaved appropriately the day before. Youth with FAS are frequently perceived as irresponsible, manipulative, and defiant. However, depending on the location and severity of their brain damage, their brain may not function identically two days in a row. Rather than being "bad" teens who *won't* follow rules, teens with FAS often *can't* do what is asked of them.

These youth may not exhibit *major* problems in a specific area (intelligence, language, reading, coordination, impulsivity), so they may not meet the eligibility criteria for special programs. However, their mild to moderate difficulties in *many* areas can still be detrimental to their functioning. When teens with FAS do receive a diagnosis, it is frequently related to their disruptive behavior (Oppositional Defiant Disorder, Conduct Disorder). Or they may be misdiagnosed as having Bipolar Disorder or Posttraumatic Stress Disorder because of their extreme mood changes.

Friendless and Frustrated

There appears to be a subgroup of teenagers who, despite being intelligent, don't seem to "get" *social interactions* the way their siblings or peers do.

Evan, sixteen, is obsessed with *Star Wars*, and has seen each movie in the *Star Wars* trilogy at least 100 times. Every holiday, he requests *Star Wars* posters, books, action figures, and other memorabilia. He has no real friends but talks with others in *Star Wars* chat rooms on the Internet. Evan's parents have tried enrolling him in a soccer league, a drama class, and music lessons, but he refuses. They are proud that their son has a high IQ and wonderful grades, but they wish that he would expand his interests. Evan seems to enjoy when his parent's friends bring their teenagers to the house, but he never develops friendships with them. Evan's brother attributes this lack of friends to Evan being a "brainiac" and "totally weird."

These youth tend to differ from other adolescents with regard to the following six factors:

- *Social Abilities.* Despite wanting friends, these teens lack the basic skills required to "connect" with others. They have difficulty providing and recognizing subtle social cues (tone of voice, eye contact, facial expression, body language, mood), which leads to awkward inter- actions and peers perceiving them as "odd" or "weird." Their relationships are often one-sided, with them talking about their areas of interest. These teens have little in common with peers, don't follow teenage trends, and are not interested in conversing about pop culture or participating in sports or other teenage activ- ities. They typically don't get other people's humor, and other people usually don't get theirs. These teens have difficulty putting themselves in other's shoes, so they don't understand when they are offensive or hurtful. This makes them seem self-centered and insen- sitive, further isolating them from others. Any sexually inappropriate comments usually stem from a lack of understanding of how to talk with the opposite sex.

- *Hobbies and Interests.* These teens have an intense (obsession-like) interest in only one or two specific subjects or hobbies. Their free time is spent investigat- ing all they can about the subject, and it is all they talk about. They have often accumulated and memorized a huge collection of facts without understanding what they have learned. Parents repeatedly find pictures of the subject of interest drawn by teens in different sizes, versions, colors, views, and depths or long essays stating fact after fact, statistic after statistic. They may spend time only with peers who share their interest and knowledge of the topic. Their intense fixation leaves little time for the ordinary tasks of adolescence.

These teens also become fixated on peculiar routines and rituals that must rigidly be followed. They may have to read their favorite comic book from front to back every night, or they cannot allow different food groups to touch on their plate. Many adolescents have ingrained habits or are particular about their food, but these teens have meltdowns if their routine or ritual is disturbed. They impose their idiosyncrasies on parents and siblings, who often become frustrated with their "eccentric" behavior. Although their behavior is similar to that of people with Obsessive-Compulsive Disorder (OCD), their rituals and routines are usually comforting to these teens, whereas compulsive behavior in OCD is usually driven by anxiety.

■ *Thinking Skills.* These teens typically are of average intelligence, if not above average or even "gifted." They learn to use language at a very young age, usually much more quickly than siblings or peers. They have extensive vocabularies, exceptional memories, and they notice and remember peculiar and idiosyncratic features that others don't. Because of their voracious appetite for reading encyclopedias or anything on science, these teens are often labeled "geeks," "nerds," or "dorks." Although overly "intellectual" during conversations, they find it difficult to remain organized and on schedule.

■ *Communication Skills.* These teens engage in limited eye contact during conversations and speak in a monotone and formal style—as if trying to sound intelligent and sophisticated. They rarely spontaneously start conversations or engage in small talk. When someone asks them a question, these teens provide much more information than was asked. Because of their long-windedness, detailed explanations, and way of talking "at" people, siblings and peers may call them walking encyclopedias or "mini-professors."

■ *Emotional Abilities.* These teens have difficulty controlling their frustration and upset, so they may throw tantrums in reaction to even small incidents. They may be extremely bothered by things that most teens don't notice (bright lights, loud music, sensation of tags inside the neck of a t-shirt). They require a great deal of comfort, support, and encouragement when things don't go their way. These youth are often sad and lonely because of their lack of meaningful friendships and sometimes develop Major Depression, Dysthymia, or Anxiety.

■ *Physical Coordination.* In direct contrast to their superior verbal skills, these adolescents are awkward and clumsy. Team sports are difficult for them, and they are often teased because of how they run or throw a ball. Their lack of coordination can affect individual forms of recreation such as riding a bike, skateboarding, or climbing trees. These teens are typically not drawn to physical activities, due to lack of interest or repeated episodes of failure or embarrassment.

Asperger's Syndrome

The characteristics described here are symptoms of Asperger's Syndrome (often referred to as Asperger's), a condition that occurs four to five times more often in boys than in girls. Although the exact cause of Aperger's is unknown, it is thought to be genetic and involves irregularities in different parts of the brain. Basic, yet essential, information-processing abilities in the brain are altered, which makes initiating and sustaining relationships a continual struggle.

Plenty of adolescents are idiosyncratic or passionate about their interests or hobbies, and plenty of bright teens have difficulty making friends. That does not mean all of these young people have Asperger's. *The diagnosis of Asperger's is given when an adolescent's unusual social behavior and intense interests are so significant they interfere with a teen's ability to form friendships with peers their own age, learn in school, or appropriately function within their family.*

This condition is present in early childhood, although the symptoms may not be as obvious. Even when very young, these children have difficulty making and keeping friends and have overly restrictive interests and activities. Parents of children with Asperger's often refer to their son or daughter as "unique," "original," or "quirky."

Teens with Asperger's are often misdiagnosed with ADHD or Oppositional Defiant Disorder.

How You Can Help Teens Who Have Difficulty "Getting" It

If any of the descriptions in this chapter sound like your teen and he or she is having difficulty at home, school, or with relationships, you should obtain a comprehensive evaluation to identify what is underlying your teen's struggles. These conditions occur on a continuum. Teens with minor difficulties may need only a few of the strategies listed here, while for those with more severe conditions you may need all of them.

- *Help them get organized.* Provide structure with a predictable environment, daily routines, and cues to help teens remember what to do. Help them organize their bedroom by setting up shelves so that teens can see where to find things and where to put things back. Designate specific places for backpacks, cell phones, keys, and other portable items that are repeatedly misplaced.

- *Help them understand.* Use short, simple, sentences and speak slowly. Give one directive at a time. Break complex activities into small tasks. Telling teens to "hang up the phone, help me set the table, put your backpack in the room, and turn off the TV" is too much for their brains to handle. Ask teens to tell you what you have asked them to do in their own words.

■ *Provide extra support.* Supervise activities. Because of their impulsivity, poor problem-solving ability, and poor judgment, these teens commonly get involved with risky and dangerous activities situations. Use a matter-of-fact tone with verbal reminders so that teens do not feel inadequate if they have forgotten to do something, and give lists of responsibilities they can check off upon completion. Provide advanced notice of upcoming transitions or changes, and provide *several* warnings as the time gets closer (e.g., "Ten minutes before dinnertime," "Tonight I won't be home until 8:00 P.M.").

■ *Help with social skills.* Work with teens on letting others speak without interrupting them, looking at the person with whom they are conversing, walking up to and joining a group of peers, and firmly standing up to peers who tease them.

■ *Seek support from others.* Investigate the wide range of special services available from the teen's school. Pairing teens with higher-functioning and responsible peers for mentoring can be positive and rewarding experience for both parties.

■ *Use effective behavior management techniques.* Don't assume that misbehavior is purposeful. Focus on success by providing immediate praise and rewards to motivate teens to try new tasks and activities. Do not use threats of punishment or restrictions, because these have little impact on these teens, who have difficulty conceptualizing future events or consequences.

■ *Encourage new interests.* Be patient and allow teens to take the time they need (no matter how long) to learn a new task or activity. Although they may be overly dependent on your support initially, they are moving toward increasing autonomy with every new skill they master. Caring for pets teaches responsibility, and companionship and affection come with no expectations of good social skills.

- *Be empathic and kind.* When you are most frustrated with these teens, imagine what it must be like to have a brain that has difficulty processing information, gets easily confused, or does not understand social nuances. If you roll your eyes, tease them, or put them down, you are giving permission to others to do the same. Model patience, understanding, and respect.

- *Don't let their size fool you.* Chronological age and physical size do not indicate teens' cognitive ability. Make sure your expectations are truly in line with teens' capabilities—be realistically optimistic. Help teens compete against their own previous performance, not against the performance of others.

Every teenager's individuality and uniqueness should be treasured and respected. However, when teens' "differences" cause them to feel chronically frustrated, anxious, depressed, or hopeless, seek out professional assistance for strategies to help them more fully participate in society (interviews for college admission, job interviews, friendships, dating, marriage). Adolescents like those described in this chapter do not outgrow their conditions, but with proper support, many of these youth graduate from high school, attend college, have careers, and start families.

CHAPTER ELEVEN

Behaving Bizarrely

Teens Who Lose Touch with Reality

*I don't want to curb my teen's individuality, but when
is outside the box too strange, or even dangerous?*

This section of the chapter describes some of the most serious symptoms within this entire book. As you read about them, don't panic. They are *much rarer* than the warning signs you have read about to this point. However, I believe they should be included because you have likely heard the terms but may not fully understand them. It is also critical that you recognize these symptoms should your teen or one of their friends begin experiencing them.

> While working as a camp counselor, Steven, eighteen, began behaving oddly. He said voices were telling him that a computer chip was implanted in his head to help the CIA track his whereabouts. Fellow camp counselors did not take this seriously until they discovered Steven sitting in one of the trees "avoiding surveillance." He believed the meals at camp were randomly poisoned, so he ate only protein bars he brought from home. When his parents were called to pick him up, they were surprised by their son's disheveled appearance and poor hygiene. He passionately told his parents about his concern over the government using "inspections, examinations, investigations, and surveys," yet they could not comprehend what he was talking about. Steven spent much of the car ride home mumbling about "analyses, inquiries, and research."

Psychosis

Psychosis is a term that refers to "losing touch with reality." It is not a particular type of mental health disorder but a constellation of symptoms that occur together. Psychosis is associated with several different mental health and medical conditions. When teens have a "psychotic episode," they are unable to distinguish what is real from what it not real. Psychotic behavior can be incredibly confusing and frightening for parents. Once they understand psychotic behavior, parents can play a crucial role in the reduction of these symptoms.

During a "psychotic episode," adolescents typically exhibit one of more of the following symptoms: hallucinations, delusions, disorganized speech/thinking, and disorganized behavior.

Hallucinations. This term refers to hearing, seeing, feeling, smelling, or tasting something that is not really there. The most common type of hallucination among adolescents is hearing "voices" that other people do not hear. Psychotic teens perceive these voices not as their own thoughts but as someone talking to them or about them. These voices may tell adolescents to take certain actions (run away, kill themselves) or may comment on the teens' behavior (telling them they are stupid or ugly, ridiculing them for something they did). Hallucinations can be influenced by an adolescent's mood. Therefore, if a teen is depressed, the voices can be critical, blaming, and pessimistic.

Although this is less common, some adolescents see things that others cannot see (people, animals, creatures). Some teens feel sensations; for example, they may believe that insects are crawling on their skin or inside their bodies. Hallucinations in which teens smell or taste things that no one else can smell or taste are fairly uncommon but do occur.

Delusions. This word refers to false beliefs that adolescents rigidly hold onto, *even though no one else believes them and there is proof that the beliefs are false or irrational.* They may think people are stealing or controlling their thoughts or reading their minds. If they are paranoid, they may believe people are plotting against them, saying mean things about them, harassing them, following them, or even trying to poison them. Delusions associated with an adolescent's body may include beliefs they are pregnant despite being a virgin or that parts of their body are diseased, decayed, or rotting away—despite normal results on medical tests. Some teens have grandiose delusions, believing they have been "chosen" in some way (by a celebrity or God) and have a special or magical gift or talent. Delusional themes are influenced by environmental factors, so teens may hold beliefs related to technology (the Internet "pop-up" ads on their computer are being sent by terrorists), celebrities (a famous athlete or actress is sending them personalized messages through the television), or the media (journalists are subliminally sending extraterrestrial messages through their news stories).

Disorganized Thinking or Speech. Much of the speech of psychotic teenagers is strange and confusing. Parents may feel they are not listening closely enough because they cannot comprehend what their son or daughter is saying. But, in truth, their teen is not making sense. Psychotic adolescents may illogically string words together ("I need to get to the mall because cancer is right around the corner"), make up words that are meaningless to the listener ("Too many kids at school are minowens"), or use sentences that are only loosely related ("My shoes are getting old and the man on the television said old people need hearing aids, but I hear fine when my Mom yells at me if I don't clean my room, which is filled with old shoes and jeans I haven't worn for years"). They may repeat certain words again and again or for no apparent reason, talk in rhymes or with a singsong tune, completely stop talking in the middle of a sentence, or parrot back what others say. On the other hand, some psychotic teenagers say little to nothing at all. Even when asked direct questions or prompted to elaborate, these teens might only use one or two words.

Disorganized Behavior. Teenagers often become restless and agitated during a psychotic episode. They may wring their hands, pace the floor, or rock back and forth for extended periods of time. Whereas some of these teens feel they must constantly keep moving, others remain still, without any movement, for hours. When psychotic, some adolescents move their bodies in unusual, and often bizarre, ways. They may crawl into and remain in tight spaces, such as under their bed or in a dark closet. These teens typically have a messy appearance and may not shower or brush their teeth for several days.

Psychosis significantly affects schoolwork, chores, and relationships with family and friends. Because of their lack of insight, teens who are psychotic often refuse help because they don't think anything is wrong with them. If anything, many of these teens believe the main problem lies with everyone else.

Psychosis can be associated with Schizophrenia, Bipolar Disorder (severe), Major Depression (severe), Medical Conditions, or Alcohol and Other Drugs (severe). Most adolescents with these conditions *do not* experience psychosis—with the exception of Schizophrenia. *Adolescents with Schizophrenia always experience at least one (and usually more than one) psychotic episode, and their psychotic symptoms tend to persist longer than in the other disorders.*

Some adolescents with Posttraumatic Stress Disorder (PTSD) or Conduct Disorder may report psychotic-like symptoms when under high levels of emotional stress. Although these teens may report hearing voices, they typically do not experience the delusions, unusual thinking and speech, and bizarre behavior seen in truly psychotic individuals. Teens with very low IQs may say they see imaginary friends or hear the voice of superheroes, though these are usually not delusions. Seeing visions of deceased relatives or religious figures is an acceptable part of some cultures. I have worked with my share of gang-involved teens who were convinced someone was trying to kill them—because of their lifestyle, these beliefs were often accurate and not "paranoid" thinking.

Schizophrenia

Schizophrenia is a serious mental health disorder associated with abnormal brain functioning, which negatively impacts every aspect of a teen's life. It occurs much less often than the other conditions described in this book. When it does occur, the onset is typically during late adolescence or early adulthood.

Adolescents with Schizophrenia experience what are referred to as "positive" and "negative" symptoms of the disorder. *Positive* symptoms of Schizophrenia tend to be *too much* of something, such as the psychotic symptoms of hearing or seeing things that are not really there, holding bizarre beliefs, speaking in strange ways, or displaying odd movements. The *negative* symptoms of Schizophrenia refer to a *lack* or *restriction* of typical behaviors: no energy, little to no speech, flat emotions, no facial expression, indifference to the feelings of others, lack of eye contact, loss of interest in people or activities that used to be important, inability to concentrate, apathy, and little to no movement. Although the positive symptoms of Schizophrenia are more peculiar, the negative symptoms often last longer and can be just as distressing.

To be diagnosed with Schizophrenia, adolescents must experience positive or negative symptoms of the disorder for at least six months, with the positive symptoms (hallucinations, delusions, bizarre speech and behavior) lasting one month or more. Teens must also show a clear deterioration in functioning or be unable to achieve what is appropriate for their age.

In addition to positive and negative symptoms, teens with Schizophrenia may also laugh or smile when nothing appears to be funny, sob for no reason, sleep throughout the day because of difficulties sleeping at night, worry excessively, or may have difficulty paying attention, concentrating, and remembering things. Clearly these issues make the condition even more disabling.

Phases of Schizophrenia

Schizophrenia often has a very slow and subtle onset. Adolescents with the illness tend to experience each of the following phases:

Prodromal Phase. Weeks, months, and sometimes years before adolescents with Schizophrenia have their first psychotic symptoms (usually called a "psychotic break"), their behavior begins to change for the worse. This is referred to as the *prodromal* phase of the illness. They may develop unusual concerns or preoccupations. Their academic or job-related skills may decline, with some of these teens dropping out of school, quitting their jobs, or being fired for unexplained and odd behavior. During this phase, teens typically withdraw from family and friends and are less concerned about their appearance and what others think of them. They may feel sad and irritable much of the time, begin experimenting with alcohol/drugs, or increase current substance use. Verbal or physical aggression can occur, as can disruptive and oppositional behavior. The prodromal phase of Schizophrenia may appear similar to a difficult phase of adolescence," Oppositional Defiant Disorder, Conduct Disorder, or Major Depression, so misdiagnosis is common.

Acute Phase. The phase acute phase of Schizophrenia is associated with the most dramatic changes in an adolescent's behavior. Hallucinations, delusions, disorganized speech, and disorganized behavior are common, and these significantly interfere with a teen's ability to function. This phase of the illness can last from one to six months, although, without effective treatment, this phase may last even longer.

Recuperative/Recovery Phase. Symptoms are much improved in this phase, but adolescents may still have difficulty fully returning to their lives due to persisting negative symptoms of the illness (isolation, no energy or motivation, depressed mood). For some teens with Schizophrenia, some of the positive symptoms may continue as well, although at a lower intensity.

Residual Phase. Adolescents with Schizophrenia may go for several months or even years without any major psychotic symptoms. Their thinking and behavior are much improved in this phase compared to when they were psychotic. Unfortunately, many teenagers with Schizophrenia continue to suffer some degree of impairment because of the continuation of negative symptoms.

The course of Schizophrenia is extremely variable. Some teens with the illness experience speech and language problems, are described as "different" or odd, and have few friends beginning at a young age. Throughout childhood and adolescence, they tend to prefer solitary activities, including fantasy-related games and books, or activities that rely heavily on their imagination. As they enter late adolescence, true psychotic symptoms can appear.

In contrast, some adolescents with Schizophrenia appear quite "normal" during childhood. At some point in late adolescence or early adulthood, their thinking and behavior begin to change, eventually leading to full-blown psychotic symptoms. It is rare for adolescents to function absolutely fine one day and become psychotic the next. The prodromal period typically occurs beforehand, in which a teen's functioning deteriorates from its earlier level.

Although a minority of adolescents with Schizophrenia go through the phases of the disorder one time only, most experience more than one cycle. The majority will have some form of lasting difficulty with school, work, and/or relationships with others. Adolescents with Schizophrenia are at higher risk of dying by suicide throughout their teen years and into adulthood. This can be a very debilitating disorder, so teens with Schizophrenia should receive an evaluation and treatment at the earliest point possible.

How You Can Help Teens with Psychosis

The strategies listed at the end of Chapter 10, in the section "How You Can Help Teens Who Have Difficulty 'Getting' It," are all applicable to teens suffering from psychosis, including Schizophrenia. The following are strategies specific to the teens described in this chapter:

- Make sure teens are taking their medication as prescribed. If they stop taking it, contact the prescribing physician.
- Create a calm and stress-free household. Reduce loud noises, including arguments among family members.

- If teens seem upset, ask them about it. Listen closely for allusions to suicide or aggression, and report any concerning statements to their therapist.

- Nonjudgmentally and calmly, ask teens if they are hearing voices or seeing things when you suspect this is the case. Answer teens honestly if they ask if you hear or see it, too.

- Don't exclusively focus on the content of their hallucinations or delusions, and instead focus on the underlying feelings (fear, anger, guilt). Don't argue with teens over the validity of their hallucinations or delusions. And never joke about these symptoms.

- Engage and support the part of the teen's brain that is not psychotic. Even when hearing voices or holding strange beliefs, these teens still respond to ordinary life issues. Reinforce their accurate assessments ("It's cold in here," "That football team sucks," "I need a lot of money to buy a house.") Ask them to help you with simple tasks.

Without question, many teens who struggle with psychosis will likely be a lifelong concern for their parents, other family members, and friends. The course of your teen's life may be different from what you once visualized, yet your child can, with medication, monitoring, and good communication with you and his or her therapist, enjoy a life full of the same joys as any other person. Some teens with psychosis, along with those who care for them, will face daunting challenges but also unforeseen gifts, such as learning to live "in the now" and treasuring what is rather than what could be. Teens with psychosis are often unique and multitalented individuals. You can help them make positive differences in their own lives and in those of others.

SECTION II

Getting Help
if Necessary

CHAPTER TWELVE

What's Going On?

Obtaining the Right Evaluation for Your Teen

Why is my teen acting this way?

You may have noticed how often I have emphasized the importance of obtaining a comprehensive mental health evaluation if you recognize worry signs from any of these chapters in your teen. When you skip the step of a comprehensive evaluation, you run the risk of not knowing what is truly causing your teen's emotional or behavioral difficulties. Someone may have already suggested that your child be evaluated. Education, juvenile justice, mental health, substance abuse, and healthcare professionals often need more information about how to best help a particular youth. Too often, parents access treatment services for their children before identifying what problem needs to be addressed (or whether an actual problem even exists!). At best, this wastes time and money on inappropriate treatment. At worst, your child's condition remains untreated and may worsen, or he or she may be placed on inappropriate medication.

Most adolescents know when something is not right but may not know how to verbalize it. They certainly don't know what to do about it. Wouldn't it be helpful for you *and* your teen to discover *why* she needs to remain so skinny, *why* he refuses to follow your rules, *why* she locks herself in her room, *why* he sets fires and destroys things, *why* he has so few friends, *why* she has sex with boys she barely knows, or *why* he doesn't seem interested in "normal" teen activities? A comprehensive evaluation is one of the best ways to discover the answers. Once you know *why*, then you know *what* type of support and assistance will likely best help your child. Sometimes an adolescent's emotional or behavioral difficulties are so complex that the *exact why* is hard to identify. A comprehensive evaluation can still provide critical information to help you and the professionals you work with design an individualized treatment plan to decrease your teen's struggles and increase peace in the family.

Key Issues with Comprehensive Evaluations

Previous Evaluations. Your teen may have already been evaluated—perhaps even given a diagnosis or two. Many families believe they have had a comprehensive evaluation when what they received was too brief and limited to permit a complete assessment of their teen's condition. By the end of this chapter, you should have a good idea of what a thorough assessment includes—and what information you should receive as a result.

For example, let's say your daughter is irritable, distractible, and suffering from slipping grades. Because she also complains of trouble sleeping, a clinician may assume she is suffering from Depression after conducting a twenty-minute interview with you and your teen. However, a comprehensive evaluation may uncover an undiagnosed Learning Disability that makes school difficult for your daughter. The daily struggle of classroom and homework assignments makes her cranky; distractibility sets in when she has a hard time understanding. Your daughter can't sleep at night because she is stressed out knowing she needs good grades to remain on the softball team. If she were mistakenly treated for Depression, her symptoms would not improve because the intervention would not target her core issue—a Learning Disability. In fact, if she were prescribed antidepressant medication and complained of continuing symptoms, a doctor may even raise the dosage of the medicine (which was incorrect to begin with).

Overlapping Symptoms. Many of the conditions reviewed in this book share *overlapping* symptoms. Take a teenage boy who appears distracted, restless, jittery, and jumpy. These behaviors may be signs of ADHD, anxiety, or drug use (particularly stimulants, cocaine, or methamphetamine). These symptoms may also occur in teens who are bullied at school, troubled by the recent separation of parents, living in a chaotic and abusive family—or none of the above. Clinicians need to have a full understanding of your teen, not just a few of his or her symptoms. This is critical in determining if there is a need for treatment and, if so, what type of treatment is best for your child, your family, and the current situation. A comprehensive evaluation helps do just that.

Concern About a Diagnosis or Label. It is natural to be unsure when considering the implications of undergoing this type of assessment. Some parents are fearful that their teen will receive a diagnosis and do not want their child "labeled." Other parents feel validated if their child receives a diagnosis, because they know they were not overreacting or being paranoid (something others have accused them of). Some parents are relieved to know they are not "causing" their child to feel or behave the way he or she does. And others are eager to learn more about their teen's condition so that they can research what to do about it. No reaction is right or wrong. And sometimes parents move from one viewpoint to another.

Support or treatment for your teen must be tailored to the problem he or she is experiencing. This may or may not require a mental health diagnosis; sometimes adolescent difficulties are purely related to family issues or specific stressors. You may discover that what your son or daughter is going through is typical during the adolescent years, and nothing to be concerned about.

Obtaining Special School Services. If you want special services from the school (at no cost) or if you are receiving these services but don't feel the school is appropriately meeting the needs of your teen, you must demonstrate what type of services your child requires. The information contained in a comprehensive evaluation may provide the evidence.

Even when significant difficulties are not present, these types of assessments can be very beneficial for academic and career planning for your teen.

Who Are the Helping Professionals, and What Do They Do?

Although several types of helping professionals, also known as clinicians, are trained to work with troubled teens, each has knowledge and skills in different areas. Some of these areas overlap, and a few clinicians specialize in services that others do not provide. For example, a variety of clinicians offer *treatment* for emotional and behavioral disorders, but only a small number have the schooling and skills to provide comprehensive *evaluations* for these conditions.

Evaluating teenagers is no easy task, because so much of their behavior can seem troubled, odd, or senseless. Moods can fluctuate daily, if not hourly, during adolescence, and rebellion and defiance are common. Teenagers can be impulsive, use poor judgment, and engage in dangerous, risk-taking behaviors. They may obsess about their looks, their weight, and what they perceive as physical flaws. Because *this is all very normal*, it is critical to have your teen evaluated by a clinician with extensive training and experience with adolescents so that they do not classify typical teen behavior as an emotional or behavioral "disorder."

One of the best ways to find a reputable evaluator is to obtain a recommendation from your teen's pediatrician or family doctor, school counselor, or religious/spiritual leader. Family members, friends, and neighbors can also be good resources. Depending on your insurance plan, you may have to choose an evaluator within a particular "network" to have the services paid for. The "Resource" section in the back of this book also lists associations and organizations you can call to obtain names of qualified evaluators in your area.

It is important that mental health clinicians who provide formal evaluation or treatment services for teens have, in addition to a four-year undergraduate education, (1) completed a specified graduate educational program, (2) obtained supervised clinical experience, (3) passed a national examination, and (4) qualified for your state's license or certification. The following categories of clinicians are the professionals most commonly utilized by parents of troubled teens.

Clinicians Who Conduct Evaluations and/or Provide Treatment

Clinical Psychologists (Ph.D. or Psy.D.). Clinical psychologists receive four to seven years of graduate training during which they gain experience in the evaluation, diagnosis, and treatment of individuals with emotional and behavioral problems. This training is followed by one to two years of additional supervised clinical experience. Clinical psychologists have *extensive* training in the administration, scoring, and interpretation of tests that measure an adolescent's intellectual functioning (including IQ), academic achievement, social functioning, and emotional and personality traits. *Comprehensive evaluations conducted by clinical psychologists provide the most complete and thorough picture of an adolescent's unique abilities, difficulties, and characteristics.* Not all clinical psychologists conduct mental health evaluations; instead, they may specialize in "talk therapy" or behavioral treatments. Clinical psychologists focus on the individual, environmental, social, and biological aspects of a teen's emotional and behavioral health.

Psychiatrists (M.D./D.O.). Psychiatrists have completed medical school and then an additional three years of specialized training in psychiatry. Because of their medical backgrounds, these physicians are trained to differentiate physical illnesses from emotional and behavioral difficulties. They are among the few mental health clinicians trained and authorized to prescribe psychotropic medication, with some psychiatrists providing "talk therapy" as well. *Psychiatrists are typically not trained to conduct intelligence, academic, or personality testing.*

School Psychologists (M.A./Ph.D./Ed.D.). School psychologists have obtained at least a master's degree and have completed a one-year internship, and some also obtain an education specialist's degree. These clinicians are trained to work in a school setting and help teens who have difficulty learning or adjusting to the school environment. School psychologists can evaluate teens for special education eligibility and conduct tests to evaluate intellectual functioning (including IQ) and academic achievement. They often consult with parents, teachers, and school administrators to maximize student achievement. *School psychologists are not typically trained to conduct emotional, social, and personality testing.* In addition, school psychologists usually do not provide mental health or substance-abuse diagnoses. However, school psychologists can be essential in the implementation of school-based recommendations resulting from a comprehensive evaluation.

Clinicians Who Provide Treatment

Social Workers (L.C.S.W./M.S.W.). Social workers usually have a master's degree and several years of supervised clinical experience. These clinicians are trained in a variety of "talk therapy" techniques and typically work with children, adolescents, and adults. In addition to looking at a troubled teen's individual issues, social workers also emphasize an adolescent's social and family system. Social workers often run therapy groups for individuals, couples, or families.

Marriage and Family Therapist (M.F.T.). Marriage and family therapists have at least a master's degree and supervised clinical experience specifically in marriage, family, and relationship counseling. Rather than focus on an individual teen's issues, they emphasize the nature and role of the family relationships in which teens exist. Marriage and family therapy is typically short-term, with specific treatment goals.

Clinicians Who Manage Associated Medical Issues

Pediatricians and Family Practice Physicians (M.D.). Pediatricians and family practice physicians have both gone through four years of medical school. Pediatricians receive an additional three years of specialized training in the medical care of infants, children, and adolescents. Because family practice physicians receive an additional three years of training in the medical care of individuals in all stages of life, they can treat everyone in your family. Both of these types of doctors can serve as your teen's primary-care physician. They have significant training in the diagnosis and treatment of a wide variety of medical disorders. They refer teens to clinical psychologists for comprehensive evaluations and provide associated testing (including basic blood tests) to rule out medical issues. *Pediatricians and family practice physicians do not conduct comprehensive evaluations or psychotherapy.* These physicians can monitor mental health symptoms and medication side effects, as well as prescribe medication refills once teen's mental health symptoms have stabilized.

Clinicians Who Conduct Specialty Evaluations and/or Treatment

Certified Alcohol and Drug Abuse Counselors/Certified Addiction Counselors (CADAC/CAC). These counselors may have obtained a bachelor's or a master's degree and completed supervised clinical experience in the identification and counseling of individuals struggling with alcohol/drug abuse or dependence. These counselors work with substance-abusing teens and also help family members cope with their child's difficulties. They often provide counseling in one-on-one and group settings.

Clinical Neuropsychologists (Ph.D.). After completing traditional training in clinical psychology, clinical neuropsychologists receive additional training dedicated to the relationship between behavior and brain functioning. Neuropsychologists use specialized tests to determine whether emotional, behavioral, or learning difficulties are due to abnormal brain functioning. A small percentage of neuropsychologists also use tests that assess teens' emotions and personality. Teens typically see a "clinical psychologist" first, and if there are questions about possible head trauma or damage to the brain, a neuropsychological assessment is then recommended.

Clinicians Who Provide Guidance and Support

School Counselors (M.A.). Most school counselors have a master's degree in school counseling (or another similar helping profession). Located in school settings, these clinicians provide assistance to a variety of students, only some of whom have emotional or behavioral difficulties. School counselors focus on teens' academics, career choices, and school adjustment. Some may handle student crises, as well as provide individual or group counseling. School counselors often refer teens and their families to appropriate community services when additional support is needed. School counselors are key to carrying out some of the school-related recommendations that come out of comprehensive evaluations.

Religious and Spiritual Leaders. Priests, rabbis, pastors, ministers, clerics, or other religious and spiritual leaders can be important providers of guidance and support to your troubled teen, as well as to the rest of your family. However, these individuals are not trained to evaluate or treat the emotional and behavioral disorders reviewed in this book. Religious and spiritual leaders can often serve as good referral sources to mental health clinicians in your community.

There is a significant shortage, particularly in low-income and rural areas, of qualified clinicians who specialize in the evaluation of children and adolescents. Therefore, you may not have access to one of them in your community; or, if you do, there may be a long waiting list for an appointment. It is often worth the wait for a quality evaluation, or you may have to drive to the nearest town or city. Once the evaluation is complete, you might be able to find a treatment professional closer to home.

Another option is to go to the nearest university to see if you can have your teen evaluated by a clinical psychology intern or a postdoctoral fellow in clinical psychology. These students have completed their graduate training and are working in the field to obtain additional clinical experience. Because they are just starting out, graduate students are often particularly thorough and conscientious. You actually have two clinicians problem-solving about your child's difficulties because students are closely monitored and supervised by licensed clinical psychologists with many years of experience. If finances are an issue, these clinicians are often a very cost-effective choice.

There is a significant shortage of qualified evaluators who speak more than one language. Large agencies and hospitals may have access to interpreters. If you or your child do not speak English fluently, it may be better to wait a little longer for an appointment with a bilingual evaluator than to go immediately to a clinician you will not be able to communicate with.

If teens are an imminent danger to themselves or others, do not wait for an evaluation. Call the crisis line in your community or a national crisis line (listed in the back of this book). They can guide you, depending on your particular situation.

How to Interview a Clinician Before Selecting One

If you have access to more than one qualified clinician, it is best to call two or three to compare. *Briefly* state why you would like to have your child evaluated and ask if the clinician has ten minutes for you to ask a few questions.

The following questions can help you determine if the clinician has the qualifications and training to conduct a comprehensive evaluation of your teen:

- Do you provide "comprehensive mental health evaluations" that assess intelligence and academics, as well as emotional, behavioral, and personality function?

- What type of training have you received in intelligence and academic testing and in the evaluation of emotional, behavioral, social, and personality functioning?

- What type of graduate degree do you have?

- Do you specialize in evaluating particular issues or problems?

- Do you use any tests in addition to clinical interviews? (Specific tests are needed for intellectual and academic functioning and are also beneficial for understanding factors related to your teen's emotions, behaviors, and personality.)

- Will I be able to get a written report of your findings with detailed treatment recommendations?

- How many adolescents have you evaluated and how many adolescents have you evaluated that were [give a few descriptors of your teen's issues]?

- How long have you been licensed in this state? (If the clinician is not licensed, choose someone else.)

Even if a clinician is not qualified to assess your teen, he or she may be useful for treatment later. If the clinician appears to meet your needs for an evaluation, assess how you felt about his or her personal style. Was the clinician arrogant or defensive? Pleasant and open? The best evaluators for teenagers are not rigid and aloof, nor are they too relaxed and laid back. Teens work best with evaluators who are warm and friendly, while still being professional and clearly in charge.

Do not get caught up in seeing the most "prestigious" clinician in town. Long waiting lists to get an appointment do not necessarily reflect superior service. In addition, it is usually better to take your teen to a clinician who evaluates a range of adolescents, unless you are fairly certain that your teen has a particular disorder and needs a specialist.

Questions to Ask About the Evaluation Itself

The answers to the ten questions listed here are essential. They can help you gauge how *thorough* an evaluation will be and narrow your selection to the type of evaluation that is the best match for your teen's need. Furthermore, you will be more equipped to answer any questions your son or daughter asks about the process.

1. How long will the evaluation take? (Comprehensive evaluations usually take a minimum of several hours.)

2. Will you assess my teen's intellectual functioning? Academic achievement? Emotional and personality functioning?

3. What is the cost of the evaluation? What insurance do you take, if any? Do you have a sliding fee scale if our family is financially limited?

4. In what ways are parents included in the evaluation? Teachers? Other significant adults?

5. What will you do if my teen is extremely nervous? Or becomes defiant?

6. Are you familiar with my teen's/family's culture?

7. How long will it take to receive the written report of your findings and treatment recommendations? (It should take no more than a few weeks.)

8. Will you meet with me to review the report? Should my teen attend this meeting?

9. What will I need to bring to the evaluation?

10. Should my teen receive a medical check-up (including basic blood work) before our appointment?

If you are satisfied with the clinician's answers, set up the evaluation appointment. Be specific with the clinician regarding what question(s) you want the evaluation to answer.

What to Expect During Your Teen's Evaluation

Comprehensive evaluations usually take several hours to complete. Older teens may be able to complete the process in one appointment. Younger adolescents (and teens of any age who are immature or who have difficulty sitting still or paying attention for long periods) may need to split the process into two or more sessions.

Clinical Interview

The clinical interview is a critical aspect of any evaluation, as parents have a wealth of information about their children. You (and/or your spouse) will likely be interviewed while your teen remains in the waiting room or on a day when your teen is not present. Your adolescent will be interviewed alone; if he or she is a younger adolescent, the evaluator may start out with a game or fun activity. The clinician will usually interview you and your teen together for a short period as well. An adolescent's *history* can hold important clues regarding *current* behavior. Thus, you will be asked about past and present issues. Generally, the evaluator must keep your information confidential, except for a few exceptions (see Chapter 13 for details on confidentiality). As soon as you meet, the clinician should clarify the confidentiality of your interview and other aspects of the evaluation.

The issues covered in clinical interviews will depend on the reason your teen is being evaluated.

Sidebar 12.1   Issues Covered in Clinical Interviews

The following issues are commonly covered in clinical interviews:

- Developmental history of teen (the mother's pregnancy, labor/delivery; the child's early childhood development, serious illnesses/injuries)

- Family structure (caregivers, stepparent, step-siblings, custody issues)

- Teen's current difficulties (and speculation as to the cause)

- Impact of teen's behavior on the rest of the family

- Impact of the rest of the family on teen's behavior

- Mental health symptoms

- Alcohol and other drug use

- Significant family stressors (parental divorce/separation/death, frequent moves, military deployment, poverty)

- Ethnicity; language spoken

- Religious and spiritual beliefs

- Family history of medical and mental health issues, involvement in the criminal justice system, and alcohol/drug abuse

- Exposure to emotional, physical, or sexual abuse (including parental domestic violence)

- Your teen's talents, strengths, abilities, successes

- Academic history, behavior at school, and vocational history (if applicable)

- Peer relationships, dating history, sexual orientation, and intimate/sexual behavior (if applicable)

- Legal involvement (arrest, incarceration)

- Usual coping skills

- Previous medical, mental health, substance abuse evaluations or treatment

- Other attempts to help your teen's difficulties (extended family, religious or spiritual resources, complementary or alternative medicine, curanderos, tribal leaders)

- Previous and current medications

- Significant recent or past stressors (relationship breakup, victim of bullying, physical or sexual assault, natural or other disaster)

- Hobbies, personal interests, goals, and aspirations

- Concussions or incidents of being knocked unconscious (sports, car accident)

- Strategies used at home or school to try to address your teen's problem, and how well they worked

The reason your teen was brought in for the evaluation will be discussed in detail. The clinician is particularly interested in how often the problematic behavior occurs, how extreme the behavior is, how long it has been going on, and in what situations it occurs. The degree to which the problem interferes with your child's functioning at home, school, and in relationships is also important.

It is essential to be as honest and straightforward as you can during the interview. The clinician is there to support you and your teen, not to criticize or judge. Don't worry about getting *everything* in during the interview; the clinician will ask questions to fill in information gaps. In addition to details about your child's problem(s), make sure to emphasize your son or daughter's unique strengths (bright, caring, creative, friendly, energetic, generous, funny).

Because teens behave differently depending on the situation and the people present, the evaluation should include input from significant adults who interact with your son or daughter in a variety of settings (extended family, school counselor, teachers, coach, tutor, youth pastor, probation officer, case manager, physician). Parental permission is typically needed before these individuals can be contacted. They are usually interviewed over the telephone but may be seen in person.

It is common for discrepancies to arise between the impressions of parents and those of other adults when they describe an adolescent's emotions and behavior. A teen's two parents might even disagree with each other. And a teen's own perception of his or her difficulties may differ from that of the adults. This is normal and expected. Adults differ in the amount of time spent with their teen and in the circumstances in which they see the teen. Adolescents are usually more accurate in reporting their internal experiences (sadness, worry, low self-worth, suicidal thoughts) or private behaviors (delinquency, cutting, sexual behavior, alcohol/drug use). Adults (including parents) are often more accurate when describing easily observable behavior (defiance, impulsivity, aggression, distractibility, restlessness, hyperactivity).

Assessment Tools

There is not one specific battery of tests that is appropriate for all teens. Numerous measures have been designed to evaluate adolescents' thinking, personality, intelligence, mental health, and use of alcohol/drugs and then compare the results to those for youth of the same age and grade level. The specific instruments used with your teen will primarily depend upon your child's age and presenting problem. No single test can determine whether or not your teen is suffering from an emotional or behavioral problem; therefore, adolescents should never receive a diagnosis on the basis of the results of one test.

Clinicians score and interpret the tests and then integrate the findings with the rest of the information gathered during the evaluation process. Clinicians typically take a "bio-psycho-social" approach, knowing that difficulties during adolescence are influenced by a teen's *biology* and *personality* and by the *social* contexts (family, friends, school, community) in which they exist. If additional information is needed, medical (if not already completed) or neuropsychological testing may be recommended.

Preparing for Your Teen's Evaluation

Above all, make sure you and your teen are ready. It is best to pick an appointment time when you and your teen will be well rested, well fed, and not preoccupied with an important upcoming event. Reschedule the appointment if your teen is hung over, high, or sick. If your son or daughter takes any type of medication, make sure to ask the clinician if your teen should briefly discontinue it for the evaluation. For example, stimulant medication (which treats the symptoms of ADHD) can be stopped for a short amount of time without adverse effects.

Spend time thinking about the issues you will likely be asked about; it can be difficult to remember everything during the actual evaluation appointment. You may need to look things up. It is often surprising how big a role a teen's history can play in his or her current difficulties.

Write down notes regarding the specific behaviors that concern you. Be as clear and detailed as possible. For example, when does the behavior usually occur? What seems to trigger it? What circumstances make it worse? What circumstances seem to make it better? What negative impact does it have on your son or daughter and on the family? What is your teen's payoff for behaving this way—does your teen get something out of it, or does it help your teen avoid something? Be sure to note the types of situations when your teen does *not* engage in the behavior. If your teen has had any particularly positive or negative experiences with a medical or mental health clinician while working on this behavior, make some notes about this as well.

In addition to bringing your notes—or a longer history—to the evaluation, bringing the following can help the evaluation go more smoothly and efficiently:

- Report cards, Individualized Educational Plans (if relevant), important school records (behavioral write-ups, suspensions) or letters home (positive or negative)

- Relevant medical records, reports from previous school, mental health, or substance abuse testing

- List of previous and current medications (including over-the-counter and prescription medicines, vitamins, and herbal supplements)

- Items to keep your teen occupied (iPod, BlackBerry, videogame, book, magazine) in case he or she needs to wait while you meet with the clinician

- Snacks or drinks so your teen has plenty of energy and brain fuel for the long session

Getting Your Teen to the Evaluation Appointment

Because adolescents have usually not asked to be evaluated, they often have mixed feelings about going to the appointment. They do not know what to expect or what will happen with the results, and they are nervous and distrustful. When teens are scared, they often put up a tough and rebellious front. Don't be fooled. Ask them what they know about "shrinks," and correct any misperceptions. Go over what will happen at the evaluation ("You will spend some time talking and the rest of the time doing different activities"). Tell them there may be some tests, but the tests have nothing to do with their schoolwork and grades—some don't even have right or wrong answers. The goal is to identify your teen's unique strengths and weaknesses. Explain that a large part of the evaluation is focused on their thoughts and feelings.

Sometimes teens are afraid they will get in trouble for revealing information about the family to a stranger, especially when it is negative. Encourage teens to say whatever is on their mind, and do not punish them for anything truthful they share. If they are embarrassed about having to be "evaluated," tell them no one outside the family needs to know about the appointment (and keep your word). The results cannot be sent to anyone else without your (and possibly your teen's) permission.

Most adolescents know when life is not working for them. Pick the issue that is most distressing to them and use that: "The clinician is going to try to figure out the reason why you [get picked on by the other kids, don't like the family rules, are tired all the time, have a hard time at school, worry even when you try to stop yourself]." Most important, explain that one of goals of the evaluation is to get good advice about the best way to help their issue improve or go away. Make it clear the evaluation is not a punishment, even if their behavior has gotten them in trouble.

The more you involve teens in the process, the more likely they will participate in the evaluation. Older adolescents in particular want to have some control in the situation.

Adolescents are often more willing to go when they discover they get to tell their side of the story ("I could tell them the situation from my point of view, but they want to hear your view of things—what you think and feel about the issue"). Ask teens to make a list of all the things that bother them about themselves and the family. If teens continue to be defiant, inform them that this is their chance to talk about how unfair you as parent have been and how you overreact to their behavior and to express their opinion that they don't need to change. Let them know that if the clinician completely agrees with your teen, you will respect that and change your behavior accordingly (keep your word, but don't worry—this usually doesn't happen).

You cannot physically force teens to go to evaluations, and even if you could, you cannot make them talk or participate. You probably know what motivates your teen better than anyone else does. As a last resort, you may need to use a bribe. Buy teens something special (CD, basketball, clothes), excuse them from doing something they don't like for a week (chores, family night), or give them something they want for the night (later curfew, car for extra two hours, no bedtime).

If given the choice, it can be helpful to let teens be interviewed before you; this puts them at ease by making them feel part of the process (especially if they do not want to be there). Don't worry about your teen manipulating the clinician by putting on a good face and minimizing his or her difficulties. You will get your chance to give your opinion. Helping teens build rapport with the clinician makes it more likely they will be honest during the assessment—which is critical to getting an accurate understanding of how they are doing.

What Should the Written Report Look Like?

Comprehensive evaluations should result in a detailed written report that integrates and summarizes the most significant aspects of the assessment process. This document is critical for accessing special services from the school, as well as having mental health and substance abuse services covered by your insurance company. Most important, the report provides you with the next steps in helping your teen overcome his or her difficulties, and it can be extremely helpful to the clinicians who will be helping your child.

There is some variation in the report format depending on exactly why a teen was evaluated. However, most written reports contain some version of the following categories.

Reason for Referral. This section typically includes your teen's basic demographic information (age, gender, race, grade level), a brief description of your teen's current situation, and the reason he or she was brought to the evaluation. This part of the report lays out what question(s) you hoped the evaluation would answer.

Sources of Information Used for the Evaluation. Typical sources used include the parent interview, child interview, telephone interview with school counselor, medical records, school records, and any previous mental health evaluation. All formal tests used to measure intelligence, academic skills, social skills, and personality are listed. Substance abuse assessment tools are listed if given, as are rating scales or behavioral checklists completed by you, your teen, or significant adults.

Relevant History and Background Information. This section summarizes information provided by parents and other significant adults regarding important aspects of a teen's upbringing and personal history.

Clinical Interview with Teen. Information from the evaluator's private interview with your son or daughter is summarized here. Your teen's view of current circumstances and important past events are noted, as are reports of any mental health and substance abuse symptoms.

Behavioral Observations. This section describes your teen's attitude, mood, speech, thought processes, energy level, and interpersonal style during the evaluation. The evaluator typically notes your teen's level of distractibility, patience, defensiveness, and concern about his or her performance. The goal is to give a picture of how your son or daughter interacted with the examiner, and to note whether he or she displayed any unusual reactions or behaviors during the evaluation process.

Don't be surprised if your teen showed *none* of the problematic behaviors you observe on a daily basis. Most teens can put on a good front for short periods, particularly around adults. In addition, because of the structured nature of the situation and the one-on-one attention, adolescents who have difficulty paying attention or controlling their impulses often behave fine during evaluations. *If evaluators relied solely on a teen's behavior during the evaluation and the information adolescents provide about themselves, they would rarely get to the bottom of what is really going on.* That is why it is imperative to obtain information from a variety of sources and also to use formal tests and rating scales.

Test Results and Interpretation. Actual scores from tests measuring your teen's *IQ and academic achievement* are listed and explained in relation to the impact they have on your child's day-to-day functioning. Next, your teen's *personality traits* are described, including his or her depth of emotion, motivation, drive, judgment, impulse control, expectations of self, coping skills, level of insight into thoughts and feelings, and ability to take responsibility for his or her own actions. Worries, sadness, anger, guilt, low self-esteem, problems paying attention, and obsessive thinking are discussed when applicable. *Social relationships* are described in terms of how your teen views and interacts with others. The potential for *at-risk behaviors* is noted, and when *alcohol/drug use* is formally evaluated, these results are listed and explained, as well.

Summary and Diagnostic Impression. This portion of the report is central to understanding your teen and deciding which next steps to take. Findings from every part of the evaluation are summarized and integrated in order to answer the initial referral question about your teen. Basically, this section describes *what's going on*—why your teen is doing what you are concerned about and what factors make it worse or better. The report will state whether your child's difficulties are a response to something or someone in particular or whether they are more chronic in nature. This section describes how your teen's strengths and weaknesses contribute to the current difficulties, including the teen's relationships with family, friends, and romantic partners. Your teen's goals and aspirations are discussed in relation to the test findings, particularly how strengths and weaknesses move him or her closer or further away from those goals. If your teen's behavior meets the criteria for a particular mental health disorder, he or she may be given a diagnosis. The potential outcomes for your child—both with and without assistance—are laid out.

Recommendations. This section of the report should contain specific and detailed recommendations of next steps to help your teen overcome (or manage) his or her current difficulties. For example, individualized recommendations for school assistance should include what type of school setting is ideal, the level of structure required, and what type of academic remediation is needed. Recommendations for "talk therapy" should include what format(s) (individual, group, family) of treatment is necessary, what type of therapy is likely to be most effective (cognitive-behavioral, motivational, psychodynamic), and which issue is most important to address first. The type of therapist who would best fit your teen's interpersonal style should also be noted. A recommendation for a medication evaluation may be made if your teen's functioning is significantly compromised at home, school, or in relationships. Factors that may potentially interfere with the treatment process (anti-authority attitude, excessive eagerness to please, distractibility, manipulative behavior, difficulty trusting others) should be recorded, as should factors that can be used to motivate and reward your son or daughter. A recommendation may be made for medical or neuropsychological testing if needed. *If the evaluator concludes that your teen is doing fine and is not in need of assistance, the clinician will list signs and symptoms to keep an eye on as your teen develops and matures.*

You should receive this report within a few weeks of the evaluation. It should be written in clear, understandable terms, without a lot of technical words, since you and other nonclinical professionals will read it. You (and sometimes your teen) will need to sign a "release of information" form if you want a copy of the report sent to the school, the juvenile court, or your child's medical doctor. If you do not want sensitive information about your family or child included in the reports sent to outside agencies, you can ask the evaluator to remove personal details. The conclusions in the report are important for them to know, but your family's private life is not.

The Feedback Session

The feedback session is an essential part of the evaluation process. After writing the report, the clinician meets with you and your teen to discuss the findings and to review information contained in the report. All statements and conclusions made about your son or daughter should be based on the information gathered throughout the evaluation process. The clinician should explain why he or she made particular inferences; any speculation in the report should be supported by the data. This meeting is the opportunity for you and your teen to ask questions, get clarification, or request additional information. Take advantage. You have hired the clinician for a service, and he or she is there to help you. Before you leave the meeting, you should understand what is going on with your teen, how it affects your family, and what you should do next.

The findings may be difficult for you to hear. Some may validate what your gut has already been telling you, and some may surprise you (even shock you). It is better to know what you are dealing with. Your teen may not agree with the findings and should be encouraged to express his or her opinion. But, teens are often relieved that someone understands what they are going through and that they are not "crazy," "stupid," or "bad."

Depending on your child's age, you may want to meet with the clinician alone to ask questions you do not want your teen to hear. In general, it is often best for your teen to be present for much or all of the feedback session. Even if you are discussing sensitive issues, it is usually important for adolescents to hear the answers.

Clarify which individuals and agencies will have access to the report. If recommendations are given for additional assessment or a particular type of treatment, ask the evaluator for names of respected professionals.

Sidebar 12.2   Comprehensive Evaluation

The following are important elements of comprehensive mental health evaluations:

- Clinical interview

- Intellectual (IQ) testing

- Academic testing

- Assessment of emotions, personality, relationships

- Written report

- Feedback session

Diagnoses: Helpful or Harmful?

Medical illnesses are classified into different categories (diabetes, arthritis, pneumonia), which enable doctors to diagnose patients on the basis of a set of symptoms. The field of mental health also has diagnostic categories (Major Depression, Oppositional Defiant Disorder, ADHD) to help classify conditions that include a specific set of symptoms. One way the field of mental health tries to standardize this classification is by using the Diagnostic and Statistical Manual of Mental Disorders (DSM), which describes more than one hundred mental health disorders, each with a specific set of criteria. This manual is purely *descriptive* and does not give information regarding causes of mental health conditions or their treatment. The DSM also reviews the associated emotional and behavioral characteristics, prevalence, familial patterns, physical and physiological findings, and the typical course of each mental health disorder.

The Importance of Mental Health Diagnoses

A clearly defined diagnosis of your teen's condition will allow you to move forward more efficiently and effectively, for the following reasons:

- Knowing the diagnosis can lead to appropriate intervention. Specific emotional and behavioral problems are known to respond to particular parenting and treatment strategies.

- Insurance companies may reimburse for evaluation and treatment services only for teens with a diagnosed condition.

- You are more likely to be able to obtain special services and academic accommodations from your teen's school if your teen has a mental health diagnosis.

- A diagnosis helps all the professionals working with your teen focus their efforts on his or her most pressing concern(s).

- A diagnosis is typically required if you want to access mental health medication for your teen's difficulties.

- Knowing your teen's diagnosis allows you to research the condition (what works, what doesn't, prognosis), as well as to find other parents of teens with similar issues.

Because of the ramifications associated with mental health labels, the diagnosing of mental health conditions should never be taken lightly. Only clinicians with the appropriate education and training should be providing diagnoses to adolescents. The more comprehensive an evaluation is, the more likely your teen's diagnosis will accurately affect his or her issues. And, remember, *it is your son or daughter's problem that is being classified and labeled, not your child.*

Mental Health Diagnoses and Culture

Lack of familiarity with a teen's culture can result in the overdiagnosis or underdiagnosis of emotional or behavioral problems. The DSM classifies mental health conditions among diverse populations around the world. To decrease the likelihood of bias when assigning mental health diagnoses to individuals from different backgrounds, the DSM includes cultural variations in the way particular mental health disorders are expressed and possible cultural explanations for an individual's behavior. Clinicians must be careful not to diagnose problems where none exists, or to overlook or dismiss symptoms they mistakenly assume are just a normal part of a teen's culture. This refers to any aspect of culture, including, but not limited to, racial or ethnic background, sexual orientation, gender, and religious and spiritual beliefs.

What to Do if You Do Not Agree with the Evaluation Findings

Most parents are surprised at how accurate the findings of comprehensive evaluations are—as if the clinician "knew exactly what my teen is like." However, every once in a while, parents find the conclusions and the diagnosis (or lack thereof) inaccurate and off the mark. When this happens, you typically have several options:

- Discuss your concerns with the clinician and ask him or her to review the findings and how they were reached. You may change your mind with additional clarification and evidence.

- Get a second opinion. Have another professional evaluator review the report, including the test results and conclusions, to see whether the second clinician agrees with the first. It is not practical to repeat the entire evaluation, as many of the tests cannot be repeated right away, and it would be very expensive.

- Disregard the results, diagnosis, and recommendations.

- Consider that the evaluation could be accurate, and follow the recommended course of action for three to six months, monitoring your teen's behavior for improvement. If you see no improvement, consider options 1, 2, and 3.

Getting the Evaluation Paid For

The cost of comprehensive evaluations varies by the thoroughness of the assessment and what part of the country you live in. They typically range from $750 to $2,500.

Ironically, medical insurance companies are more likely to pay for mental health treatment than the evaluation that determines whether or not treatment is necessary. Insurance companies often make determinations on what services to cover based on "medical necessity." Emotional and behavioral problems among adolescents are often bio-psycho-social in nature (caused by the interaction of biological, psychological, and social factors). Therefore, when the need for a comprehensive evaluation arises, you should make sure to include the *biological* aspect of your teen's difficulty when working with insurance companies. For example, clearly state that you are concerned about whether your child is depressed or anxious, has an eating disorder, or is thinking about suicide, rather than discussing the consequences of these conditions (slipping grades, delinquency, running away from home). If your insurance company requires a referral for the evaluation by your teen's pediatrician or family practice physician, use the same language so that the doctor understands the issue is not something you or the school can take care of. *If you do not have insurance, see the section "Public Insurance" in Chapter 13.*

Contact your insurance company to find out exactly what types of evaluations are covered and what copay you will be expected to pay. Sometimes comprehensive evaluations will be paid for, but you must jump through a few hoops first. If coverage for your teen's evaluation is denied, find out why and see if you can appeal. Sometimes resubmitting your claim with the "right" information (including evidence of medical need) can reverse the initial decision.

If you have to pay for the evaluation out of pocket, ask the clinician if you can make monthly payments or if he or she offers a sliding fee scale for families with limited income. You can often write your payment off as a medical expense on your taxes.

Although the thought of a comprehensive evaluation can be intimidating, I hope it is clear that it is *one of the first and most important steps toward your teen's recovery—and the possibility of a healthy, peaceful home.*

The next chapter is devoted to helping you understand the variety of treatment services available for your teen. The clinician who completes your teen's evaluation may or may not be the best person to carry out the treatment recommendations. A clinician's academic and clinical training and area of expertise, the cost of services, and your insurance plan will likely dictate whom you will work with next. The section at the beginning of this chapter that describes helping professionals and their areas of expertise can serve as a general guide to which clinicians provide "talk therapy," medication, and other types of support services.

Sidebar 12.3   Did You Know?

Having a comprehensive evaluation of your teen's situation can help in a number of ways. Here are some things to keep in mind as you consider your options:

- *Comprehensive evaluations* reduce the chances your teen will be over-, under-, or misdiagnosed.

- Comprehensive evaluations conducted by *clinical psychologists* provide the most complete and thorough picture of an adolescent's unique abilities, difficulties, and characteristics.

- Psychiatrists are the primary mental health professionals trained and authorized to prescribe *medication* for emotions and behavior.

- Pediatricians and family practice physicians are one of your best *referral* sources for comprehensive evaluations.

- The clinician who *evaluates* your teen may not be the best qualified person to *treat* your teen.

CHAPTER THIRTEEN

Help Is on the Way

Obtaining the Right
Treatment for Your Teen

Can anything be done to help my child?

Mental health disorders, including substance abuse disorders, are caused and sustained by a variety of factors, making it unlikely teens will "just grow out of them." When left untreated, these disorders usually result in significant problems in relationships and school.

Families suffer when their children do. The good news is that mental health disorders are *treatable*. The sooner parents obtain treatment for adolescents, the sooner teens get well. The bad news is that 80 percent of mentally ill teenagers do not receive treatment for their condition.

Just as teens suffering from a physical health disorder (pneumonia, strep throat, asthma) need treatment, teens suffering from mental health disorders *need* treatment, as well. When physical illnesses are ignored, they tend to worsen, which can have disastrous, long-term consequences that can be truly disabling. The same is true for illnesses that affect an adolescent's emotions and behaviors. Fortunately, there are more effective treatment options available today for adolescents than at any other time in history.

Treatment of mental health conditions is similar to treatment of physical conditions such as heart disease—even if doctors cannot always *cure* heart disease, they prescribe a variety of strategies to help *manage* symptoms so that individuals can fully function and participate in their lives. The same is true for teens suffering from ADHD, Depression, Bipolar Disorder, Eating Disorders, Anxiety Disorders, Substance Abuse, or any other condition reviewed in this book. Solely changing one's diet is not likely to be as effective as treating heart disease on several different levels. By the same token, simply taking medication for a mental health condition is not likely to be as beneficial as combining medication with talk therapy that teaches teens new skills, including effective ways of problem-solving, managing their anger, and communicating with their parents.

Sebastian, thirteen, was out of control. He always seemed annoyed, refused to follow his mother and stepfather's rules, acted up in class, and continuously harassed his little sister, physically assaulting her twice. After two attempts at individual therapy were unsuccessful, Sebastian's parents felt hopeless and resigned. They basically gave him run of the house, since it was too exhausting and draining to argue with him. After hearing about a family therapist who had helped some close friends, Sebastian's parents decided to give professional treatment one more shot. This time everyone from the family participated.

Within the first few sessions, it became clear that Sebastian's behavior had taken a turn for the worse a few weeks into the school year. This was the same time his mother remarried and Sebastian's stepfather moved into the family home. His stepfather was a strict disciplinarian, while his mother rarely held him accountable for his behavior. She felt tremendously guilty over her divorce and did not like to discipline her children because "they've been through so much already." Within several sessions, the therapist helped Sebastian's mother and stepfather compromise about disciplining both children, and Sebastian and his sister got a chance to negotiate, so they felt they had some say in the household rules.

After a few months in therapy, during one of the sessions, Sebastian told his mother that he missed his biological father and felt that she was not letting him come around. He also admitted that he hated school because it was "too hard" and "gets confusing a lot of the time." It was only through therapy that he was brave enough to tell his mother, "You married my stepdad; I didn't. So you can't force me to like him." The therapist helped Sebastian's mother realize the importance of supporting his relationship with his biological father and of giving Sebastian and his stepfather time to get to know each other and develop their own relationship. When the therapist suspected Sebastian might be suffering from ADHD, she asked the family to have him evaluated. (I would have recommended a comprehensive evaluation **before** the initial attempts at individual therapy for Sebastian.) After an ADHD diagnosis was confirmed, Sebastian was placed on a low dose of stimulant medication that helped him focus in school and better control his behavior in the classroom. He was also found to have a learning disability in reading (Dyslexia). Sebastian's mother met with his teachers and guidance counselor to begin the process of obtaining services from the school to help Sebastian succeed in the classroom. Today, Sebastian's parents are in charge and running the home, he is much better behaved, and family members actually enjoy spending time with each other.

There are a variety of treatments available to today's teenagers to assist them with their emotional and behavioral difficulties. Some are more applicable to your teen than others, depending on age, severity of condition, and what approach you, as a parent, are most comfortable with. The goal of each treatment approach is to help teens better manage their thoughts, feelings, and actions—as well as their ability to function in school, relationships, and the family.

If you have not read Chapter 12, on obtaining the right evaluation for your teen, please do so now. Correctly identifying your teen's difficulties is the first step in finding the right type of help. Depending on what the evaluation reveals, your teen may or may not need professional treatment. If your teen receives a mental health diagnosis and requires professional assistance, the results of the evaluation should directly guide the treatment plan.

Psychotherapy (aka "Talk Therapy")

Psychotherapy, often referred to as "talk therapy" or "outpatient treatment," is one of the most common approaches to treating adolescents who suffer from the troubling conditions described in this book. Trained professionals work closely with adolescents one-on-one to help alleviate emotional problems and behavioral difficulties and to facilitate good mental health. The therapeutic relationship between adolescents and their therapist is critical, and teens must feel safe and supported by the clinician. Therapists do not *do* anything to their clients in psychotherapy; instead, a therapist and teenager work together on goals (and aspirations) for the teen that both parties agree upon.

Within the first few sessions, specific treatment objectives (tailored to the unique needs of your child) should be set. For example, teens who are skipping school will attend classes daily, those who are starving themselves will eat three meals a day, teens who are smoking marijuana will stop using the drug, teens who are staying out all night will be home by curfew, and teens who are shy and withdrawn will participate in three social activities. Goals set at the beginning should be monitored throughout the treatment process and modified as necessary. This helps you determine whether or not treatment is effective, and specifically how your teen's emotional and behavioral symptoms are—or are not—improving.

Cognitive-Behavioral Therapy (CBT)

Cognitive-behavioral approaches focus on teens' *thoughts*, while also teaching them more effective coping *behaviors*. This approach is based on the underlying assumption that an adolescent's actions are significantly influenced by his or her thoughts and perceptions—that teens react to situations primarily on the basis of their *evaluation* or perception of an event, rather than on what actually occurs. When a teen's perceptions are distorted or inaccurate, negative reactions can result. As teens' flawed beliefs and patterns of thinking become more accurate—and in line with what is truly happening—their behavior improves.

In addition, teens who lack the skills to effectively deal with difficult situations tend to feel frustrated, upset, or angry. Learning coping behaviors—such as anger management, frustration tolerance, emotional control, relaxation, problem-solving stressful situations, and negotiation and compromise—can help teens be more successful.

Although CBT is individualized to the particular needs of each adolescent, it usually contains the following components: (1) educates teens and their families about a teen's condition, likely causes, and how to treat it; (2) investigates which negative "thoughts" and "behaviors" are contributing to a teen's difficulties and designs a treatment plan to target them; (3) models new skills, has teens practice them, and provides feedback about their new behavior; (4) prepares teens for "high-risk" situations so that they do not fall back into old ways of thinking and behaving; and (5) monitors treatment goals to determine which strategies are most effective.

Because Cognitive-Behavioral Therapy is structured, practical, skill-based, and focused primarily on adolescents' *current* behavior and situation, treatment gains are typically made within months. Any discussion about a teen's past is used to connect previous events to current feelings, thoughts, and behaviors. Attending treatment sessions is not enough; active participation is required, and teens must be able to *demonstrate* newly learned skills. Between sessions, teens are frequently given assignments that encourage them to *practice* their new ways of thinking and behaving and that help them *generalize* to home and school what is learned during therapy sessions.

Cognitive-Behavioral Therapy is one of the most effective psychotherapy approaches for teenagers. Depending on the severity of an adolescent's difficulties, cognitive-behavioral treatment is sometimes combined with medication.

Interpersonal Therapy (IPT)

An underlying assumption of Interpersonal Therapy is that positive, supportive, and caring relationships are critical to an individual's mental health. When teens have problematic relationships with family, friends, romantic partner, teachers, employers, or others, they may experience low self-esteem, sadness, and hopelessness. Teens with relationship difficulties often repeat the same mistakes, which prevents them from forming close bonds with those they care about. Interpersonal Therapy helps teens *recognize* the self-defeating ways they interact and then *change* their behavior. Some teens need to learn how to communicate their needs, express their emotions, or behave more assertively. Interpersonal Therapy is particularly helpful for adolescents suffering from depression.

Dialectical Behavior Therapy (DBT)

This approach is a modified version of Cognitive-Behavioral Therapy. Treatment focuses on the contradictory techniques of helping teens change their behavior, while at the same time validating and accepting teens as they are. DBT blends Eastern worldviews with Western therapy strategies. Teens are taught how to more effectively manage their emotions, interact with others, control their thoughts, and tolerate being upset. DBT is particularly effective for adolescents who repeatedly engage in suicidal or self-injurious (cutting) behavior.

Motivational Interviewing/Motivational Enhancement Therapy (MET)

Motivational Interviewing/Motivational Enhancement Therapy is a supportive approach that helps teenagers explore and move beyond their resistance or ambivalence about participating in treatment (and needing to change their behavior). An underlying assumption in MET is that many teens do not view their behavior as problematic, and therefore the therapist must *engage* them into the treatment process and *motivate* them to make the decision to change. As part of the MET strategy, therapists (1) subtly sidestep teens' denial or attempts to minimize their behavior, rather than directly confront them; (2) make teens feel understood by viewing the world through their eyes; (3) convey that change is possible, emphasizing that teens can absolutely turn their lives around; (4) encourage teens to identify problems in their life and the potential solutions to fix them (nothing is forced on adolescents, so there is no reason for them to be resistant); and (5) help teens see the discrepancy between their current behavior and what they want to achieve, and how their present choices are moving them further from their desired goals.

MET can be particularly beneficial for teens who typically do not seek treatment on their own, tend to be rebellious, and often drop out of treatment. It is especially effective with substance-abusing teens. MET can be used alone but is often used in combination with cognitive-behavioral approaches.

Psychodynamic Therapy

Psychodynamic therapy focuses on past experiences to help teens achieve *insight* into how their emotional or behavioral problems developed. An underlying assumption is that current difficulties are usually the result of negative experiences in the past, unconscious conflicts, and avoidance of painful feelings (by the use of defense mechanisms such as denial and repression). Early childhood experiences are usually discussed and then related to the way the teen currently feels and behaves (depressed, worried, controlling, lonely, angry, ashamed). Once teens become aware of their inner struggles, they can learn to manage their emotions and behaviors more effectively.

Group Therapy

Each of the psychotherapy approaches just described can also be provided in a *group* setting. Teenagers are often more open to feedback about their behavior when it comes from same-age peers who can "relate" to their experience, than when it comes from authority figures. Therapists use the group interaction to demonstrate treatment issues the group is discussing. Teenage treatment groups can quickly become chaotic and disorganized, and seriously mentally ill teens may unintentionally monopolize group sessions. Adolescents who have trouble learning may not be able to grasp treatment concepts as quickly as their peers and may become confused and frustrated in group therapy.

The decision to send an adolescent to group therapy should be carefully considered, with specific attention given to the number and particular mix of group members. Placing oppositional, aggressive, or delinquent teens in a group with similar members is likely to result in a *worsening* of behavior. Clinicians leading treatment groups should be well-equipped to manage teenagers, especially if they become unruly. Group therapy can be less costly than individual therapy, but the trade-off is less specialized attention. Most teens benefit from group therapy *in addition* to individual therapy.

Family Therapy and Parent-Focused Approaches

Family-focused treatment is based on the notion that family relationships are an important factor in mental health and that an adolescent's difficulties are at least partially related to problematic relationships within the entire family system. Therapists identify and develop the unique strengths of each family and teach specific strategies to improve the way the family functions. Therapists typically meet with parents, the teen, and often the teen's siblings to focus on the interactions among all family members. The entire family is viewed as the "client," even if a teen's behavior was the initial reason the family sought therapy.

Most family-focused treatments seek to accomplish the following goals: (1) increase positive interactions and feelings of closeness among family members; (2) clarify the roles of family members, with parents as authority figures; (3) teach conflict resolution and negotiation skills so that family members can reduce the frequency of arguments and fights; (4) educate family members about appropriate physical and emotional boundaries and help them effectively set boundaries with one another; (5) work with family members on ways to meet one another's needs in healthy and adaptive ways; (6) educate parents about effective behavior management strategies (reinforcing positive or prosocial behaviors and disciplining negative or harmful behaviors); and (7) assist parents in developing specific and strategic behavior modification plans for their children

Even when trying to do what is best for their child, parents can *unintentionally* say or do things that worsen their teen's worries and fears, sadness, hopelessness, weight concerns, defiance, anger, or alcohol and drug use. Learning effective ways to manage their teenager's mental health symptoms and to react strategically and constructively to problematic behavior helps parents feel empowered and usually results in a significant improvement in their child's difficulties.

Some therapists specialize in one treatment strategy; others are more eclectic in their style, utilizing techniques and strategies from two or more approaches. Regardless of the specific type of therapy, teens must feel they have some type of "connection" (no matter how small) with their treatment provider. Expert credentials and proven therapeutic techniques are of little value without a trusting, supportive, collaborative relationship between adolescent and therapist. You may even find yourself getting jealous of their relationship, because your son or daughter seems to tell the therapist "everything," while you seem to get "nothing." Do not take it personally. It is because this adult is *not* their parent that teens are able to share much of the information they do. Supporting your teen's private relationship with the therapist is key to your teen complying with treatment recommendations.

That being said, parents should be involved with their teenager's treatment; this is even more essential if your teen is in early adolescence. Involvement can range from initially meeting with the therapist and providing important background information, to receiving general updates on a regular basis, to attending some (or all) sessions with your troubled teen. Much will depend on the severity of your son or daughter's issues, how involved your child wants you to be, and how necessary the therapist believes your involvement is. It is essential that you participate if the therapist or your teen requests your attendance. Although all families are different, the chances of your teen's emotional and behavioral changes lasting for the long term are much higher if you take part in your son or daughter's treatment process.

Questions to Ask Potential Providers of Psychotherapy

Before making an appointment for your teen, you should call a few mental health professionals and "interview" them. Ironically, in our society, most people research new cars more thoroughly than they do the treatment of their child's emotional and behavioral health. Even with a referral from a trusted source, you should still do your homework. There is great variability among clinicians and mental health agencies. You want an adolescent's first shot at treatment to be successful, as you may not get another chance.

Most treatment professionals, or clinicians, will be in session with clients when you call, so you will probably have to leave a message. *Briefly* state what the mental health evaluation revealed about your teenager, and say that you would like to speak with them about possible treatment services. When they call back, ask if you can have five to ten minutes to ask some questions about the type of treatment they provide. Set up a time to talk if they are unable to do it at the moment. If the clinician is unwilling, he or she is not the right therapist for you.

Important questions to ask include the following:

1. What professional degree do you have and where did you receive your training? Are you licensed?

2. Do you use any tests or conduct comprehensive evaluations?

3. How many teenagers have you treated? How many with conditions similar to my child's?

4. Do you focus more on helping teens process their feelings or on learning new skills? (Focusing on feelings is fine, as long as it is related to helping teenagers learn new skills.)

5. Will you require my teen to completely stop using alcohol and other drugs? Why or why not? (A rigid adherence to abstinence may prevent your teen from attending treatment after the first session.)

6. How do you develop a treatment plan specific to my teen's needs? How soon will that occur? How do you monitor progress? At what point, if ever, will the plan be modified?

7. Do you involve parents? Are you willing to communicate with my teen's school?

8. How will you ensure that my teen's emotional or behavioral changes translate outside your office?

9. What do you do if treatment is not working? How long until we know?

10. What happens if treatment ends and my teen's symptoms return or worsen?

11. What is your fee? What type of insurance do you take? What happens if my insurance runs out before my teen is ready to stop treatment?

If a clinician has appropriate credentials, as well as training and clinical experience in treatment approaches known to be effective with teenagers similar to your child, you are halfway to your decision. The other half of the decision-making process is more subjective. Were you satisfied with the answers to your other questions? Did you like the clinician's style during the phone call? Do you think this individual is a good match for your son or daughter? If so, make an appointment for both you and your teen to have a face-to-face meeting; it is important that your son or daughter feel reasonably comfortable with the clinician. Trust may not be there immediately, but most adolescents can tell you if the possibility exists for trusting the person sometime down the road.

Although some adolescents feel relieved after the first few sessions of psychotherapy (particularly if they feel listened to and understood), teens who have spent months or years avoiding painful thoughts or feelings may actually feel worse before they feel better. Psychotherapy is not about quick fixes—your teen is learning life skills to help him or her cope long-term.

Go to www.whentoworry.com *for suggestions on how to find a qualified mental health treatment provider.*

In-Home Services

In-home services deliver treatment in an adolescent's "real-life" environment—the family home. Therapists typically meet with youth and their families several hours each week and are available to them 24/7. Therapists also coordinate teens' treatment, schooling, medical services, and juvenile justice involvement (when necessary). The following are the primary goals of most in-home services: keeping teens living at home rather than in out-of-home treatment settings; remaining flexible in order to address the particular needs of different families; improving parenting skills; increasing positive interactions between family members; increasing teens' involvement in prosocial activities; improving teens' school or vocational functioning; and broadening and developing a support network for teens and their family (extended family members, neighbors, and friends) to help make and maintain positive changes.

Multisystemic Therapy (MST) is one home-based approach that has been helpful for delinquent teens, including those who have mental health disorders. Although MST is family centered, it also emphasizes other social networks in which teens and their families interact: school, neighborhood, church, peers. Important components of treatment are increasing teens' association with prosocial youth and decreasing teens' association with negative youth. This approach typically blends aspects of Cognitive-Behavioral Therapy, Family Therapy, and Motivational Enhancement Therapy; medication is used as needed. Family members are also taught how to interact effectively with various systems and agencies so that they can maintain treatment goals, even after formal MST treatment ends.

Temporary Out-of-Home Placements

Adolescents with serious emotional or behavior problems may be difficult for parents to handle at home, even with the help and support of treatment professionals. In these situations, a temporary out-of-home placement may be necessary to provide your teen with a more structured and intensive treatment setting. This also removes your adolescent from his or her current environment (including negative influences); without these distractions, some teens are better able to engage in treatment. A quality out-of-state treatment facility may be more effective than an inadequate local placement. However, family involvement is a critical part of the treatment process, and distance makes participation a significant challenge.

There are a variety of out-of-home placements available to teens. Before you can know whether this drastic measure is truly necessary, seek a thorough and comprehensive evaluation and a detailed discussion with a qualified professional. Both steps should indicate that an out-of-home placement is needed. The goal should be to return teens to a less restrictive setting as soon as their behavior allows it.

Juvenile Boot Camps

Boot camps that have been beneficial for defiant or uncontrollable teenagers typically offer much more than military-style, boot-camp programming. Helpful programs offer treatment-related activities such as educational assistance, individual and group therapy, and substance abuse services. The programs also provide supervision and intervention services after teens return to the community.

Boot camps with a confrontational, in-your-face style are typically not appropriate for adolescents suffering from the majority of mental health dis-

orders described in this book. Even with "treatment" services and comprehensive aftercare, these programs are often too physically and emotionally intense for teenagers with serious emotional and behavioral issues. Make sure a particular boot camp program is a good fit for your teen and his or her particular issues. At the very least, an inappropriate fit can delay your teen's access to appropriate services; at the very worst, it can significantly exacerbate his or her mental health symptoms.

Wilderness Programs

Wilderness programs have become increasingly popular over the past decade. Although these programs vary in the types of activities they offer, most provide a personal growth experience through living in a remote, natural-wilderness setting. The underlying assumption is that a unique environment, separation from negative influences, a lack of distractions, participation in emotionally and physically challenging activities, and individual and/or group counseling can help adolescents develop self-esteem, responsibility, teamwork, and communication skills. An important goal is for teens to become aware of their self-defeating beliefs and behaviors and to begin making important attitudinal and behavioral changes. Some teens find wilderness camps an empowering experience, one that helps them gain self-awareness and clearer goals. These programs tend to be most effective for adolescents who exhibit "at-risk" behaviors (defiance, rebellion, experimentation with alcohol/drugs) rather than those suffering from major mental health disorders or serious substance abuse problems.

Day Treatment/Partial Hospitalization

This type of program provides adolescents with significant structure and intensive treatment services all day, with teens returning home to their families in the evening. Specialized school programs and individual, group, and family therapy are common. This type of treatment is more comprehensive than outpatient psychotherapy but not as restrictive (or costly) as residential treatment centers or psychiatric hospitals.

Residential Treatment Centers (RTC)

These twenty-four-hour treatment facilities provide a structured and predictable environment where teens are taught new ways of managing their emotions and behavior. RTC programs vary widely. Some are nurturing and home-like, while others are similar to hospital settings. Many offer individual, group, and/or family therapy. Educational groups focused on mental health or substance abuse issues are also common. A range of activities may be offered and used therapeutically, including but not limited to caring for animals (horses, dogs), arts and crafts, wilderness adventures, gardening, and wood carving. Specific parent-oriented support groups or workshops are usually offered—and sometimes required.

Therapeutic Foster Care

This type of temporary out-of-home placement is designed to combine a therapeutic environment with a family and a home-like setting. Adolescents with emotional or behavioral problems are placed in private homes with specially trained foster parents. Most foster families accept one teenager with special needs into their family at a time. Parents in therapeutic foster homes usually receive significantly more training, supervision, and support than do traditional foster care parents. Teens typically continue to receive mental health services from community providers while they are living in the foster home. Therapeutic foster care tends to be one of the most effective types of out-of-home placement.

Therapeutic Group Homes

Therapeutic group homes are typically staffed with two or more adults specifically trained to work with troubled teens. Most of these placements house four to ten teenagers at one time. Therapeutic group homes are usually very structured, and many offer individual and/or group therapy. Some group homes are heavily focused on behavior management and accountability, while others are more nurturing and relationship oriented. Teens residing in therapeutic group homes usually attend school (and sometimes receive mental health services) in the community.

Inpatient Treatment/Psychiatric Hospitalization

Inpatient psychiatric hospital programs are typically staffed with a variety of medical and mental health professionals. To be admitted, adolescents must have a mental health disorder that results in their being a danger to themselves or to others or unable to take care of their basic needs.

Because of the range and intensity of services offered, parents frequently view psychiatric hospitals as one of the most desirable treatment options if their son or daughter suffers from a serious mental health disorder. Although hospitalization may be necessary to keep an adolescent safe during a crisis, long-term behavior change resulting from inpatient hospitalization is rare. Recent changes in insurance and managed care have significantly limited the amount of time teenagers can obtain inpatient mental health services, and these programs are used primarily to "stabilize" a teen's behavior. Today, the current length of stay in most psychiatric hospitals is one to two weeks—clearly not enough time to "treat" conditions as complex as mental health disorders.

Due to potential "medical" concerns, specialty hospital/inpatient treatment programs exist for teens with serious substance abuse disorders, eating disorders, and self-injurious/cutting behaviors.

Questions to Ask Potential "Out-of-Home" Placements

Finding an out-of-home placement for troubled teens is easy; finding the right program for your particular teen (and family) is the challenge. Sharp, glossy, and colorful marketing brochures and pamphlets do not necessarily translate to a quality treatment program. Ask the professionals you are working with for recommendations. Then contact the agencies and ask the questions below, as well as any other questions you have.

- Is this program licensed? By whom?

- What is the program's overall philosophy about troubled teens and behavior change?

- Is the facility locked, or can teens leave the premises when they choose?

- Does the facility work with teens who have problems similar to those of my son or daughter? What other types of teens will my child be interacting with?

- What is the overall tone of the program: nurturing, militaristic, structured, therapeutic, rule-based? (One tone may be better than another, depending on your teen's particular issues.)

- What types of therapy do you offer? How will it be individualized for my teen? How often would my teen participate in these therapeutic activities?

- How much and in what way do you include family members in the treatment process? (The answer should be "a lot," and specific examples should be provided.)

- Will my teen have access to a Ph.D.-level psychologist? A child psychiatrist?

- What is your view on medication for adolescents?

- Will my teen attend an accredited school while enrolled in your program? Are special education resources available if my teen needs them?

- How long do most teens stay in the program? (Shorter is not necessarily better; teens need an adequate time to truly make behavior changes. However, the *average* length of stay should not be more than a year.)

- What is the total cost? Is treatment covered by my insurance? Is there any financial assistance available?

- Have any studies been done on the effectiveness of your program? If not, what studies have been done on the treatment approaches you use?

- If my teen has an alcohol/drug problem in addition to a mental health disorder, does the facility have the resources to treat *both* conditions?

- If my teen becomes defiant and/or aggressive, how will the facility handle this behavior? What will you do if my teen runs away from the program?

- How much opportunity will my teen have for recreation, physical activity, and "play"?

- How often can I visit? Can my teen come home for weekends or holidays?

- How will your staff help me develop an "aftercare" plan that includes schooling and treatment services? (Aftercare is *critical* to long-term emotional and behavior change.)

- Do you have a list of parents I can contact who sent their teen through the program?

If a program is unable to answer these basic questions, you should search for one who can. If you are satisfied with the answers, *take a tour of the program* (anyone can make promises over the phone). You want to know if the adolescents in the program are happy or miserable. Are they active or just hanging out in their rooms? Are a variety of constructive activities offered? Is the staff friendly, helpful, and respectful to teens—or harsh and punitive?

Once you find a treatment program you believe is a good fit for your teen (and one you can afford), you need to remain confident you are doing the right thing for your child. Your son or daughter will likely—and understandably—be very resistant to placement outside the home. He or she will likely beg, plead, and promise you the world "as long as you don't send me." If other, less-restrictive treatment alternatives have repeatedly failed, stay committed to your decision. Watching a child explode in anger or cry uncontrollably is heartbreaking for any parent. Fortunately, this reaction is usually temporary; once teens adjust to a program and meet other teenagers they can relate to, most youth are able to acknowledge they really did need help.

Crisis Programs

Parents whose teen is in an emergency situation may need to access a crisis program to avoid hospitalizing their child. Crisis services are typically available twenty-four hours a day, seven days a week. Crisis programs provide very brief but intensive treatment to stabilize youth and then link teens and their families with mental health services in the community. Crisis staff is usually trained to manage urgent situations, screen adolescents for emotional and behavioral problems, and provide assistance to parents. Walk-in crisis centers, mobile crisis teams, shelter services, and telephone crisis hotlines are examples of these types of programs. Larger communities often have a variety of these services, while smaller communities may only have one or two.

Support Groups

Support groups for both teens and their parents can be a powerful addition to traditional therapeutic approaches. Individuals meet in small groups to discuss their difficulties, as well as to share their strength and hope. Because members are in similar situations and experiencing many of the same thoughts and feelings, individuals typically gain a sense of understanding and relief. They also learn new ways of coping with current challenges (as well as potential actions to take) from one another. Support groups are usually based on unconditional, nonjudgmental support and encouragement. Most follow a structured format; some are led by trained facilitators, and others are led by a volunteer from the group.

Support groups have popped up around the country for many of the specific conditions described in this book. Troubled teens benefit from sharing their experiences with similar peers; parents obtain the same benefit from sharing their experiences with other parents who are raising teens with emotional or behavioral difficulties.

Twelve-step programs (Alcoholics Anonymous, Narcotics Anonymous) are the most popular type of support groups for individuals suffering from alcohol/drug abuse. Teens can attend adult meetings, or, depending on their community, they can attend twelve-step meetings specifically designed for young people. Because a teenager's substance abuse affects an entire family, parents can get assistance from *Al-Anon Family Groups*, a twelve-step program for individuals affected by someone else's alcohol/drug use. Alateen (part of Al-Anon) is a twelve-step group specifically for youth affected by someone else's drinking. *Alateen* can be particularly helpful for siblings, close friends, and girlfriends or boyfriends of teenagers struggling with substance abuse. In addition, churches, temples, and community mental health centers often offer their own support groups for teens recovering from substance abuse and/or mental health difficulties.

You and your teen have the freedom to talk or remain quiet at support group meetings. Everything discussed is confidential, and there is no cost to attend.

Psychotropic Medication

More teenagers take psychotropic medication today than at any other point in history. Psychotropic medicine affects the brain chemicals (neurotransmitters) that affect an adolescent's thoughts, emotions, and behavior. Treatment with psychotropic medication has its benefits and dangers; placing a teenager on this type of medicine is a personal decision that should be made on a case-by-case basis, with families carefully weighing the issues. *It is just as dangerous to rigidly rule out medication as a treatment option for your teen as it is to blindly accept a prescription without considering the potential consequences.*

Psychotropic medication should be considered only when teenagers are:

- Experiencing significant distress or emotional suffering
- In danger of harming themselves or someone else
- Having difficulty functioning at home, at school or work, or in relationships, because of a mental health disorder

Medication should not be sought solely because a teenager is loud, annoying, or defiant.

Is Medication Necessary?

Are today's teens overmedicated? Yes and no. There are definitely adolescents who have been prescribed psychotropic medication without needing it, and that is wrong. But, believe it or not, there is probably an even *larger* number of teenagers who are suffering from mental health disorders but who are not receiving medication that could relieve their suffering and help them function more successfully at school, at home, and in relationships. This is just as wrong. Obtaining comprehensive evaluations before medication is prescribed is one way to help teens get appropriate treatment and prevent unnecessary prescriptions. If you are contemplating medication treatment for your son or daughter, you should also take into account the following additional factors: the duration, severity, and intensity of your teen's mental health symptoms; your teen's willingness to take psychotropic medication; your teen's willingness to refrain from alcohol/drug use while taking medication; and your own willingness to dispense medication to your teen (daily or several times a day), if needed.

Taking psychotropic medication is like taking cough syrup for a cold, using inhalers for asthma, or taking aspirin for a fever or insulin for diabetes. Although the medicine does not "cure" the underlying illness, it can control symptoms and lessen an adolescent's burden. Less severe mental health conditions do not always require the use of medication. For example, teenagers suffering Anxiety, Eating Disorders, and mild Depression have been effectively treated with cognitive-behavioral psychotherapy.

That being said, teenagers suffering from Schizophrenia, Bipolar Disorder, and *severe* cases of the other conditions covered in this book will likely require psychotropic medication (in addition to psychotherapy) for symptom relief. Medication can stabilize mood and behavior; skill-focused groups, behavior management strategies, and psychotherapy are much more effective when teens can sit still, pay attention, think clearly, or manage their intense and overwhelming emotions.

Medication is typically not effective for treating defiance, delinquency, or substance abuse, although it can help mental health conditions that frequently co-occur with these disorders.

For medication to be helpful, adolescents must take it as prescribed for an adequate amount of time, without combining it with alcohol or other substances of abuse. Too often, medications are thought to be ineffective with particular adolescents, when in reality the teens stop taking the medicine prematurely or because physicians change the medication too hastily. Medications that treat depression can take up to four to six weeks before their full effects are evident. How long teens will need to remain on medication depends on their condition and the severity of their symptoms. Some adolescents may need to be on medication for a year or less, while those with serious illnesses may need medication for much longer.

Even when psychotropic medication is used appropriately, it should be viewed as one component of the treatment plan, not the only treatment approach. These pills are not magic, and taking them does not "fix" a troubled teen. Just as adolescents with diabetes need to make dietary and exercise changes in addition to taking insulin, treatment for adolescents with mental health conditions also requires a multifaceted approach. Because mental health symptoms may return once medication is discontinued, teens must learn new coping skills to manage their emotions and behavior. Even with a reduction in mental health symptoms, adolescents with emotional and behavioral difficulties often have academic and social problems that also need to be addressed.

Medication Side Effects

All medications have side effects; some are frequent and mild, while others are less frequent but more dangerous. Some unpleasant reactions to psychotropic medications may lessen or completely diminish after an adolescent's body has adapted to the medication; other reactions may remain throughout the entire course of treatment. The following are common side effects associated with psychotropic medications: headaches, drowsiness or insomnia, weight gain or loss of appetite, stomachaches or nausea, rapid heart beat, constipation, dizziness or lightheadedness, skin rashes, irritability, nervousness or anxiety, blurred vision, dry mouth or chronic thirst, and akathesia (inability to sit still, rocking, fidgeting, tapping feet continuously).

How teens experience side effects from psychotropic medication is extremely variable. Some teens experience several side effects at once, and others experience none at all. Because adolescents may not associate physical symptoms with their medication, you and the doctor should directly ask your teen if any "unusual things are happening" with his or her body. Lowering the dose or switching to a different yet comparable medication can often alleviate discomfort; when it comes to youth and dosages of psychotropic medication, physicians should "start low and go slow." Abruptly stopping psychotropic medication is dangerous; these medicines should always be discontinued under the supervision of a medical professional.

Medications: Helpful or Harmful?

Safety is clearly a concern when you are considering placing your child on psychotropic medication. The majority of psychotropic medications used with teenagers have not been thoroughly studied in young people. Although many lack approval by the Food and Drug Administration (FDA) for use in adolescents, the FDA does not prohibit physicians from prescribing these medications to adolescents. At this point, we know little about:

- The long-term side effects of these medicines (including the effects on the developing adolescent brain)
- Which medications work best for which teenager—and at which dose
- The potential risks of these medications when not taken as prescribed (such as skipping doses for days or weeks at a time, which is common among some adolescents)
- The most effective way to treat adolescents with more than one mental health disorder
- The potential effects of mixing psychotropic medication with alcohol and other drugs
- The interactive effects when two or more psychotropic medications are taken simultaneously

Taking any medication (particularly one that affects the brain and nervous system) carries some amount of risk. The FDA now requires pharmaceutical companies to label selective serotonin reuptake inhibitor (SSRI) antidepressants with a "black box warning" stating that antidepressants can increase the risk of suicidal thinking and behavior in children and adolescents. Keep in mind that *this effect is seen in only a very small subset of young people,* usually within the first few weeks or months after starting this type of medication or after a change in dosage. Families should closely monitor teenagers placed on antidepressant medication and immediately report any unusual behavior or increased symptoms of depression (agitation, irritability, restlessness, insomnia, thoughts of suicide) to the prescribing physician. Stimulant medications carry warnings of sudden death in children and adolescents with heart problems, and some antipsychotic medications can cause significant weight gain, as well as raise an adolescent's risk for diabetes and hypertension. Talk to your teen's psychiatrist or physician regarding the specific risks and benefits of *any* prescribed psychotropic medication.

When considering medication, always consider the risk of NOT treating your teen's mental health disorder. Think about the answers to these questions:

- Is your teen so depressed that he or she wants to die? (Untreated depression is one of the biggest risk factors for suicide among adolescents.)

- Is your teen's judgment so compromised that he or she continually participates in physically, sexually, or emotionally dangerous situations? Is your teen constantly miserable and upset?

- Are other people at risk from your teen's aggression?

- Does your teen cut or burn himself or herself?

- Is your teen's ability to perform in school, keep a job, maintain friendships, or fully participate in the family significantly compromised by excessive fear, worry, food or weight obsession, hyperactivity, impulsivity, distractibility, defiance, uncontrollable moods, bizarre thinking, or erratic behavior?

- Is your son or daughter self-medicating a mental health condition with illegal drugs and alcohol?

Because of advances in psychotropic medication, many adolescents who might otherwise have needed to live in hospitals or residential treatment centers can now live at home with their families and attend school in their communities. Medication has helped teens with serious mental health disorders hold down jobs and have fulfilling relationships instead of being completely consumed by obsessive thoughts, erratic and overwhelming moods, urges to die, or strange and peculiar beliefs.

Some parents worry that placing teenagers on these medications increases the chances their teen will abuse alcohol/drugs in the future. In fact, it appears that the opposite is true. When their mental health disorder is appropriately treated (with medication or psychotherapy), teenagers are actually *less* likely to abuse substances. The exception to this is teenagers who have *already* begun abusing alcohol/drugs. Parents and professionals must carefully monitor substance-abusing teens who are prescribed psychotropic medication (especially Ritalin, Adderall, and the other stimulants). When aware of the issue, doctors can often use medications with less potential for "abuse."

Skipping or Refusing Medication

Teenagers vary in their attitudes toward taking psychotropic medication. Some are willing to take what is prescribed because they believe "the doctor knows best," they recognize the beneficial effects of the medication, or they have already taken psychotropic medication for years and do not question it (common among teens with ADHD). However, a significant number of adolescents refuse to take what the doctor prescribes. Others skip doses and do not take their medication regularly. Many adults assume that defiance or a power struggle is behind a teen's refusal to take medication. However, the issues in Sidebar 13.1 are more commonly at play.

Sidebar 13.1   Why Teens Skip or Refuse Psychotropic Medication

Teens skip or refuse psychotropic medication for the following reasons:

- They don't want to be viewed as "crazy" by friends or siblings.
- They are experiencing physically uncomfortable side effects.
- Previous treatment with medication was unsuccessful, and they do not want to try again.
- They do not think the medication helps them.
- They believe medication makes their behavior worse.
- They hate or are unable to swallow pills.
- They forget to take their medication.

- They do not want a substance "controlling" their mind or body.

- They do not want to become dependent on medication.

- As part of their natural striving for autonomy, they want to make independent decisions about what they put into their body.

- Family members opposed to psychotropic medication tell teens not to take it.

Teens who abuse alcohol or other drugs are often willing to take psychotropic medication for a co-occurring mental health disorder. Some are motivated by the improvement in symptoms; others are happy to take any substance that alters their state of mind.

Regularly asking teens about how their medication impacts their moods and behavior involves them in the treatment process and can increase medication compliance. You should monitor and track your teen's behavior before *and* after he or she begins taking psychotropic medication, to provide specific, concrete feedback to your teen (and the doctor) about emotional or behavioral changes you observe.

Questions to Ask the Doctor About Medication

If a comprehensive evaluation and the resulting mental health diagnosis indicate that medication may be helpful for your teen's condition, take your teen to a child psychiatrist (if one did not do the evaluation), as these physicians have the most knowledge and training in psychotropic medication for adolescents. If you are unable to find a child psychiatrist (or even a psychiatrist who treats young adults), see your teen's pediatrician or family practice doctor. Your son or daughter must inform the doctor of *all* medicines or drugs (vitamins, herbal supplements, over-the-counter medications, alcohol, illegal drugs) he or she currently takes, because the interaction of the substances can be dangerous.

To educate yourself on the psychotropic medication pre-scribed for your teen, you should question the physician, as well as do research on your own.

You should know the answers to the following questions:

- What is my teen's diagnosis, and why is this the best medication to treat it?

- What non-medication approaches are available to effectively treat my teen's condition, if any?

- What specific emotional or behavior changes are expected to occur from the medication? How soon can we expect them? How will you monitor them?

- What are the most common side effects of the medications, and what are some ways of minimizing them? Are there any rare, but potentially serious, side effects?

- What are the risks of *not* placing my son or daughter on this medication?

- What medical tests will my teen need before starting this medication? How often will he or she need to have these tests done?

- How long will my teen need to take this medication? How will we know if the dosage should be changed or the medication should be stopped?

- How often should my teen be seen and monitored by you?

- Where can I find out more about this medication? Do you have any material I can read?

- Can you recommend a quality clinician to provide psychotherapy or other helpful treatments for my teen's condition?

Complementary and Alternative Medicine (CAM)

Treatments that fall in the category of Complementary and Alternative (CAM) health care include products and practices not currently considered part of mainstream conventional medicine. Treatment providers typically hold degrees other than the M.D. "Complementary" treatment approaches are usually combined with conventional approaches, whereas "alternative" treatments are often used in place of more mainstream treatments. Because this type of health care has become so popular over the past decade, the National Institutes of Health has developed a specific division to study these approaches—the National Center for Complementary and Alternative Medicine (NCCCAM). Each year, Americans spend more than $36 billion on CAM treatments.

Some parents find that conventional treatments for their teen's emotional or behavioral problems are not working as well as they hoped, have too many negative side effects, or are too expensive. They may be attracted to treatments that are more "natural." A number of CAM approaches are relatively inexpensive and easy to access. Most of the CAM treatments listed in this section have some scientific data to support their effectiveness, although they are supported mainly by numerous case studies and anecdotal reports. Until now, the infrastructure and funding to conduct large-scale, high-quality studies of CAM were unavailable. This has recently changed, and many more studies investigating the nature of CAM approaches—including their safety and effectiveness—are going on today.

CAM approaches may help your teen, but they are typically not enough to completely alleviate his or her condition. Because of the multifaceted nature of most mental health disorders, adolescents almost always require at least some conventional treatment (psychotherapy, behavior management, psychotropic medication). Relying *solely* on CAM can delay teens' obtaining help they need.

Good Nutrition

Nutritional strategies are some of the easiest and least invasive ways to help teens with emotional and behavioral difficulties. After trying the changes for a month or so, you (or your teen) will know if the modifications are helpful. These strategies are part of an overall treatment plan and are not meant to be the sole method for eliminating symptoms. A nutritionist, family practice physician, or naturopath can help develop a program specifically tailored to the needs of your teen, as well as your family.

Healthy and Balanced Eating. For some teens, even minor changes in their nutritional intake may positively affect their mood and behavior. Help your teen eat more fresh fruit and vegetables, whole grains, and lean meats; limit sugar, processed foods, and caffeine. Take a gradual approach, and include the whole family. Healthier eating also helps prevent obesity and other physical health issues.

Food Sensitivities. A small number of teens experience a worsening of emotional or behavioral symptoms after consuming foods or beverages with artificial colors, artificial sweeteners, preservatives, or dyes. Some teens are sensitive to particular foods, usually one (or more) of the following: dairy products, wheat, corn, soy, egg, chocolate, or nuts.

Sugar, Sugar, Sugar. Different teens appear to metabolize sugar in different ways, and some adolescents appear to be "sugar sensitive." Sugar is often listed on ingredients lists as corn syrup, fructose, sucrose, dextrose, honey, or cane juice. Sugar does not cause ADHD, Major Depression, or other mental health disorders. However, ingesting large (or even small) amounts of sugar may worsen symptoms in some teens who already have emotional or behavioral issues. Even if your son or daughter is not "sugar sensitive," reducing his or her intake of high-sugar cereals, snacks, and beverages can be beneficial, particularly in preventing obesity and oral cavities.

The Mighty Vitamin. When teens are not adequately nourished, they may experience academic and behavior problems. This may partly be because they are missing nutrients necessary for optimal brain functioning. Studies have found that some teens with mental health disorders have lower-than-average levels of certain vitamins and minerals. Supplementing your teen's diet with appropriate amounts of these nutrients (a daily high-quality multivitamin and mineral supplement) may result in positive effects on their thinking and behavior. Very high doses of one or more vitamins or minerals (sometimes known as "mega-dosing") is *not* recommended, as this can be toxic and cause serious side effects.

Essential Fatty Acids (EFAs).   Essential fatty acids are fats that the body requires for optimal health. They are critical if an adolescent's brain and nervous system are to function properly, yet most teens do not get enough of them, due to repeated dieting or heavy consumption of processed foods. The easiest way to supplement a teen's diet with EFAs is with fish oil or flaxseed oil, either in liquid or in capsule form. Buy a high-quality fish oil from a reputable manufacturer to ensure that the product does not contain high amounts of Vitamin A or D and that it has been tested for mercury, as these can be toxic.

Exercise and Physical Activity

Too many teens fill their days watching television, playing videogames, and e-mailing friends on the computer. Exercise is helpful not just for physical health; it is also beneficial for a teen's mental health. Physical exercise can enhance self-esteem, decrease depression, and provide an overall sense of well-being. Exercise frequently reduces stress, tension, and irritability. Do not worry if your teen is overweight or out of shape; the less fit adolescents are before an exercise program, the more likely they will experience benefits. The more regular and intense the exercise, the more effective it will be. The positive effect of exercise on mental health is likely a result of the following responses to physical effort: feelings of accomplishment and success, a sense of control over one's body, feelings of relaxation that follow exercise, and distraction from current stresses.

Exercise also changes chemicals in the brain (including those associated with depression) and helps teens sleep better at night.

Participation in an individual or team sport can give adolescents a chance to be successful, as well as burn off high levels of energy. Utilizing a personal trainer or a workout buddy often helps adolescents get started on an exercise program.

Light Therapy

Exposure to bright light (including sunshine) can help improve the moods of individuals who are depressed. Light therapy involves individuals sitting very close to a light box each morning for 20 to 60 minutes. This technique has also been shown to be as effective as antidepressants, although many use a combination of the two treatments.

Herbs

Due to concerns about safety, and because of the uncomfortable side effects associated with prescription drugs, many parents are opting to give their teens herbal supplements instead of traditional medications. Because the active ingredients in herbal formulas can vary from one manufacturer to another, obtain guidance in choosing the most reputable brands. *Herbs should always be taken under the care of a naturopath or another health-care professional who is knowledgeable about herbal medicine.* Even though they are "natural," herbal supplements may not always be safe—and more is not necessarily better. Some herbs can cause serious side effects, and some may have dangerous interactions with conventional medicines.

Acupuncture

Acupuncture is a common practice in traditional Chinese medicine. During an acupuncture session, very thin needles (much thinner than straight pins) are painlessly placed on the body in strategic areas to unblock or balance the energy paths. Brain chemistry, including neurotransmitters, may also be altered. Because of the success of this type of treatment, many insurance plans now cover acupuncture, and it has become a part of some substance abuse treatment programs.

Homeopathy

Homeopathic treatment is specifically tailored to an adolescent's unique emotional or behavioral issues and personality traits. Minute dilutions of plant, animal, or mineral extracts are taken orally.

Eye Movement Desensitization and Reprocessing (EMDR)

During EMDR sessions, adolescents recall traumatic events or memories while the therapist stimulates rapid back-and-forth eye movements by moving his or her fingers in front of the teens' eyes. EMDR is most effective with individuals who have experienced a significant trauma or major loss, including those diagnosed with Posttraumatic Stress Disorder (PTSD).

Neurofeedback

Neurofeedback trains adolescents with ADHD to control their brain activity through immediate feedback—similar to biofeedback for the brain. Learning to regulate brain activity is thought to improve teens' ability to focus and control their behavior. This treatment is controversial and can be quite costly.

Removal of Heavy Metals

Chronic, low-level exposure to lead, cadmium, and mercury can cause subtle neurological difficulties, resulting in a variety of emotional or behavioral symptoms. Testing for heavy-metal exposure is usually done with blood, urine, and hair samples. If high levels are detected, detoxification techniques are used to remove them from a teen's body.

Other CAM Treatments

Therapeutic massage, meditation, music therapy, and art therapy have also been shown to help teens with emotional and behavioral problems.

Complementary and Alternative Medicine (CAM) Practitioners

CAM practitioners believe that the body can heal itself from any illnesses or injury. Therefore, they prefer not to use prescription medications or invasive surgery unless absolutely necessary. The goal is to treat the "whole person," find the underlying cause of an adolescent's difficulties, and restore overall health. Examples of such practitioners include naturopathic physicians (NDs), licensed acupuncturists (LAcs), and licensed dieticians/nutritionists (LDs/LDNs). These practitioners work collaboratively with conventional healthcare professionals and make referrals when appropriate.

Teens involved with CAM should be supervised by a qualified healthcare or CAM professional, and all alternative and complementary treatments should be coordinated with other health or mental health care your teen receives. CAM should be viewed as one piece of the treatment puzzle—the beneficial effects of which may be subtle, dramatic, or nonexistent.

If a Treatment Seems Too Good to Be True, It Probably Is

Be wary of products advertised or discussed on television, on radio, in magazines, or on the Internet that promise "amazing" results and "miracle cures." It's easy to be tempted by these claims if you are frustrated and disappointed with conventional medicine. However, if these products truly were miraculous, they would be used by healthcare professionals around the world and would sell for a lot more than $39.95.

When investigating treatment approaches (and there are many in addition to those covered in this chapter) for your teen, consider the following: the out-of-pocket cost (high cost does not necessarily equal high quality), the time commitment for your teen and family, the degree of invasiveness of the approach, the risks it poses for your teen, and the benefits it has offered to similar teens.

Do your homework. Talk with people whose adolescents have benefited from an approach; do not rely solely on promises of the healthcare provider. Ask for references, call them, and ask questions.

Culture Counts

Mental illness and substance abuse affects teenagers from all ethnic, racial, and cultural backgrounds. Yet, American adolescents of African, Hispanic, Asian, and Native descent use formal treatment services at much lower rates than white adolescents.

It is important that the clinician understand your family and your teen's culture—including your family structure, beliefs about mental illness and substance abuse, values, traditions, life experiences, where and how you live, and how much you identify with mainstream society. Cultures differ in the way they express emotional distress, in which behaviors they consider abnormal, and in their ideas about what "treatment" should look like. This may mean you have to make clinicians aware of cultural differences. For example, if in your culture it is polite not to look doctors directly in the eye out of respect, if you prefer to engage in small talk before jumping into psychological issues, or if you are particularly respectful of the father or elderly family members during family sessions, you may need to tell the doctor. If tangible services, such as childcare, housing, transportation, or school intervention, are needed before your family can focus on abstract mental health material, this should also be conveyed so that treatment can incorporate these issues. Psychotropic medication can be metabolized differently among various ethnic groups, so bothersome side effects should be reported in case a lower dose is more appropriate for your teen.

Although you may prefer to work with professionals of your own race and background, this is not always possible because of a shortage of formally trained, degreed, and licensed mental health professionals of color. Matching minority teens with clinicians from backgrounds similar to their own is important, but not at the expense of training, knowledge, and experience.

Extended family members should participate in treatment when appropriate. These individuals can provide critical information and are often vital to carrying out intervention strategies and influencing teens' compliance with treatment recommendations. Depending on your background, treatment can also be greatly enhanced when prayer, natural healers (curanderos, shamans), or religious or spiritual leaders are integrated into the treatment plan.

Communication is at the core of traditional mental health treatment. If you or your teen do not speak English fluently, request a bilingual clinician or an interpreter, if one is available. You should not have your child interpret for you; parents need to be in the role of authority, and your teen may take liberties regarding exactly what is communicated.

A holistic approach that examines the physical, spiritual, and psychological aspects of a teen's presenting problem usually works best for teens and families of color. Because ethnic and racial minorities may encounter racism, discrimination, and poverty (all stressful events that can act as risk factors for mental illness and substance abuse), the role of external events in your teen's distress should be explored. Family conflict can arise when teens take on characteristics of mainstream society and their parents are committed to traditional cultural values and customs. If this issue is negatively affecting your family relationships, inform the clinician so that it can be addressed in treatment.

Minority Under- and Overrepresentation

Minority adolescents are usually not referred for mental health treatment as often as white adolescents. Even when experiencing similar levels of emotional and behavior problems, teens of color are more likely to be seen as "bad" and in need of punishment, whereas white teens are more likely to be seen as "sick" and in need of treatment. Because of this racial bias, the juvenile justice system is filled with undiagnosed and misdiagnosed minority youth in need of mental health services. On top of being *underrepresented* in treatment systems, minority teens with these problems are *over-represented* in the juvenile justice system. Making matters worse, being labeled as an "offender" negatively affects teens' self-image and self-worth, placing them at risk for further distress. Furthermore, once stigmatized by involvement with the juvenile justice system, teens may find that accessing quality treatment services can be difficult, if not impossible.

Another reason that teens of color are sometimes not referred for treatment is that, in an attempt to be culturally sensitive and not overpathologize "normal" cultural behavior, treatment professionals may be slow to realize when unusual behavior among minority youth indicates an emotional or behavior problem. This conservative approach may result in clinicians mistakenly assuming that troublesome mental health symptoms are an expected characteristic of an adolescent's ethnic background. Teens of color often have to exhibit much more dramatic and extreme behaviors than white teens to be perceived as needing treatment services.

When services are responsive to their culture, minority teens and families often find treatment for mental health difficulties very helpful. If you are not familiar with formal treatment services, ask to be educated on how the process works (length of treatment, length of each session, role of psychotherapy, role of medication, ways treatment can help), if this is not automatically done. Present-focused and practical approaches that are relevant to your family's everyday life will likely be most helpful. You and your teen should know why certain information is being gathered and how it will be used in the future. Let the therapist know if you feel that any of the recommendations go against your cultural beliefs or values. You and your teen should communicate what you believe is causing your child's emotional or behavioral difficulties so that clinicians can integrate this information into their formulation of what is going on. If you or your teen do not feel your needs are being met, discuss these concerns with the professionals from the treatment program or with the treatment provider, who may be able to remedy the situation. Do not just stop going to treatment. If things still do not improve, you can work with the provider or program to find alternative services that are a better match for you and your son or daughter.

All of the factors that are important for African American, Hispanic American, Asian American, and Native American teens also apply to white American teens. In addition to race and ethnicity, *every* adolescent has a culture and several subcultures associated with his or her gender, sexual orientation, religious and spiritual beliefs, and community. No two teenagers are alike, regardless of what "group" they belong to. Therefore, treatment providers must truly get to know each adolescent and family they work with in order to individualize care to their particular needs, strengths, and goals.

What if Treatment Is Not Working?

Because many parents view treatment providers as "experts" who are all-knowing, they are uncomfortable questioning or disagreeing with them. Clinicians are experts in their subject area; however, parents are experts on their teens and can offer critical observations and information. When they employ the services of a plumber or a computer technician, most parents expect specific results (no more leaks, virus removed from computer) and voice their concerns if these expectations are not met. Mental health professionals also provide a "service," and parents enter the relationship to receive certain results. Just as plumbers or computer technicians explain at the outset what *realistic* outcomes are possible, clinicians should clearly explain their treatment goals and a *realistic* prognosis.

Your teen's problems did not instantly appear, so do not expect them to immediately vanish—regardless of how "good" the treatment is. This is particularly true when teens experience problems in more than one area. There is no magic medication or therapy technique. It takes time to discover which approach (or combination of approaches) will meet the unique needs of your child and family. If it feels like treatment is moving too slowly, communicate your concerns to the treating professionals and ask about expected time frames. If *some* positive change is not seen after an adequate period, your son or daughter's diagnosis should be reviewed, alternative reasons for symptoms should be explored, and perhaps another approach (psychotherapy technique, type of medication) tried. Patience is important, but unwavering commitment to an approach that is providing little to no benefit wastes time, energy, and money; it also keeps adolescents from receiving the care they need.

If you or your teen feel uncomfortable with a treatment provider or a particular treatment approach (and if you are feeling blamed, criticized, or spoken down to), you should voice these concerns. It is crucial to directly address and resolve these issues, instead of suffering silently or impulsively stopping treatment. Clinicians are typically flexible and responsive to this type of communication, and they are motivated to modify treatment so that it best meets the needs of the client; if modifications cannot be made or are not satisfactory, you may decide to seek services elsewhere for your teen.

Before you come to the conclusion that treatment is "not working," evaluate the potential reasons why. Is your teen actively and regularly participating in treatment? Are *you* doing everything that has been asked of you? Does the treatment provider seem knowledgeable and committed to helping your child and family? Sometimes even when all participants are doing their part, there is just not a good "fit." On the other hand, if the involved parties are not putting forth 100 percent effort, 100 percent improvement is unlikely.

What Is Said in Treatment Stays in Treatment (for the Most Part)

Adolescents are unlikely to participate in treatment if everything they say is reported back to their parents or other authority figures. Teenagers generally want privacy and autonomy, and this concern is even greater where their inner thoughts and secret behaviors are concerned. In fact, the level of trust that develops between teens and their treatment providers is usually directly proportionate to how confidential their conversations remain. Teenagers are typically surprised—and relieved—to discover that treatment professionals are *not allowed* to reveal what is told to them during the course of therapy, with a few exceptions.

At the outset, treatment providers should be very clear with both you *and* your teen regarding what types of information will remain private and what types will be shared—and with whom. For example, you may not automatically be privy to your teen's confidential communication if your teen is old enough to request treatment without parental permission (often known as the "age of consent"). In some states, teens can consent to treatment at thirteen or fourteen years of age; other states do not allow teens to obtain mental health treatment without their parent's permission until the age of eighteen. If teens are of consenting age, they must typically give their written approval by signing a "release of information" form, which specifies exactly what information can be disclosed, to which individuals, and within what time frame, before private information can be disclosed.

That being said, in most cases treatment providers encourage adolescents to tell their parents important information and may even practice and role-play challenging conversations during treatment sessions to help teens become more comfortable sharing difficult information.

In situations where parental permission is required for teens to enter treatment, you usually have a legal right to the private communications between your child and the therapist. However, you should use caution when exercising this right. Teens who do not have the safety and security of confidential conversations are much less likely to discuss their true thoughts and behaviors during therapy, which basically defeats the purpose of treatment.

However, there are specific instances when confidential information can be revealed *without* an adolescent's permission, and in some states treatment providers are *required* to disclose certain information to parents, social services, individuals at risk of serious harm, or the police. Although states vary regarding exceptions to confidentiality, the most common reasons for *exceptions* include these:

- If a teen is suicidal and is likely to make a suicide attempt

- If a teen is going to seriously harm someone
- If a teen is being physically or sexually abused
- If a teen is being seriously neglected
- If the teen's health is in jeopardy and there is a medical emergency

Depending on the reporting requirements of the clinician, confidentiality may be breached if teens are having sex with someone several years older than themselves (even if it is consensual) or are involved with serious criminal activity.

Adolescents feel betrayed by treatment providers when confidentiality is broken, and this can significantly damage the therapeutic relationship. Treatment providers should inform teens and their parents if information will need to be disclosed and communicate it only to individuals who need to know in order to keep the teen (or a potential victim) safe.

Who Is Going to Pay for This?

At this point in the chapter, it is natural to be wondering about potential costs. You should not feel guilty for thinking about money when considering treatment for your teen—this is a legitimate concern. Lack of health insurance and expense of treatment services are two of the most common reasons parents are unable to obtain mental health services for their children. Fortunately, most people (though certainly not all) are covered by some form of health insurance issued through their job or their spouse's job. Many of these plans cover mental health treatment, but there are often significant restrictions on the amount and type of services. If you recognized your son or daughter in one or more chapters in this book, you should call your healthcare plan to ask *exactly* what "mental health" benefits and "substance abuse" benefits your family has and what *specific types of services* are covered.

Many healthcare plans now restrict access to advanced-level treatment providers, limit the number of psychotherapy sessions, utilize group rather than individual treatment, approve only short stays in residential programs, and rely on quick fixes (such as medication alone) for clinically complex problems. These factors make it difficult for families to obtain long-term solutions for their teens' emotional and behavioral difficulties. In addition, if insurance benefits run out before treatment is complete, parents have to pay for services out-of-pocket or apply for public insurance to help cover treatment costs. Parents often need to be assertive with primary-care physicians to obtain referrals to specialists. They may also need to demand that insurance companies cover necessary mental health services for their children. Obtaining quality treatment can be frustrating, exhausting, and expensive for families without excellent healthcare benefits. *Please do not give up.* Treating your teen's mental health disorder is one of the best investments your family can make. Consider the "cost" of *not* getting treatment for your child—to his or her emotional health, friendships, academics, and future career.

Families of teens suffering from serious physical illnesses frequently receive financial help (and other types of support) from extended family, friends, and even neighbors and houses of worship. Parents do whatever it takes to reduce physical suffering and help their children heal. Because of the potentially devastating impact that untreated mental health disorders can have on every area of an adolescent's life, it is critical that these conditions be viewed similarly.

What if My Teen Does Not Have Private Insurance?

If you do not have access to or cannot afford private insurance, you may be able to qualify for government or public insurance plans. These programs are free, and payment for mental health services is made directly to treatment providers. In some cases, you may have a small copayment. To be eligible for public insurance, teens must be both U.S. citizens (even if their parents are not) and state residents of the state providing the insurance and must reside with a family with low income. You should apply for public insurance if your teen is under the age of eighteen and your family income is limited. Even if you have private insurance, you may still qualify for public insurance if you have excessive medical or mental health bills. More information on eligibility can be found at U.S. Department of Health Services Center for Medicare and Medicaid Services (www.cms.hhs.gov).

Medicaid   Medicaid is the largest public insurance program serving children and families with low incomes and few resources. It is a federally mandated program and is collaboratively funded by federal, state, and local monies. Each state runs its own program and determines who is eligible and what types of services are covered. Most Medicaid programs offer coverage for mental health and substance abuse disorders, including mental health evaluations, outpatient psychotherapy, inpatient hospitalization, and psychotropic medication. Families do not have to pay any deductibles or co-payments. The challenge with Medicaid is that many treatment providers do not take public insurance, so finding quality mental health services can be difficult. Most *community mental health centers* take Medicaid, although they often have long waiting lists and high staff turnover. Some nonprofit counseling centers and university teaching hospitals take Medicaid as well.

State Children's Health Insurance Program (SCHIP)   SCHIP is a public insurance program for teens of working parents who make too much money to participate in the Medicaid program but who do not make enough to afford private insurance. Mental health services are typically covered, although there may be low-cost monthly premiums and low copayments. Although SCHIP is available in all fifty states and the District of Columbia, each state varies in the amount of coverage the program offers.

Providers Who Do Not Take Insurance

Because of the growth of managed care and the associated demands for detailed documentation and preapproval for necessary treatment and other administrative requirements, some experienced treatment providers no longer take insurance as payment for their services. If parents want their teen to receive services from one of these providers because of their expertise, they will need to pay all costs out-of-pocket. Many treatment providers offer a sliding fee scale, which adjusts their rates according to a family's ability to pay. Some treatment programs offer scholarships and other types of financial aid to help ease the financial burden. Always ask about these options.

Getting Help from the School

Expectations for today's students are higher than they have ever been. Besides having to pay attention and focus, read, organize, compute, and memorize for hours throughout the day, teens must deal with a variety of social demands—initiating and maintaining friendships, coping with romantic relationships, wanting to fit in, obeying authority, and possibly being bullied or teased. Due to shrinking budgets, schools are providing fewer opportunities for recreation and creative expression but are mandated to improve student test scores. Teenagers (even those who appear not to care) want to learn and succeed at school, and school success is crucial to becoming responsible and productive young adults in the working world. *If your teen is struggling academically, emotionally, or behaviorally at school, you may be eligible for support services at no cost to you.* But first you need to learn some key acronyms.

> *Individuals with Disabilities Education Act (IDEA).* There is a national special education law called the Individuals with Disabilities Education Act (IDEA). Because all adolescents are entitled to a "free and public education," students with disabilities are entitled to the same educational experience as students without disabilities. IDEA helps students receive additional school services to help them be successful. Your teen will not neces-

sarily be required to attend "special education" classes. Services must be provided in the "least restrictive environment," which often means that students obtain extra help while remaining in regular classes. Teens in public, private, and charter schools are eligible for assistance.

To be eligible for extra school assistance, it must be established that your teen has a disability and that it is adversely affecting his or her learning. If the findings from your teen's comprehensive evaluation specify that your son or daughter suffers from an emotional or behavioral disorder, you are halfway there. Some districts may also require that the school conduct its own assessment of your child. Your teen needs to suffer from a "specific learning disability" or a "serious emotional disturbance" (often referred to as an "emotional disturbance"). An emotional disturbance typically refers to one of these problems: (1) major problems learning or building relationships; (2) displaying inappropriate behaviors or emotions; (3) having a persistent unhappy or depressed mood; (4) exhibiting fears or physical symptoms related to personal or school problems; (5) having Schizophrenia. Thinking of your son or daughter as "disturbed" can be unsettling, but try not to get caught up in the label. Focus on the helpful services your teen may be able to obtain and the academic and social improvements he or she is likely to make.

You and a team of school professionals (teachers, counselor, school psychologist, district representatives) will get together to review your teen's situation and decide on a course of action. It can be overwhelming and scary for parents to advocate for their child among so many professionals (especially if you disagree with their decisions or have a hard time asking for things). You may want to ask the clinician who conducted your child's comprehensive evaluation to join you, along with anyone else that can provide important information about your teen.

Individualized Education Program (IEP). If your son or daughter is eligible for services, an *Individualized Education Program* is developed. This written plan is jointly developed and contains detailed and clearly stated information regarding specific goals for your teen and what support the school will provide to help your teen achieve these goals.

Because teens spend more time at school than anywhere else (other than home), educational professionals are in a prime position to observe adolescents over time and in a variety of settings. This information is key when developing the IEP, and it is helpful if you access treatment for your teen in the community. That being said, educational professionals are not allowed to diagnose your son or daughter with an emotional or behavioral condition or require your child to take psychotropic medication as a condition of attending school or receiving special services.

If your teen's emotional or behavioral difficulties are not serious enough to qualify as a disability, your child may still receive some assistance from the school under a Section 504 plan.

Educate yourself on the laws regarding special services at school to ensure your teen has access to appropriate services when eligible. The National Information Center for Children and Youth with Disabilities (NICHCY) can provide details on IDEA, Section 504, your legal rights, and organizations and parent groups that can help guide you through the process of working with schools to get your teen's needs met. Additional resources about accessing school services for teens are located in Appendix A.

You are your teen's best advocate; however, you must work with the school if your son or daughter is to receive an IEP that best meets his or her needs. It is never too late to access special services from the school—even if your teen is a senior!

Relapse Prevention

Even after making substantial progress in treatment, a teen's problems may suddenly *worsen* or *return* after the teen has been symptom-free for some time. Parents may discover that their teen drank alcohol, cut himself or herself, committed a crime, or restricted or vomited food. Or the teen may appear increasingly worried, depressed, oppositional, or aggressive. Do not panic if this is your teen; this is referred to as a "relapse," and it is very common (particularly within the first six months after treatment ends). Relapse does not "just happen"—teenagers have their own unique set of warning signs indicating they are heading down a negative path. Parents, treatment providers, and teens should collectively identify those warning signs, as well as what must happen to help teens return to their prior level of functioning. *The reappearance of previous symptoms or behaviors should be viewed not as a treatment failure but as a signal to reconsider or reinstate treatment strategies.*

Treatment for mental health difficulties must focus on high-risk situations that are most stressful for adolescents, and should help them develop effective skills to cope in those circumstances. Every time teens successfully cope with a high-risk situation, they gain more confidence. The more times they cope effectively, without returning to past inappropriate behaviors, the less chance they will relapse in the future. Conversely, if teens are unable to handle difficult or stressful situations, they are likely to resort to prior negative behavior, which reinforces their belief they are weak and will never change. These thoughts become even more ingrained if significant others hold these beliefs and utter them aloud. The worse adolescents feel about themselves, the more likely they are to engage in further destructive behavior to make themselves feel better. In general, the longer treatment lasts, the less the chance of relapse.

Sidebar 13.2   Reducing the Chances of Relapse

To reduce the chances of relapse, treatment should contain the following components:

■ *Realistic Expectations.* Expects realistic and achievable treatment gains and behavior change. Educates teens and their families about the possibility of relapse and problem-solves how everyone will respond.

■ *Focus on High-Risk Situations.* Identifies high-risk situations or stressful events unique to each child. Validates adolescents' desire to fit in, while teaching skills to resist peer pressure to engage in problematic behaviors.

■ *Education and Reinforcement of New Coping Skills.* Helps teens think through their emotional and behavioral reactions rather than relying on their automatic responses of the past. Teaches teens how to manage negative emotions (anger, frustration, disappointment, worry, sadness) and handle conflict with family, friends, or a romantic partner. Encourages teens to practice new coping skills *before* treatment ends and provides feedback.

■ *Focus on Associated Issues.* Assesses and treats co-occurring substance abuse or mental health disorders when present. Involves family members and helps them parent more effectively, and may address untreated emotional, behavioral, or substance abuse issues among parents.

■ *Management of Physical and Emotional Health.* Encourages healthy eating, adequate sleep, physical activity, and reduction of stress. Makes sure teens are taking prescription medication exactly as prescribed. Encourages teens to spend their leisure time in positive activities with healthy and positive peers.

> ■ *Motivation and Support.* Motivates teens to maintain their positive behavior changes. Provides support during periods of relapse and encourages teens to attend support groups in the community *during* and *after* formal treatment. Teaches teens how to ask for help from family, friends, romantic partners, and professionals when faced with difficult situations or overwhelming emotions.

Many outpatient therapists offer "booster sessions" to help teens stay on the right course after treatment ends. Residential treatment programs may allow teens to return for a brief stay to gain extra support during difficult times. These treatment "tune-ups" may be all teens need to get back on track.

Recovery is a process, and errors and setbacks should be expected as adolescents learn new ways of coping and behaving. A relapse does not mean that an adolescent will not recover or does not *want* to recover; it is usually a sign that he or she needs to learn additional skills to deal with high-risk situations. Although it may be difficult in the moment, acknowledge and praise teens for any actions they take to reduce the severity or length of a relapse. Keep them motivated and moving forward.

SECTION III

Family Matters

CHAPTER FOURTEEN

You Make a Difference

Positive Parenting for Teens with Special Needs

I feel so helpless when I see my teen struggling.

Teenagers still need their parents, and this is particularly true for the adolescents described throughout this book. As they mature, adolescents are faced with increasingly complex demands within the family, at school, and in relationships. Because teens with emotional and behavioral disorders are at increased risk for early sexual behavior, teen pregnancy, car accidents, trouble with the law, dropping out of school, and unemployment, they require extra support and guidance. I hope you see the benefit of obtaining professional help when necessary. However, I also hope it is clear that formal treatment is not a cure-all. Depending on the treatment provider and type of service provided, professionals may meet with your teen once a week, once a month, or maybe only once a year. Therefore, your role in your teen's recovery is indispensable.

In previous chapters, I have included parenting tips associated with specific emotional and behavioral conditions. This chapter includes additional strategies to keep in mind during day-to-day interactions. Whether your teen is already experiencing one of the conditions described in this book or is teetering on the edge of one, positive parenting can significantly help relieve your child's suffering—or even prevent it. *Never underestimate the power of your parenting.*

Educate Yourself

We now know more about emotional and behavioral conditions in adolescents than at any other time in history. Just a few clicks on the Internet can open up a wealth of information on the issues your teen and family are dealing with. Libraries and bookstores are filled with books that specifically focus on each of the topics in this book. Your goal is to gather as much information as you can, not to find a quick fix (promises of immediate cures should actually be avoided). If you gather enough material, you will find what resonates with you and what doesn't. Focus on what is a good fit for your teen and family. A good place to start is the resource section in the back of this book or the www.whentoworry.com Web site.

Talking to Teens About Their Diagnosis

If a comprehensive evaluation indicates that your teen's behavior meets the criteria for a specific diagnosis, the clinician will discuss this during the feedback session and your teen will have ample opportunity to ask questions. However, your teen will likely have thoughts and feelings about the information for some time afterward. If your child does not broach the topic, you should initiate it to gauge how he or she is adjusting. Although you may be concerned that a "label" will negatively affect your teen's self-esteem, most adolescents with emotional and behavioral difficulties already suffer from a poor self-image. In fact, many youth take comfort knowing there is an explanation for the unusual feelings or urges they experience—and that it actually has a name, which tells them they are not the only ones suffering from this disorder. Discovering that their behavior is associated with a particular condition can remove feelings of guilt and frustration after months or years of believing they were stupid, did not try hard enough, or were *choosing* to behave a certain way.

The clinician may have spoken to your teen about brain chemistry or the way your teen's brain is "wired." Reassure your teen that there is nothing *wrong* with his or her brain—but that it works differently from the brains of some of their friends. Your teen needs to know that he or she can still likely participate and succeed in his or her typical activities and personal interests. Emphasize that the diagnosis helps the family, school, and professionals better understand your teen and know exactly which steps to take to help him or her achieve personal goals.

Make sure your teen understands that a diagnosis describes a *condition*—not a person. An adolescent has ADHD, just like he has brown hair, likes motorcycles, and comes up with funny jokes. *It describes one part of them, not who they are as a whole.*

Teens who become involved in treatment can also share their thoughts and feelings about their diagnosis and condition with the therapist. The more adolescents understand about how their condition affects them and what they can do to help themselves, the more active teens tend to be in getting well. Over the past decade, a number of books have been specifically written for teenagers dealing with mental health conditions. Once again, knowledge is power.

You, your teen, and the clinician should discuss who should be told about the diagnosis and exactly what will be said. To the extent possible, an adolescent's desire for privacy and control should be respected. If teens are embarrassed about their diagnosis, share with them the famous and successful individuals who have suffered from the same condition and achieved great things (see Chapters 2, 5, and 7). Many of these individuals have spoken publicly about their struggles because they want the world to better understand mental health conditions.

What Is Your Parenting Style?

Each parent has a unique approach to parenting, but in general, most rule-making parenting styles fall into one of several categories. Each style has a different effect on how teens learn to handle the stressors and temptations of adolescence. What follows is a brief description of the most common parenting styles.

> *Easygoing and Agreeable.* These parents relax about rules. They allow teens to make their own decisions and do not make a big deal out of rude comments or missed curfews. Their overriding philosophy is that if you allow children freedom, they learn from

the natural consequences of their actions. Many of these parents believe childhood and adolescence are meant to be enjoyed and so do not make many demands of their children. Or they may believe that adolescents can handle adult responsibility, so they allow them the privileges of adulthood. These parents shy away from punishment so as not to damage the parent-teen relationship; it is important that their teen's "like them." If raised in strict and rigid homes, these parents make a conscious effort to do the opposite of their own parents.

One category within this parenting style is *indulgent.* These parents believe you can never do too much for or give too much to your own child. If raised with little material wealth, they make sure their children have access to everything they did not. Or they may feel guilty over a divorce or another family stressor. This category also includes parents who use an *uninvolved* parenting style. Because they are overwhelmed with everyday responsibilities or struggling with their own issues, they are unable to closely monitor and regularly discipline their teens.

Teenagers raised in an easygoing and agreeable household often have difficulty in school and are at high risk for becoming involved with alcohol/drugs, delinquency, and early sexual behavior. When teens do not receive rules and accountability, they may rebel (sometimes to the point of being out of control) to force their parents to provide some structure. In addition, adolescents parented under the indulgent style often end up selfish and self-centered and expect to be given things rather than earn them. They commonly become incensed when they don't get what they want. These teens often manipulate their parents, as well as those around them. Teens of uninvolved parents fare most poorly, often ending up with problems in several areas of their lives.

Strict and in Charge. In these families, parents are boss, and everyone knows it. Respect is demanded from children, and teens are expected to comply with all rules. Questioning parents is seen as backtalk and is unacceptable. The term "because I said so" is often heard in these households and punishment is provided when adolescents disobey parental wishes. Importance is placed on how the family appears to the outside world, with emphasis on tradition, order, and conformance to parental expectations. The family is similar to a dictatorship.

Imposing excessive restrictions on teens can set up power struggles and push them to rebel. These youth are more likely to want to taste the "forbidden fruit" or engage in risky behaviors as a way to show their parents that they cannot be controlled. The harder parents clamp down, the more adolescents rebel. When these teens are respectful and well behaved, it is usually because they fear their parents—but these exemplary behaviors often disappear when their parents are not around. In addition, teens who comply just to avoid getting in trouble don't learn to think for themselves and may become followers in life. In contrast, others become driven to obtain approval from a parent who seems impossible to please. Teens raised in strict, authoritarian homes are at increased risk of alcohol/drug use, delinquency, low self-esteem, and depression.

Firm and Open. These parents are definitely in charge, and their teenagers do not always get their way. However, there is more balance in this approach than in the other two parenting styles. Parents set rules and have the final say—yet allow teens to question them and express dissatisfaction. *If safety is not an issue*, parents are often willing to give choices and negotiate expectations and restrictions until they are acceptable to parent and teen alike. Adolescents *earn* parental trust in order to gain increased freedom and privileges, and parents support them in doing so. When family rules are not followed, consequences result. These parents know they can never fully *control* a developing adolescent, so they provide the structure and guidance to help them make good decisions. Individuality is encouraged as long as it does not hurt the adolescent or others. This family is similar to a democracy; a leader sits at the helm, yet everyone contributes to the decision-making process.

Adolescents want rules and guidelines to help them manage the temptations of the teenage years. When parents strike a balance between being too strict and being too permissive, teens are less likely to rebel and more likely to resist pressures to use alcohol/drugs and try other risky behavior.

Firm and open is the most effective parenting style for all adolescents, but it is essential for those with emotional and behavioral difficulties.

Build Your Teen's Esteem

Teens with emotional or behavioral problems often have low self-esteem due to academic struggles, difficulty maintaining friendships, and repeated reprimands for their behavior; in addition, they may hear adults talking about what's "wrong" with them. Parents must make a special effort to point out what is "right" with their teens, as well as how much they appreciate and like (in addition to love) them. These adolescents need a strong sense of self to maneuver the temptations, complexities, and obstacles they will face as they transition to young adulthood.

Understand That Words Are Powerful

Words help teens define who they are. Use *people-first* language and politely correct other adults when they refer to your teen by their diagnosis or difficulty. For example, teens are not "anxious," "addicts," or "antisocial." Instead, they are "adolescents who have high levels of anxiety," "teens with an addiction to alcohol or drugs," or "someone who engages in antisocial behavior."

Having parents want to "fix" you can feel pretty awful. If seeking professional treatment, be clear with your teen (and yourself) that assistance is needed for your child's *difficulties*—not because *your teen* is difficult. These language differences are subtle, but the role they play in your teen's self-image can be huge. Do not compare teens to their siblings or peers—or even to yourself when you were their age. Criticizing, yelling at, or making fun of your teen in front of others shames your child, though they'll never tell you.

Take a New View

Some of your teen's most annoying behaviors may actually help them be successful in life: *stubborn* means persistent, determined, committed to beliefs, and having a strong sense of self; *hyperactive* means energetic, passionate, spontaneous, exciting, and entertaining; *needy* means loving, affectionate, and devoted; *fragile* means gentle, compassionate, caring, and kind; *nosy* means concerned and curious about the world; and *daydreamer* means imaginative and able to tell wonderful stories. At a specified time each day, take one minute to write down three things you love or appreciate about your son or daughter—give specific concrete examples such as "filled the dog's water bowl," rather than abstract traits like "helpful." This exercise helps balance out any focus on negative behaviors. *Give this list to your teen each year on his or her birthday so that your teen develops a balanced self-perception.*

Broaden Your Definition of Success

Make sure your family has a broad enough definition of success so that your teen can be a winner. Does your family value academic achievement, body size, or athletic prowess? Encouraging your teen to become involved in the science club, school newspaper, a religious or spiritual program, or a 4–H club, or to volunteer after school may lead to triumphs you never dreamed of.

Highlight Your Teen's Talents

Many of the teens described in this book feel badly because they cannot do things as well as their peers. Identify what they are good at and build from that foundation. Teens with emotional and behavioral conditions are among the most artistic, musically gifted, dynamic, creative, bright, and funny teens around. If they have an abundance of energy, help them channel it constructively. Help them find their passion and then go for it!

If It's Important to Them, Make It Important to You

It means the world to teens when you attend back-to-school nights, sporting events, performances, and presentations. Show up, keep quiet, and keep it about *them*.

Realize That Mistakes Are a Part of Life

Tell teens about mistakes you have made and what you learned from them. Help them accept mistakes as a part of life and an opportunity for learning. When adolescents repeatedly experience failure, guide them in setting more practical goals so that they can experience some success. When teens mess up, they need support, not criticism; they feel badly enough already.

Distinguish Between Different and Bad

If your teen is different from his or her peers, don't deny it. Rather, point out how peers are also different (have one parent, don't have a car, are extremely rich, have braces, have blue hair, haven't gone through puberty)—the message is that different doesn't mean bad. Differences are what makes life interesting.

Celebrate Good Times

Celebrate teens' accomplishments. Welcome them home from camp, take them out after a big test, and give them a card when they try out for band, choir, or the school play. Celebrate adolescents' efforts and positive risk taking, not just achievements and successes. Make homemade signs or cards saying "You Did It" or "We're Proud of You." Put sticky notes with congratulations in their lunch bag or backpack or on their bedroom door. It's cheap and easy, and it keeps teens motivated to keep putting themselves out there despite negative experiences.

Help Them Be Comfortable in Their Bodies

Team sports such as football, baseball, and basketball are not always the best choice for adolescents who have poor coordination, who have difficulty getting along with teammates, or who find competition too stressful. Help teens explore alternative physical activities such as swimming, bowling, martial arts, horseback riding, rollerblading, biking, gymnastics, ice skating, running, and noncompetitive soccer. In addition to the health benefits, these activities can prevent their spending excessive time in front of front of the television or computer or talking on the phone. In addition, coaches and other adults are often around to provide guidance and support.

Love a Lot When Things Get Rough

During difficult times, remember to say "I love you," even if your teen is misbehaving or doing awful things. The teens described in this book frequently use unhealthy (and sometimes dangerous) behaviors to cope with overwhelming emotions and stress. If parents tell their teen that they hate what the teen is doing to the family or to himself or herself, they should make it clear they still love the teen. Believe they are doing the best they can with the skills they have, and let them know you are there to help. Emphasize that you will not give up, even if it seems like they have.

Take Action Against Bullying and Teasing

Teenagers with emotional and behavioral problems are at risk of being bullied and made fun of; some are likely to be the bullies themselves. Boys may taunt and mock their victims, sometimes becoming physical. Girls can be cruel by ostracizing, humiliating, or verbally terrorizing their targets. At a time when the importance of fitting in and being accepted is at an all-time high, being bullied or teased can devastate an adolescent's self-esteem. Take action regardless of whether your teen is the victim or the perpetrator.

Small actions like regularly hugging teens (despite their resistance) and proudly introducing them to friends and colleagues *as your daughter or son* communicate acceptance of teens just as they are. If you and your teen are struggling, directly ask what you could say or do to show how much you care. You may be surprised at how little it takes.

Stay Connected

Believe it or not, today's adolescents would prefer to spend *more* time with their parents than they currently do. It is up to you to create opportunities to spend time together: watch television or go to the movies (even if the subject matter isn't what you would choose); research topics of interest with your teen on the Internet; hike, bike, play sports, or lift weights; engage in religious or spiritual activities; go to a concert or shopping for CDs or clothes. Find out what teens are interested in—and give it a go. Ask your son or daughter to teach you something—Instant Messaging (IM), taking pictures with your cell phone, updating your make-up or hairstyle, or choosing new genres of music. You may find yourself spending time in activities that are of little interest to you; however, you'll also find the time spent with your teen invaluable.

Eating dinner together (with the television off) is the perfect opportunity to hear about what your teen has been up to. If your son or daughter does not naturally open up, have everyone go around and say one thing that "sucked" about the day. Most teens jump on this—and will probably be shocked you even suggested it. However, using reverse psychology, follow this question by asking everyone to then say one good thing that happened that day. If regular family dinners are unrealistic for your family, have a family meeting once a week where all family members talk about what they have been up to and what they have planned for the upcoming week.

Have a "Technology Time-Out" for an hour each evening (even fifteen minutes for starters). When families refrain from using the TV, computers, stereos, a BlackBerry, or the phone, they tend to talk to each other!

Although family time is important, teens with emotional and behavioral problems often thrive during one-on-one interactions. Make sure to find something special only the two of you do together, whether once a month or once a year. If your teen does not want to spend time with you, don't force it. Instead of making teens feel guilty or wrong, let them know they are missed and say how much you would love for them to join you and/or the rest of the family.

Staying connected to your teen also makes it easier to monitor him or her.

Monitor, Monitor, Monitor

Risk-taking behaviors and the desire to fit in and be accepted by peers reach a peak during adolescence. This combination can lead teenagers to engage in troublesome—and sometimes dangerous—behaviors. Know where your teen is and what he or she is doing. Weekdays between the hours of 3:00 P.M. and 6:00 P.M. are a particularly high-risk time for adolescents, so check in with them after school. Have a curfew, especially on weekends, and enforce it. Know where they will be and whom they will be with. Get to know their friends by inviting them over to the house or taking your teen and a friend shopping or to the movies. Meet their parents or guardians.

Monitor the television shows and movies they see, video games they play, books they read, and music they listen to. Keep computers out of bedrooms so that you can keep an eye on your teen's Internet activities. Purchase an Internet filter that restricts access to harmful Web sites, specifies times when the Internet can be used, and generates reports on Web sites visited. Get a quality product, even if it costs a little more. Today's teens are sophisticated and can bypass most standard Internet filters. Emphasize the importance of not giving out personal information online, and make it clear that meeting anyone from the Internet without parental permission is unacceptable.

Monitoring teens is not the same as keeping them under surveillance. Adolescents need autonomy, so gradually give them increasing amounts of freedom and privacy. If teens abuse the freedom given to them, supervise them more closely until they *earn* your trust again. Remind them that your increased presence is a direct consequence of the choices they have made.

Adolescents want you to pay attention to what they are doing. If they don't think you are, they will engage in behaviors that will force you to take notice.

Effectively Communicating with Your Teen

Just a few changes in your awareness and parenting can go a long way toward helping your teen.

Talking Less, Listening More

Adolescents with emotional and behavioral problems have a lot to say to someone who truly listens to them. When speaking with (not *at* or *to*) your teen, you should provide your full attention without distractions: let the phone ring, put down your magazine, or serve dinner a few minutes late. Most teens find brief interactions with parents who are offering their full attention more satisfying than lengthy interactions with multiple interruptions. Brief, nonjudgmental follow-up questions ("Then what happened?") keep conversations flowing. Adolescents are less likely to open up if you sit them down to "talk." Instead, converse during simple activities such as riding in the car, eating a meal, shopping, setting the table, or shooting basketballs. The goal is to help teens feel understood by accepting how they think and feel about situations or experiences—this is particularly important when they are angry or upset.

Knowing What Not to Say

When teens are upset, the following responses can make teens feel *less* understood:

- *Advising.* "Call your boyfriend and tell him you aren't going to stand for that." "You shouldn't have gone after that job in the first place." "Give him back the money."

- *Philosophizing.* "Life isn't fair." "We don't always get what we want; we get what we need."

- *Denying.* "I saw you laughing earlier; you aren't as sad as you think." "You don't look upset to me." "It's not that big of a deal."

- *Disagreeing.* "That's not what she was trying to do." "That's not what happened."

- *Underreacting.* "You're blowing this out of proportion." "I'm sure it's not as bad as you think." "I don't see why it's so terrible."

- *Pacifying.* "I'm sure that's not what he meant." "It will all blow over." "I'm sure they will forgive you."

These responses are typically an attempt to be helpful, but they can unintentionally invalidate the adolescent's thoughts and feelings and make the teen feel worse. Teenagers want you to understand their experience, regardless of whether or not you agree with them. If they ask for advice, by all means give it. If they don't, bite your tongue.

Tips for Talking with Teens

The following strategies can help you and your teen communicate more effectively regardless of whether you have a close relationship or haven't spoken in days. Although some suggestions seem obvious, the majority of us don't use them as often as we think we do.

Preparing for a Talk   Before entering an important talk with teens, decide on the outcome you are trying to achieve so that you don't

get distracted by unrelated topics. Be open to what teens are asking for, and negotiate. Strive for a win-win situation—neither
party may get exactly what it wants, but both will get an outcome
they can live with.

Do not attempt to communicate if either of you is angry or upset. Wait until both of you calm down. If things get heated during
the conversation, take a time-out. It is okay for parents and teens to
agree to disagree. Don't talk if either of you has been drinking alcohol or using any other type of drug. You will get adolescents to
open up much more when others aren't around. Even the possibility that people will overhear them can shut teens down. If, after repeated attempts, your teen is not comfortable talking with you
about sensitive issues, encourage him or her to talk with another
responsible adult (school counselor, mentor, "sponsor"). Don't feel
badly or take it personally.

Listening   When teens open up—take advantage of the moment,
even if it is late, you are heading out the door, or need to finish
a task. You don't know when the opportunity will arise again. Let
teens finish their thoughts before you respond—parents often
respond—or even interrupt—before their teen gets to the meat of
the issue.

Although it is difficult to see your child upset, encourage
teens to express all emotions, including anger, fear, and sadness.
Listen. You don't need to have all the answers to fix their problem. It may be best not to comment. Remember, teens pay more
attention to nonverbal messages than your words. Are your arms
crossed (defended, angry); are you looking around the room (impatient, distracted); does your voice sound bored (discounting
your teen's need)?

Talking   Talk about trivial, day-to-day matters to connect. Communication doesn't have to include heavy-duty topics. Adolescents
want parents to be straightforward and direct; otherwise, they often
miss your point. If you hear something troublesome about your
teen, ask him or her about it. Over time, not all at once, initiate
conversations about tough topics such as smoking, alcohol/drug

use, sex, date rape, abusive relationships, fighting, gangs, and bullying. Communicate your feelings and values. Ask about your teen's thoughts, beliefs, and experiences. Take a deep breath before the teen answers, and remember to *listen*. Apologize if you react and bring the conversation to a halt.

Ask open-ended questions that are specific ("What happened with your science project?") rather than general ("How was school?"). Be willing to *briefly* share struggles you faced growing up. Despite rolling their eyes when you are talking, teens often find that this helps them feel that you can relate to what they are going through. Acknowledge and empathize with your teen's pain, even if you cannot understand why he or she is so upset (e.g., "That must have been really difficult.").

Using "I" Statements   Express your thoughts and ideas directly ("I worry that your anger is going to get you in trouble or physically hurt") whenever you want to convey how your teen's behavior affects you. Avoid using "You" statements to tell them what they are doing wrong: "You're going to end up in jail or physically hurt if you don't get control of your anger."

Avoiding Unhelpful Responses   Don't speak continuously for more than one minute. Time yourself if you have to. You lose teens after that. Don't jump in to fill the silence. Let your teen have enough time to process what is being said and add more to the conversation. You will be surprised at some of the jewels you may have missed by jumping in.

Communication is a two-way street. If you get loud, so will they. If you are calm, caring, and respectful, chances are better they will be, too. Don't correct grammar or criticize the use of profanity if a few bad words accidentally slip into their story. Avoid the use of *always* and *never*—they usually are not accurate, anyway. Don't ever give your opinion on something without asking for your teen's opinion, as well. It is fine to say you do not agree with their opinion, but convey respect for it.

When Your Teen Won't Talk

If your teen does not want to talk with you, step back and let him or her know you are available when the teen is ready. Approach your teen again in a few days if he or she has not approached you. If you and your teen have conflicting schedules, write messages on a dry erase board, leave sticky notes, or hang a calendar in the kitchen to communicate family members' whereabouts.

When frustration sets in, just remember: if teens don't get information and guidance from you, they'll seek it out from others. Do you really want them getting advice from their friends? It's natural for parent-teen communication to go through peaks and valleys as they move through different phases of adolescence. What is essential is that you *keep showing up, asking the questions, listening, and letting them know you are there when they are ready*. As with any other skill, communicating effectively takes practice. As long as you are trying to do the right thing, teens get that.

Siblings: What About Me?

Being the sibling of a teen with an emotional or behavioral problem can be challenging. Parental attention, worry, and time are frequently tied up with the brother or sister with special needs, which can cause siblings to feel rejected, abandoned, angry, or resentful. If they attend the same school or share similar friends, siblings may be embarrassed by their brother or sister's unusual or unruly behavior. Or they may be angry that family outings or trips get compromised, or cut short. Even though they love each other, some siblings engage in intense arguments with their brother or sister with special needs. Others may react in the opposite manner by swallowing their feelings to avoid stressing an already stressed-out family.

Siblings should be encouraged to talk about their emotions and not made to feel guilty for those that are negative. These youth are at risk of depression or becoming overly responsible and perfectionists to balance out the "troubled" teen in the family. There are now books specifically written for siblings of teens with special needs to help them feel less alone.

Siblings need to understand (at the level appropriate for their age) why their brother or sister behaves the way he or she does, particularly if it is unusual or scary or if they have been victimized by it. Reassure them that the situation is being taken care of and that they are not to blame. Siblings should not be expected to always include their brother or sister in social activities or to take on parental responsibilities. Keeping the family routine in place, to the best of your ability, provides siblings with a sense of predictability and safety. It is important to spend quality one-on-one time with siblings so that they feel important and valued. Otherwise, they may believe they need to act up or break down to get your attention.

Siblings look to parents for how to view their brother or sister with special needs. If you view emotional or behavioral problems as a burden and hardship, so will they. If you view all your children as having different needs, including their own unique strengths and limitations, that's how they'll see it as well. *"Fair" doesn't mean that each child gets the same thing; it means that each gets his or her individual needs met.*

Have a Crisis Plan

For a small group of adolescents with emotional or behavioral problems, no rules or discipline seem to work. When someone confronts them with their negative behavior or holds them accountable, they respond with increasing agitation, anger, or aggression. If this is your child, you need a crisis plan in place in order to respond strategically to urgent and potentially dangerous situations.

Should your teen become belligerent, family members and close friends may be able to help you de-escalate the situation. Some will even allow your child to stay with them for a day or two to provide a cooling-off period. The contact numbers of these "helpers" should be easily accessible; they should be alerted if your son or daughter begins showing signs of agitation to prepare them to assist if circumstances worsen. You may need to call the police or 911 if your teenager becomes assaultive. When help arrives, alert officials to your child's emotional or behavioral condition and express that you need help managing his or her behavior.

Having the police enter your home and interact with your teen can be heartbreaking and frightening; however, many law enforcement officers have experience interacting with and de-escalating out-of-control adolescents, including those with emotional and behavioral issues.

If necessary, your teen may need to be transported to a secure facility for his or her protection and the protection of others. Depending on the circumstances, this may be a hospital, residential crisis center, or a juvenile justice facility. You should investigate local adolescent treatment programs at the hospitals in your community prior to a crisis. Most adolescents never require this extreme level of care, but if they do, parents need to be prepared.

When it comes to parenting teens with special needs, there are good days, not so good days, and downright awful days. This is to be expected. Raising adolescents is no easy task, and teens with emotional and behavioral problems require even more time and energy than the typical teen. Not surprisingly, there is little left of either for you and your needs. Taking care of yourself is a necessity—not an option. Take a deep breath; the next chapter is all about *you*.

CHAPTER FIFTEEN

Don't Forget *Your* Oxygen Mask

The Importance of Self-Care

I'm just so tired . . . all the time.

Raising an adolescent with emotional and behavioral problems elicits a variety of emotions—all of which are very normal. Fear, frustration, confusion, anger, disappointment, relief, excitement, and joy can occur throughout one month, one week, and sometimes even one day. Your teen's behavior may be the least of your stress. Family, friends, neighbors, and even professionals may blame you for your child's noncompliant, unpredictable, or unusual behavior. Dealing with appointments, the school, insurance companies, and medication for your teen can be overwhelming on top of an already crazy-busy schedule. Each day may feel like a whirlwind of activity, and then you have to get up the next day and do it again. And you do.

I spend a lot of time on airplanes. One of the phrases flight attendants always say prior to takeoff is: "Should there be a sudden loss of cabin pressure, an oxygen mask will drop from above. If you are traveling with a child, *be sure to secure your own mask first before placing one on a child traveling with you.*" Even the airlines know that it is a parent's instinct to put their child's needs before their own— but if you don't take care of yourself, you will be of no help to your son or daughter. What fantastic advice for parents of adolescents with emotional or behavioral difficulties, where the pull to put your teen's needs before yours can be even stronger.

Asking for Help

You may be one of the superhero parents who pride themselves on "never asking for help." I hate to burst your bubble, but this can actually be detrimental to your health, your happiness, and your family. It is actually a sign of strength, as well as commitment to your teen, to seek help when stressed, exhausted, or burned out. There are a number of individuals and agencies that can provide assistance and relieve some of your burden. Most won't come to you, so you will need to go to them and ask. For holidays, think about skipping traditional gifts and ask friends and family for ways to free up your time: take your teen to sports practice or dance lessons, do your grocery shopping, pick up a takeout meal, or take your teen to a movie. They may be willing to do this once, or maybe even monthly. If you happen to be fortunate enough to have people offer to help out, take them up on it. Get rid of thoughts related to inconveniencing them; they would not have offered if they didn't want to do it. People who care about you want to help but often don't know how. Allowing them to contribute to you and your family is a gift you give to them.

Who Is in Your Village?

Are you having a hard time thinking of people you could ask for help? We often hear the phrase "It takes a village to raise a child," and having a village around your adolescent is essential if he or she has an emotional or behavioral problem. But, you may feel as if you are alone in your village. In today's world, parents get divorced, family members live across the country, and good friends and neighbors move away. Broaden your idea about who is in your village to include school personnel, clergy, physicians, therapists, parents of your teen's friends, coaches, neighbors, colleagues, and close friends. Contact organizations that match adolescents with responsible adults who can provide guidance and support, such as Big Brothers/Big Sisters, as well as mentoring, tutoring, and coaching programs. If you have recently moved to a new town, keep in touch with old friends, but start creating a new village for you and your family.

And don't rule out family members who aren't nearby. Teens often prefer *strange relatives* to *relative strangers*. Being part of a larger "family" can mean the world to adolescents who feel isolated, alone, and different from their peers. Ask relatives to write, call, and send e-mails of support; your teen needs cheerleaders from all over the world, as do you! In today's technological age, it's never been easier for family to keep in touch.

Some village members may initially make unkind and insensitive comments about your teen if they are unfamiliar with (or misinformed about) emotional and behavioral conditions that affect adolescents. When compassionately educated, these individuals can become some of your biggest allies.

Clusters of Support

Support groups composed of other parents who understand your struggles can provide reassurance, encouragement, and practical assistance. Why reinvent the wheel when there are others who have been in your shoes and can help you avoid the mistakes they made? You can often get referrals to highly regarded professionals and services, as well as advice on effective parenting strategies, from parents who have "been there and done that" with teens similar to your own.

In-person support group *meetings,* such as those run by the National Association for the Mentally Ill (NAMI), allow you to physically see and connect with others. *Internet* resources (chat rooms, message boards, listservs) allow you to access support at a time that is convenient for you. Some parents use a combination of methods, particularly during challenging periods. If the first support group you try isn't a good fit, try another one. Each has its own personality and culture. If you can't find one you are comfortable with or can't find one at all, think about starting your own support group with at least one other parent. Once you put the word is out, your group will grow.

Let It Go

Many parents blame themselves for their teen's condition. It's not your fault. You didn't cause it. Emotional and behavioral problems are the result of complex interactions among an adolescent's unique biology, personal attributes, and life experiences. Even if you played some role in your teen's current situation, blaming yourself does not help matters. Take responsibility, make apologies where necessary, and then move forward. Your energy is much better spent focusing on what can be done now to help your child.

What Do *You* Need?

Taking time to unwind looks different to each person, so it is important to identify how *you* like to relax. Do you prefer to spend your down time taking a bath, getting your nails done, watching TV, or reading a magazine? Perhaps you need to crank it up to rejuvenate, such as working out at the gym, going for a bike ride, or dancing all night. You may want a night out alone with your significant other—or maybe a night away from your significant other. It's possible you don't know what you need to relax because you haven't thought about it for so long. That's okay; think about it now. Really. Specifically identifying what helps you unwind is the first (and most important) step toward getting there. Then, take the time, and make it happen. The dishes might not get done, the floor might stay sticky, or your teen may have to eat cereal for dinner. This is nonnegotiable. Children aren't happy when their parents are miserable, so if feelings of guilt creep in during your alone time, remember that *you are supporting your teen by supporting yourself.*

Body, Mind, and Spirit

Parents need to be in good shape to effectively parent teens with emotional or behavioral problems. I'm referring not to your body size but to your emotional, physical, and spiritual health. That means making healthy food choices, exercising, and getting enough sleep. If you have spiritual or religious beliefs, rely on them for guidance and strength. Forgive your teen if he or she has hurt you;

forgive yourself if you have made poor choices. If you feel stressed out and feel like you are barely getting by each day, take an honest look to see if some unhealthy coping behaviors have crept into your life. Repeatedly relying on shopping, food, alcohol/drugs (including prescription pills), cigarettes, or gambling to relax can be problematic for you and your family. *Everything you say and do your son or daughter sees and will likely do some day.*

Frequently feeling tired and irritable can be a sign of depression, especially when associated with problems sleeping, difficulty concentrating, and a lack of motivation. If these symptoms impact your work performance, relationships, or daily responsibilities, please seek help for yourself. Talking with a therapist can provide a safe place where you can discuss your emotions, as well as learn adaptive ways to manage intense and demanding child-rearing situations.

Putting their own oxygen mask on first allows a parent to continue breathing and thinking clearly—important skills needed in ensuring that their teen's mask is put on correctly. Think about what could happen if a parent were to forget the instruction and immediately went to put an oxygen mask on a wiggly, screaming, terrified child. This could take a very long time and put the parent's (and therefore the child's) life on the line.

I urge you to use the resources in the appendices of this book. There are plenty of organizations, agencies, and associations to choose from, so if one doesn't work, please try another.

Throughout the book I have used the cliché that knowledge is power. Now that you have made it to the end, you are one powerful parent! You now have the tools you need to recognize when your teen needs help—and you know what steps to take if necessary. That doesn't mean it is going to be smooth sailing from here on out. But, your family can be on the right path in no time. Parenting a teen with emotional or behavioral difficulties is the hardest job you will ever love. Thank you for letting my book contribute to your efforts.

Special Note

Please let me know if *When to Worry: How to Tell If Your Teen Needs Help—And What to Do About It* provided you with "aha" moments, helpful advice, or useful recommendations. Your success stories may end up on the *When to Worry* Web site or in future *When to Worry* projects. At this moment, millions of parents are struggling with a troubled teen—let them learn from you. I guarantee you have lots to share.

Lisa Boesky, Ph.D.
www.whentoworry.com

Resources and Support

Crisis hotlines (24 hours a day, 7 days a week)

- National Crisis Hotline: 800-273-TALK (8255)
- National Suicide Hotline: 800-SUICIDE (784-2433) *or* 877-SUICIDA (784-2432)
- Covenant House Nineline Hotline: 800-999-9999
- Self-Abuse Finally Ends (SAFE): 800-DONTCUT (366-8288)
- National Runaway Switchboard: 800-RUNAWAY
- Girls and Boys Town National Hotline: 800-448-3000

- Befrienders Worldwide: www.befrienders.org (numbers listed for forty different countries)

Mental Health Information

- Mental Health America: 800-969-6MHA (6642); www.nmha.org
- National Alliance for the Mentally Ill: 800-950-NAMI (6264); www.nami.org
- National Institute of Mental Health: 866-615-6464; www.nimh.nih.gov
- National Mental Health Information Center (SAMHSA): 800-789-2647, or, for international calls, 240-747-5484; www.mentalhealth.org *and* www.samhsa.gov
- American Psychological Association (APA): 800-374-2721; www.apa.org
- American Academy of Child and Adolescent Psychiatry (AACAP): 202-966-7300; www.aacap.org

Specific Conditions
Depression, Dysthymia, and Bipolar Disorder

- Depression and Bipolar Support Alliance (DBSA): 800-826-3632; www.dbsalliance.org
- The International Foundation for Research and Education on Depression (iFred); www.ifred.org *or* www.depression.org

Attention-Deficit Hyperactivity Disorder (ADHD)

- Children and Adults with Attention Deficit Disorder (CHADD): 301-306-7070; www.chadd.org
- National Resource Center on ADHD: 800-233-4050; www.help4adhd.org
- Attention Deficit Disorder Association (ADDA): 856-439-9099; www.add.org

Oppositional Defiant Disorder and Conduct Disorder

■ National Youth Violence Prevention Resource Center: 866-SAFEYOUTH (723-3968); www.safeyouth.org

■ Stop Bullying Now: www.stopbullyingnow.hrsa.gov

■ National Runaway Switchboard (NRS): www.nrscrisisline.org

Anxiety, Social Phobia, Obsessive-Compulsive Disorder, and Trauma

■ Anxiety Disorders Association of America: 240-485-1001; www.adaa.org

■ Obsessive Compulsive Foundation: 203-401-2070; www.ocfoundation.org

■ Freedom from Fear: 718-351-1717; freedomfromfear.org

■ National Center for PTSD: 802-296-6300; www.ncptsd.va.gov

■ The Social Phobia/Social Anxiety Association: www.socialphobia.org

Alcohol and Other Drug Use

■ Partnership for a Drug-Free America: 212-922-1560; www.drugfree.org

■ Parents—The Anti-Drug: 800-729-6686; www.antidrug.com

■ Substance Abuse and Mental Health Services Administration (SAMHSA): 800-662-HELP (4357); www.samhsa.gov

■ National Institute on Drug Abuse: 301-443-1124; www.drugabuse.gov

■ Al-Anon: 888-4ALANON (425-2666); www.al-anon.alateen.org

Eating Disorders

- National Eating Disorders Association (NEDA): 800-931-2237; www.nationaleatingdisorders.org
- National Association of Anorexia Nervosa and Associated Disorders (ANAD): 847-831-3438; www.ANAD.org

Self-Injury (Cutting)

- Young People and Self-Harm: www.selfharm.org.uk
- Secret Shame: www.selfharm.net

Suicide Prevention

- Suicide Awareness Voices of Education (SAVE): 952-946-7998; www.save.org
- Suicide Preventon Action Network USA (SPAN USA): 202-449-3600; www.spanusa.org

Learning Disabilities, Traumatic Head Injury, Fetal Alcohol Syndrome, and Asperger's

- Learning Disabilities Association of America: 412-341-1515; www.ldaamerica.org
- LD Online: www.ldonline.org
- Brain Injury Association: 800-444-6443; www.biausa.org
- National Organization on Fetal Alcohol Syndrome (NOFAS): 800-66NOFAS; www.nofas.org
- Online Asperger Syndrome Information and Support (OASIS): www.aspergersyndrome.org

Schizophrenia

- Schizophrenia Resource: www.schizophrenia.com

APPENDIX B

Psychotropic Medication Chart

Generic Name	*Brand Name*	*Medication Class*	*FDA Approval for Age and Condition*
Stimulants			
Methylphenidate	Ritalin, Concerta, Metadate	Stimulant	6 & up, ADHD
Dextroamphetamine	Dexedrine, Dextrostat	Stimulant	3 & up, ADHD
Amphetamine, Dextroamphetamine	Adderall	Stimulant	3 & up, ADHD
Dexmethylphenidate	Focalin	Stimulant	6 & up, ADHD
Nonstimulants			
Atomoxetine	Strattera	Non-stimulant	6 & up, ADHD
Clonidine	Catapres	Anti-hypertensive	12 & up, High Blood Pressure
Guanfacine	Tenex	Anti-hypertensive	12 & up, High Blood Pressure
Antidepressants			
Fluoxetine	Prozac	SSRI	8 & up, Depression 7 & up, OCD
Sertraline	Zoloft	SSRI	6 & up, OCD 18 & up, Depression, Social Anxiety, Panic, PTSD
Paroxetine	Paxil	SSRI	18 & up, Depression, Generalized Anxiety, OCD, Panic, Social Phobia, PTSD
Escitalopram	Lexapro	SSRI	18 & up, Depression and Anxiety
Fluvoxamine	Luvox	SSRI	8 & up, OCD
Venlafaxine	Effexor	SSRI	18 & up, Depression
Duloxetine	Cymbalta	SSNRI	18 & up, Depression
Bupropion	Wellbutrin	Atypical antidepressant	18 & up, Depression
Trazodone	Desyrel	Atypical antidepressant	18 & up, Depression

Generic Name	Brand Name	Medication Class	FDA Approval for Age and Condition
Antidepressants (continued)			
Mirtazapine	Remeron	Atypical antidepressant	18 & up, Depression
Clomipramine	Anafranil	Tricyclic antidepressant	10 & up, OCD
Imipramine	Tofranil	Tricyclic antidepressant	6 & up, Bed-wetting
Nortriptyline	Pamelor	Tricyclic antidepressant	18 & up, Depression
Mood Stabilizers			
Lithium Carbonate	Lithium, Eskalith, Lithobid	Mood-Stabilizing Salt	12 & up, Bipolar
Divalproex, Valproic Acid	Depakote, Depakene	Anticonvulsant	10 & up, Seizures 2 & up, Seizures
Carbamazepine	Tegretol	Anticonvulsant	Any Age Seizures
Gabapentin	Neurontin	Anticonvulsant	3 & up, Seizures
Lamotrigine	Lamictil	Anticonvulsant	2 & up, Seizures 18 & up, Bipolar
Topiramate	Topamax	Anticonvulsant	2 & up, Seizures
Oxcarbazepine	Trileptal	Anticonvulsant	2 & up, Seizures
Anti-Anxiety			
Alprazolam	Xanax	Benzodiazepine	18 & up, Generalized Anxiety, Panic
Lorazepam	Ativan	Benzodiazepine	18 & up, Anxiety
Diazepam	Valium	Benzodiazepine	6 months & up, Anxiety
Clonazepam	Klonopin	Benzodiazepine	All Ages, Seizures; 18 & up, Panic
Buspirone	BuSpar	Atypical Anti-Anxiety	18 & up, Generalized Anxiety
Zolpidem	Ambien	Non-benzodiazapene Anti-Anxiety	18 & up, Insomnia

(continues)

Generic Name	Brand Name	Medication Class	FDA Approval for Age and Condition
Antipsychotics			
Risperidone	Risperdal	Antipsychotic (Second Generation)	5 & up, Irritability Associated with Autism 18 & up, Bipolar and Schizophrenia
Quetiapine	Seroquel	Atypical Antipsychotic (Second Generation)	18 & up, Bipolar and Schizophrenia
Olanzapine	Zyprexa	Atypical Antipsychotic (Second Generation)	18 & up, Bipolar and Schizophrenia
Ziprasidone	Geodon	Atypical Antipsychotic (Second Generation)	18 & up, Bipolar Disorder and Schizophrenia
Aripiprazole	Abilify	Atypical Antipsychotic (Second Generation)	18 & up, Bipolar and Schizophrenia
Chlorpromazine	Thorazine	Antipsychotic (First Generation)	2 & up, Severe Behavior Disorders
Trifluoperazine	Stelazine	Antipsychotic (First Generation)	6 & up, Schizophrenia (closely monitored or hospitalized); 12 & up, Schizophrenia
Haloperidol	Haldol	Antipsychotic (First Generation)	3 & up, Schizophrenia, Severe Behavior Disorders, Tourette's

OCD = Obsessive Compulsive Disorder
PTSD = Posttraumatic Stress Disorder
SSRI = Selective serotonin reuptake inhibitor
SNRI = Selective norepinephrine reuptake inhibitor
SSNRI = Selective serotonin and norepinephrine reuptake inhibitor

Acknowledgments

I am grateful to the many people who supported me as I researched and wrote this book. My literary agent, Cathy Fowler, who believed in the project from the moment she heard about it. I so appreciate her wise counsel. My acquisitions editor at AMACOM Books, Christina Parisi, who shared my vision of reaching as many parents as possible. Christina's guidance has been *invaluable* every step of the way. Polly Bowman's editorial help was excellent, and Elizabeth Lyon at Editing International went beyond the call of duty on all counts. I am indebted to Mike Sivilli, Penny Makras, and the rest of the staff at AMACOM Books for all their hard work, attention to detail, and amazing attitudes. I feel blessed to be a part of their "team."

I thank my family and friends from the bottom of my heart for their love, support, and understanding about my time constraints. This is particularly true of Stephen Milley, who cleaned the house and cooked his own dinner more times than any new husband should. His unyielding patience, partnership, and belief in me and this book are the reasons he is truly my prince charming.

And finally, to the thousands of teenagers, parents, family members, and youth-serving professionals who have personally shared their stories and lives with me over the years. I am humbled and inspired by their depth, resourcefulness, and strength. They have changed me forever.

INDEX

About the Author

Dr. Lisa Boesky is a Clinical Psychologist, National Speaker and Author who is a nationally reconized authority on teenagers with with emotional and behavioral issues. She has worked with a wide range of adolescents—from mildly stressed teens to the most troubled, challenging, and dangerous youth in psychiatric hospitals and juvenile correctional facilities. You may have seen "Dr. Lisa" on *CNN, Fox News, CBS, ABC* or in *Family Circle, USA Today* and other media outlets.

For the past decade, "Dr. Lisa" has captivated, educated, and inspired tens of thousands of parents and professionals across the country with her high-energy and interactive presentations. Dr. Lisa consults on mental health policy for a variety of agencies and is regulary sought by legal professionals to serve as an expert witness on cases involving mental health or suicide.

She is also the author of *Juvenile Offenders with Mental Health Disorders: Who Are They and What Do We Do With Them?*, as well as numerous book chapters, articles and a DVD. Dr. Lisa's excellent reputation and popularity are due to her passion, warmth, humor and unique ability to make complex information interesting and easy-to-understand.

For more information about Dr. Lisa Boesky, including having her speak to your group, please visit www.drlisab.com.